SWAN

JACKS

CONGRATULATIONS ON YOUR MARRIAGE

Andrew Tooze

FROM

with

Martin King

HEADHUNTER BOOKS
www.headhunterbooks.co.uk

Head-Hunter Books
www.headhunterbooks.co.uk
www.myspace.com/headhunterbooks

Contents

TOOZEY'S ACKNOWLEDGEMENTS

This book would not have been remotely possible without the assistance, enthusiasm and goodwill of a multitude of people. If there are any whose names I have failed to mention, I apologise profusely.

My good mates:

Lee Wallis (co-writer of this book), Alan Roberts (co-writer of this book), Neil Cooney, Carl Evans (brother-in-law), Stacko, Tracy, Aggis, John The Bank, Mike Buller, Craig Buller, Mark Buller, Kev Newt, Simon Ivy, Duffy, Mojos, Tebays, Big Roger, Gypo, Kano, Paul Neale, Dai Lloyd, Dai Porter, Peter Paton, Watsy, Whitey, Grayo, Owain, Magsy, Giovanni, Thomo, Wayne Gorsh, Nobsy Boxer, Nipper, Little Dai, Martin Arthur, John Longdon, Matty, Bone, Chilli, Ricky, Chris Aberdare, Clivey, Dai Hammacot, Pinto, Davis, Eddy Eyes, Aggis Junior, Jason Ryan, Jez, Jonesy, Laddy, Max, Mucca, Nick Paintbox, Oxo, Rees, Rodney, Dustbin, Young Stacko, Trev Bond, Tony Jenkins, Sion, Barry, Payno, Mark Simpson, Daz, Edge, Max, Budgie, Muffers, Priddy, Les & Carl Brain, Hank, Mayo, Oakers, Ross, Jinksy, Terry Davies, Ginger, Abe & The Herberts, Psycho Karl & Andrew & The Monkey Jacks and Townhill Youth.

Many thanks to Martin Johnson for his camera work.

RIP to some good lads who include Nutty; Alan; Baileys; Alan Gorton; Robbie Mathews; Chrissy; Jason "Cheesey" Angus; Dai Nicholls; Carl Pitson and Noel James.

Also to my lovely wife, Claire and kids Luke, Emily, Georgia and Elliot; and Alan's kids, Bradley and Kelsey. In addition, this book really would not have been possible without the support of my family who have had to put up with being ignored for the past 14 months while I have been working on it. Toozey.

Thanks to Helen Wallis for many hours of typing and to my lovely children, Amelia & Jac. Love Lee.

CHAPTER ONE
TOOZEY

Before the original stadium was built, there was a patch of dirt where the local children would play. On it grew a cabbage like vegetable called Vetch which was used to feed cattle. The area was traditionally a rugby union area. In 1912, Swansea Town Football Club was formed and played their first game as a professional outfit against archrivals, Cardiff City with the game ending in a 1 - 1 draw. In that first season, the club won the Welsh Cup and went on to be the first Welsh club to play in the FA Cup proper. In 1926, while on tour, they beat the legendry Real Madrid, 3 - 0. In 1971, we were granted 'city status' and the football club then became Swansea City. Season 2005-2006 saw the club move from The Vetch Field to the new 20,000 seater Liberty stadium on the outskirts of the city and, to me and lots of the other boys, that's when going to football and watching the Swans changed. You no longer had the crowd in the opposition's faces. That intimidating atmosphere was lost and, with the all-seater venue, the singing and chanting fell away. It's now more like being at the ballet or the opera. If you dare stand up and voice your opinion or swear, you stand a good chance of being thrown out by the stewards and maybe even face a banning order. It's just gone crazy. Teams no longer fear coming down here. It's no longer the fortress it once was. It's too family orientated and too politically correct for my liking. Bring back the old days, I say.

Natives of Swansea are often referred to as 'Swansea Jacks'. Some people believe this stems from the famous black retriever dog which rescued 27 people from the waters around the Swansea coast in the 1930s; others prefer the explanation that 'Swansea Jacks' stems from the times when the area around Swansea had a very busy port and a reputation as excellent mariners.

I'm 41 now and I first went to watch the Swans play with my Dad when I was about 13 years old. We played Chesterfield at home; it was hardly an exciting fixture. My Dad was old school and we used to stand on the North Bank which is the home end. We'd stand down the front with all the singers and the chaps huddled together at the back. My first impressions, to be honest, were that the place was a cold, dingy shit hole. I went with my Dad to a few more games down at the Vetch and after a while I started going down there with a few school friends. I then went on a few away trips with the official supporters club. It was then, as

I tagged along, that I first noticed a certain element that weren't just there for the football. A few faces like Hank, Michael B, Billy Pridmore and the Smuto brothers were our frontline firm in those days. The Smutos, as they were called, were the Smith brothers, Dai and Charlie, a right pair of scruffy fuckers - they stuck in my mind for some reason. Trinny and Susanna would have had a field day with them. That's after Kim and Aggie had given them a scrub down with a tin of Vim.

The house I lived in backed onto Swansea railway station and one Saturday morning, me and a mate were just pissing around and getting up to no good when we saw a train stopped short of the station. Hanging out of the windows were hundreds of youths hurling abuse at any locals within earshot. The police arrived and emptied the train and lined everyone up at the side of the tracks. I was fascinated by what was happening. It turns out it was a Football Special and it was full to the brim of Chelsea fans. Many of the windows on the train had been smashed but the fans didn't seem to give a fuck that the Old Bill was there. They just carried on singing and chanting in their strange accent. Even in those days I could see some nasty looking guys I wouldn't want to get on the wrong side of; still, that didn't stop me picking up a brick and throwing it towards them. Although it landed well short, I got a right buzz out of it.

Soon after, I started hanging around with some of the boys that liked a punch up and from then on I found out the boys' hatred of fellow Welsh club, Cardiff City. Not just the football side of things but anything to do with Cardiff itself. It really runs deep. There's a real hatred on both sides. The mention of them makes the hairs on the back of the neck stand up. Many people find them arrogant. Without a shadow of a doubt, they think they're above anyone else in Wales. When it comes to their firm at football, they're bullies. They have huge numbers which you can't take away from them. Eighty percent of their fans don't even come from Cardiff; they come from the surrounding towns and the valleys. They're the Man U of Wales. I don't want to harp on about them because even talking about them gives me the hump. We've had some right run-ins with them over the years and, believe me, they've not always had it their own way. Far from it.

My first brush with the law at football was in 1980 against Liverpool at home. There were Liverpool fans everywhere. I was walking along the Mumbles Road and a group of our boys were having a bit of a scuffle with some gobby Scousers when a vanload of them screeched to a halt, jumped out and came towards me. I was caught in no man's land. As they ran towards the Swansea boys, my instinct for survival kicked in so I picked up a brick and threw it through the windscreen of their van. The police came from everywhere and I was pinned to the floor by a police dog. It bit my hand and there was blood everywhere. I've still got the scars to this day. I was arrested and thrown into the back of a police van, laying on the floor with a copper's foot on my chest. At the nick, the arresting officer would not believe I was a juvenile. I was only about 14 but was a big lump for my age. When it came out I was the age I'd given, the other coppers took the piss out of the one that had arrested me. I ended up going to court and getting a £50 fine with a conditional discharge. I did hear on the grapevine that the police dog died after it had bitten me ! Besides that, I haven't got into a great deal of bother with the law when it comes to football although I did end up in prison after fighting with Cardiff fans out in Italy.

I went out to Milan with a few other Swansea boys to watch Wales play Italy. We arrived on the Friday afternoon, dropped our bags off at the hotel and went straight out to get something to eat; we didn't even unpack. We headed for the main square and, straight away, we bumped into a dozen or so Cardiff fans. Millsey, one of their boys, started gobbing off so we told them we're here, do something about it. There were words exchanged and off they went. Their excuse was that the Old Bill were in the square with guns. We told them that we didn't give a fuck so let's get it on. We left it like that. There was only a dozen of us and all we could hear were the hundreds of Cardiff fans milling about saying they were looking for Jacks. In our hotel were Piper and Vinny and about 50 Newport lads, who are a good bunch. Cardiff were looking for them as well as us. The Newport lads, rightly so, were a bit on edge and you can't blame them. But they sort of distanced themselves from us. Everywhere you went, Cardiff lads were on the lookout for us. Every bar we went into, we seemed to bump into the Newport lads who, as soon as we appeared, would drink up and move off to another bar. We seemed to be bad news. They just wanted to have a few beers and enjoy themselves without any hassle. In the end, we went into a restaurant and had a pizza. I think I plumped for the Margherita with extra cheese while the rest of the boys went for the cheese and ham and mushroom with a mixed side salad and a few bottles of the house red. Anyway, who gives a fuck ? This isn't a book on culinary delights. What I am trying to say is that the only Italian males we'd seen so far were the waiters in the restaurant with no sign of the infamous Italian Ultras. We came out and there was a bit of a scuffle going on. Vinny from Newport had been stabbed by some Cardiff supporter and had a couple of nasty looking wounds to his side. We found that there'd been trouble between Newport and Cardiff boys down by the canal. The Newport lads said they'd been attacked by a huge 400 strong Cardiff mob who were on the lookout for us lot. They hadn't yet found us so they bullied the Newport lads. What we didn't know was that the Newport lads had been followed up the road by a mob of Cardiff and walked straight into us. Our numbers were now down to about eight as a few of our boys had had a bit too much to drink of the old vino and had headed back to our hotel.

"Come on you Jack bastards !" shouted the Cardiff boys as they came straight into us.

Me, Stacko and Gypo stood our ground and had a set-to with them. Stacko took up a boxing stance and was laying them out as they came into us. Stacko was a good amateur boxer in his younger days and Gypo was one of our youngsters who was as game as fuck. Three or four of them came around me and we exchanged blows as they tried to get me down. I'm a bit bigger than the average guy so they weren't having a lot of luck. If I had gone down, I would have been dead. Also I was very worried about being stabbed after just hearing what had happened to the Newport lad. They're dirty bastards who, over the years, have not been afraid to use weapons against us. I looked around and four of our boys had disappeared. It was a scary situation to be in, let me tell you. It was fight, run or go down and take a kicking. Next to me, Stacko was still pinging them for fun. About four times, he knocked down this big lump of a guy wearing a black Stone Island jumper but this bloke kept getting up and coming back for more. It seemed Stacko had drawn an imaginary circle and just planted his feet in it. He was like an old-fashioned boxer going toe to toe. Gypo also stood and was as game as fuck but we were getting overrun by their superior numbers.

Max, one of our boys, had had too much to drink and he lay on the floor sparked out by a punch. Laying next to him were his false teeth that had been knocked out. In the end, he came round, realized what was going on and dived into a doorway where the shopkeeper pulled down the metal shutters and saved him from further punishment. Kano, one of ours, was bringing up the rear by launching bottles through the air at the Cardiff hordes. I could hear a few of them shouting "Get Toozey".

We still never moved and, at one stage, we backed them off. This was the respite we needed. I picked up one of the moped type scooter bikes the Italians whizz around the streets on and hurled it into the middle of the Cardiff mob. Then the sirens started and we could hear them getting closer. All the locals were now out with many hanging out of their windows watching what was going on. I had my brother-in-law, Carl, with me so I told him to fuck off as the fighting hit a lull. I pushed him up a side street and we all headed off in different directions. The police turned up and we'd all dispersed. I looked over my shoulder and I could see them talking to some locals who were pointing in my direction. Next thing, a police car pulled alongside and the driver shouted something in Italian at me. I took no notice and carried on walking. He got out and whistled and called me to them. I carried on walking and then another whistle. I looked around and the copper had his gun pointing at me. At that stage it made perfect sense to stop. They spoke to me in broken English and slapped the handcuffs on. I'm taken back down the road to where the fight had taken place and was identified by a group of Italians.

Swans fans are arrested in Italy

THREE Swansea City fans were arrested in Milan early today during violent clashes between rival Welsh gangs.

A dozen arrests were made ahead of the Wales v Italy clash in the San Siro Stadium where up 8,000 Welsh supporters were expected to back the

team. South Wales Police, who have experts on football hooligans in Milan, estimate 40 known troublemakers from Swansea, Neath, Port Talbot and Llanelli have made their way to Italy.

Thirty-seven yobs who are banned from games have had their passports confiscated and had to report to police stations in Swansea today.

Most of the arrests in Milan were made in a series of violent clashes between gangs from Newport and Cardiff.

The Swansea supporters who were detained were involved in a clash early today. The circumstances surrounding the arrests were not immediately clear. Constable Lyn Phillips, football

liaison expert for Swansea City, is in Milan with four other police hooligan spotters from Cardiff and Wrexham. He said in Milan today: "Most of the trouble last night was between Cardiff and Newport supporters. We have been informed three Swansea fans have been arrested but it not clear yet what they were doing."

At this point I think I'm the only one that's been nicked. Inside the police station, Stacko and Gypo are already there and smile and look pleased to see me. My brother-in-law has got away which pleased me as he's not a fighter and has only really come for the piss-up and the football. We were held in a holding room in chains for a couple of hours with various Italians coming in and having a look at us. At this stage, a few of the Cardiff lads were brought in and I was chained up to Christian Thomas, one of their lads who'd been arrested for fighting with the Newport boys earlier that evening. Next thing, the football liaison officer from Swansea, Lyn Phillips, arrives.

"Oh my God. What have you boys been up to ?" he said, sounding concerned.

Now, Lyn's one of the nicest men you could ever wish to meet. He's old school when it comes to coppers and he's a real gentleman. He turned up with Simon, Cardiff's football liaison officer who ain't a bad bloke either. Lyn tried his best to sort things out for us by getting an interpreter or someone to come down from the British Consulate. We'd seen him in plain clothes down in the main square where he'd tipped us off to be careful as Cardiff were out in huge numbers. The row had to come sometime, be it before, during or after the game. We would have clashed with Cardiff no matter what. If we had got inside the stadium they would have killed us with the numbers they had.

After a while, we were moved into another cell and in the morning we were loaded up in chains and shackles onto a bus with metal bars on the windows. We were taken to court, laughing and joking, thinking we would get a slap on the wrist and be home in time for dinner in Swansea as heroes. The only word I understood in the whole proceedings was 'Jail'. I looked from the cage used to house Mafia bosses and noticed Lyn Phillips standing at the back of the courtroom shaking

Three in court after soccer

THREE Swansea men were due to appear before a court in Milan today following violent clashes before the Wales-Italy football match.

They were arrested in the canal area of the city on Friday night as gangs from Newport, Cardiff and Swansea fought a pitched battle.

Police sources in Milan named the three as Andrew Tooze, Paul Stack and Jason Griffiths.

Mr Tooze and Mr Stack are understood to be in their 30s and Mr Griffiths in his 20s.

They were remanded in custody at the weekend accused of the Italian equivalent of the British charge of violent disorder.

They were believed to be among a group of around a dozen Swansea City supporters who had been drinking at a bar close to where fans from Newport and Cardiff fought a pitched battle.

They were among up to 12 people, including a woman, who were arrested.

The arrests were part of a disastrous weekend for Welsh football with many of the 10,000 travelling fans being terrified at the San Siro Stadium as they were pelted with missiles, including bottles of urine, as Mark Hughes's men lost 4-0.

At one stage Welsh fans charged at police who were penning them into a lower deck at the ground to make escape routes for frightened women and children.

Up to 400 fans were also stranded in Italy last night after a jumbo jet due to fly from Cardiff to collect them was hit by lightning.

his head. He mouthed to me, "It's bad news, boys". That soon took the smile off my face and I came back down to earth with the reality of the situation. Panic set in as we were taken away to a nearby prison.

We were driven in through the gates and unloaded. Straight away the noise and the smell hit you. It turns out this prison only housed foreign prisoners like Moroccans, Albanians and Africans and now Welsh was added to that list. The screws ushered us inside and my first impression was that they were scabby-looking, arrogant misfits with gelled back hair and smug looks on their faces. Basically they looked horrible cunts. Our chains were taken off and we were given a T-shirt and a pair of shorts as we were processed into the jail. A few of them in broken English said ...

"English hooligan. You English hooligan ?"
"I'm fucking Welsh, not English," I replied but they didn't get it.

It went straight over their heads as did the fact that we'd been sent to prison for fighting our own countrymen. There were no Italians involved and they could not work that out.

We were in the jail for a few days and we still had no idea how long we were going to be banged up. It could be a year, it could be two years - we had no idea. No British Consulate had been to see us and we weren't allowed to make any phone calls so my wife, Claire, as far as I knew, had no idea where I was. I found out afterwards that she'd had news where I was and was relieved that I was still in one piece. The prison was a hell hole with a daily ration of a cup of warm milk, a plum and a scabby stale bread roll. What had happened to fine Italian cuisine? No seafood tagliatelle or bowls of mussels in garlic and white wine sauce. You wouldn't get fat on this gear. At the time, I was bang into weightlifting and body building so I was quite a lump. A couple of times, the guards saw me with no shirt on and in broken English inquired about my physique. In the night you could hear these scabby Albanians coming

£26,000 fine over Wales Italy game

THE ITALIAN football association has been fined £26,000 by UEFA for their role in the crowd trouble which blighted the recent Wales versus Italy game.

The Welsh FA could face a similar fine for not making sure its fans behaved while at the match in Milan on September 6.

In a separate incident on the Friday night before the European 2004 qualifier, three Swansea men, Andrew Tooze, Paul Stack and Jason Griffiths, were arrested and later given suspended jail sentences after fighting with Cardiff City supporters.

Following the game, UEFA announced they were to launch an investigation into crowd trouble at the San Siro stadium in Milan.

The Football Association of Wales made an official complaint about the treatment of their 8,000 supporters following their 4-0 defeat and some Welsh fans reported being pelted with missiles from Italians in the upper tier of the stand.

down off the heroin and they would scream and shout and bang their cell doors as they went through cold turkey.

One morning, we were put back in chains and loaded onto a bus and taken back to court in our shorts. Lyn was in court and relayed a bit of info to us so we found out what was going on. The trial started but this time there was an interpreter who explained to us what was being said. A year's jail was mentioned and our arses dropped to the floor. Then, five minutes later, the court added that the sentence was to be suspended. There was no fine and we were taken back to the prison, given our clothes, held in a room for three or four hours and then released out onto the streets of Milan. That was it. Nine of us were released. The Swansea boys, the Cardiff lads and the boys from Newport - all let out together.

Lyn Phillips had gone to our hotel and collected our stuff and handed it to us as we came out. Now we had the slight problem of getting back home. We had some money but not a great deal. My phone and the cash I'd left at the hotel had gone missing. Lee, my mate I was meant to be sharing a room with, had managed to pack up most of my clothes and my wife, Claire, booked a flight for me her end with British Airways back to Heathrow that night. It cost £550, first class, back to London. Only me and Vinny from Newport flew home. The rest of the boys stayed in some cheap hotel and got a cheaper flight home the next day. I had to get back because my job was on the line. They paid £70 but I had to get home. We made the flight I was booked on with five minutes to spare. I kept my job, just, and Claire was as good as gold. She never moaned and didn't nag me or give me a bollocking. She was very understanding but then, that's why I married her. She's a lovely girl, one in a million. To tell you the truth, that was a wake-up call for me and made me think that there was more to life than football. This happened in September 2003, not that long ago. But football hooliganism is just in your blood although I did stay out of trouble for a hell of a long time. That was until the Swans played up at Mansfield.

We arrived there in a minibus which I was driving, only to find out that the game had been called off. Then someone hit on the idea to stop and have a drink in Cardiff on the way back home. I thought it would be a good idea as I could call in and have a drink with Christian who is one of Cardiff's main boys in the Soul crew and someone I'd been banged up with out in Milan. I'd kept in contact with Christian since our release and found him a decent geezer - like Simon Needs and Macca, another couple of Cardiff faces, I've got a total respect for. The rest of them are shithouse bully boys who I have no time for. As we left Mansfield, I got on the blower to Christian and told him we were coming back to Cardiff. "It'll be nice to see you, Toozey," he replied.

So two minibuses of Swansea set off for Cardiff. Christian did point out to me that Cardiff had played Nottingham Forest at home that day and, as we spoke, he said "They had a 150 strong mob still hanging about in the pub well after the game had finished." Half way back, I called him and told him we were a 150 handed mob now. "Not to worry, our numbers have swelled to over 200," he replied. I knew he was exaggerating and he knew I was but who gives a fuck. We'd told him now. We were coming, so there was no turning back.

We arrived in Cardiff and drove past their pub, The Royal Exchange. It didn't look that busy so we drove up the road, turned around and had a second look. I parked up and my brother-on-law, Carl, in the second minibus pulled up behind me. We were about 300 to 400 yards away from the pub and, to my knowledge, nobody had noticed our arrival. We were out of view of the local CCTV so we strolled towards the pub in a nice tight little mob. Me, Stacko and Divvey led the way. One of our lads was so out of his nut he was being held up by my mate, Al. This geezer was a huge lump and we really needed him fighting fit and at the front but, in his present state, he was no good to anyone. We reached the pub doors and there's now only about 15 of us and the booze and the bravado had started to wear off. It's twitchy bum time as the rest of the lads bring up the rear, all strung out along the road. Divvey and Tebay go through the doors and walk up to the bar and look around. Max, one of ours who's a right character, even gets served and has a cigar and pint in his hand.

A couple of locals look at us a bit strange but so far nothing's been said. The pub's sort of set out in an L shape. Standing next to the pool table is a group of lads so we moved towards them. I then notice Simmo, one of Cardiff's main faces and his son coming towards us. Then the barmaid asks Max if we're on a stag night or are we Forest fans ? Simmo is now standing in front of Tebay, along with about 15 others in his group. More appear from a corridor inside the pub which connects to another bar. So now they have the numerical advantage. We still have 20 lads outside who never set foot in the pub. They can say what they

FANS CLASH IN PUB PUNCH-UP

Fighting spills out on to city centre street

RIVAL football fans fought in the street after a brawl spilled out of a pub over the weekend.

The punch-up began in the Royal Exchange pub in Cowbridge Road East, Canton, Cardiff, on Saturday night.

It came just hours after Cardiff City's goalless draw against Nottingham Forest in their First Division match at nearby Ninian Park.

The warring groups of fans involved some from Cardiff and some from Swansea, whose scheduled fixture at Mansfield Town was postponed because of bad weather.

Police said the fighting started at around 10.30pm as closing time approached.

Witnesses said around 40 people were involved in the incident at the pub.

But police were today unable to confirm if anybody had been arrested as a result of the fight, in which some of the pub's windows were smashed. Three police vans were called to the scene.

One person who saw the fight said: "Some fans came into the pub and threw some chairs around, then the fight moved out on to the road.

"None of the staff who worked for the pub was hurt, although there were some injuries among the fans."

There were no arrests following the game between Cardiff and Nottingham Forest.

■ **Cardiff City report: See Monday Sport.**

want but they stayed put outside for whatever reason. Simmo then asks Tebay if he's Toozey. I come to the front and inform him that I'm Toozey. "Have you been on the weights ?" he asks. I replied with a smack in his mouth and then cracked his son. I did the pair of them with a right and a left and down they went. I smashed the pair of them with two punches. From then it just went mental and for a moment I thought my life was over. It was scary, as all sorts of stuff rained down on us.

One of our boys punched the windows through from the outside and we backed off towards the door. As we're trying to get out, some of our lot are trying to get in. So there's a human jam of bodies near the main doors. I'm still in there throwing punches but finally we end up outside. A table hits me on the head and Tebay's on the floor looking for one of his shoes which has come off. To this day, the Cardiff lads still claim to have his shoe and it's supposedly hung up behind the bar as some sort of war trophy. It was like a fight from the OK Corral, with glass, chairs and bottles flying through the air, Wild West style. I came out and crossed over the road and that's when I noticed the CCTV cameras. I hadn't been drinking so I was more aware than the other boys. A few Cardiff came out and threw bits of broken glass in our direction but wouldn't come out in any numbers.

By this stage, you could hear the police sirens heading in our direction. One of our minibuses had loaded up already and had gone so we were left with about 15 of us. Now Cardiff started getting a bit brave and followed us up the road. We got within sight of the van, had it on our toes, jumped in and started up the engine. Cardiff caught hold of a couple of our back stragglers and gave them a bit of a pasting. Every one of them Cardiff bastards were carrying some sort of weapon. They had bottles, lumps of wood, chair legs, pool cues - the lot. The police arrived as the Cardiff lads were banging on the back of the bus telling us to get out. I put the bus in gear and tried to drive away but the Old Bill put a stop to that by taking the keys out of the ignition. The situation got worse as more Cardiff boys turned up from everywhere. Obviously someone had made a phone call and the news that we were in town spread like wildfire. The police cordoned off the road and held back the baying hordes. The police agreed that the best thing to do was to allow us to leave town as our presence was inflaming the locals' anger. I explained to the police that I was in fear of my passengers' safety and it worked a treat as we were sent on our way. We all fully expected to be pulled over on the motorway as we headed back to Swansea but nothing. We all got back safe and sound.

Six weeks later that all changed when the police turned up at my house at four o'clock in the morning and smashed my front door down. They didn't bother knocking, they just took the door straight off its hinges. Me, the wife and the kids were all fast asleep when they burst in. They came up the stairs but, by this stage, I'm at the top of the stairs wondering what the fuck was going on. Six Old Bill grabbed hold of me but, to be fair, they weren't heavy-handed with me, they didn't wake the kids and they didn't turn the house upside down or go through any of my possessions. I was taken to the police station in Swansea and interviewed by the Cardiff CID. They'd code named the operation 'Javelin'. The Cardiff Old Bill were very upfront and honest with me and laughed at my story of meeting up with my mate, Christian, for a reunion drink. They thought it was a load of bollocks. They just didn't believe it, even though there was no CCTV footage from inside the pub. They weren't very happy about the pub being smashed up but, all in all, they were pretty fair. I was held for 20 hours in the cells before the interview and was the first person to be arrested. Unknown to me, there was half a dozen of us arrested. We went to court three times in Cardiff where the case eventually was thrown out but Kano, one of ours, got 18 months in jail for smashing the windows and Viking, one of theirs, got a 6 months jail sentence. We later learnt that the big lad who was with us and was stoned out his head had his arm broken after being hit by a chair but just laughed at the bloke that clobbered him. One of them come up behind him, kicked him, tripped him up and he fell on his arm and broke it. He then lost us, didn't have a clue where we or the minibus was and staggered into town and got a cab home. Not a good night for him. At the end of the day, we know who took it to who. Even though Simmo and his pup deny I decked the pair of them, it's no good mouthing off in front of the Old Bill. As I say, I know the truth and so do they. They have never been to a Swansea boozer on a non-match day and tried it on and that's a fact.

After that I picked the games I went to away from home. I now have a season ticket at the new stadium but, as I said, the atmosphere isn't anything like the Vetch. It's a lovely stadium but it just hasn't got the intimidating atmosphere. Those days are long gone. It's a different type of audience now. The boys' day out for a few pints and a row is almost over. The fans have been taken out of football now and replaced with expressionless robots. It's a whole new world. We now have a bit of a youth movement who are trying to get things going but it's more about designer clothes and bravado than having a punch up. They wouldn't have survived at places like West Ham and Liverpool in the 80's. We took 12,000 fans up to Anfield for a game when we were top of the old First Division and when we had the likes of Leighton James, Robbie James and Chris Murustik who is a cousin of mine who played in that team. But he then went on to play for Cardiff so I stopped speaking to him. These young boys today, as I say, wouldn't survive at places like West Ham and Spurs and Newcastle - it would probably be too much for them. Plus now, if you get caught fighting, it's no longer a £50 fine and a slap on the wrist and sent off on safari to Kenya for rehabilitation; it's a bit of bird or a hefty fine and a banning order. Over the years I've been to most lower league grounds with the Swans and these so-called smaller clubs sometimes have nasty tight little firms. Take Lincoln City, who I give total respect to, they only have 50 or 60 boys at home but they could mix it with the best and fair play to them. Bristol Rovers and Hull City are another two that spring to mind. Mansfield are not bad, as well as Wolves and West Brom and the other Bristol club, City. Plymouth are not bad at their place but never travel to Swansea where we play a lot of teams - excuse is it's too far to travel to Swansea for a game. But look at it from our point of view, every game away is a long way for us. Most games we have to leave at 6 o'clock in the morning. Now that's dedication. We recently took 150 lads to Hull which is eight hours away and two weeks later we took a firm up to Carlisle which is another long old haul for a small club. We have a decent support both home and away. I think, if we ever made it into the premiership, a lot of firms coming to Swansea would have a shock. If we played the likes of Tottenham or Arsenal or Chelsea we'd take 400 to 500 boys up to London. We'd give the likes of Everton and Man Utd and Liverpool a run for their money on our day. I'm blowing our trumpet but, on our day, we can live with anybody. But saying that, nowadays the police in most parts of the country have the trouble sewn up. At one stage, we had over 70 boys on these banning orders. Plus drugs, nowadays, takes a lot of the boys. We've lost a few good lads to drugs. We've had boys die as well as go off the rails. It seems Charlie has taken over the planet .

FIRST CLASS THUGS

The idea began on a night out with friends. Whilst sat in the St George pub in Swansea, the talk soon turned to the forthcoming derby versus Cardiff. The ban on the away fans had been in place for nearly ten years and the only way to see the game was in the police operated 'Bubble trip'. We were talking about all sorts of ways we could get into Cardiff unnoticed when, all of a sudden, my wife Claire suggested "Why don't you use limo's ?" It was a stroke of genius, it had never been done before and, if executed correctly, I was sure it would get us past the police's ring of steel. I was so excited about this plan and was dying to tell all the boys but, for this to work and for us not to be rumbled by the Old Bill, I was gonna have to keep quiet and keep it to myself.

The plan was set. Claire booked six limousines from different companies in her name to throw the police off the scent and we were set to leave from the Marquis Arms which was close to the northern exit of the M4; away from police spotters. The limo's would leave two at a time at fifteen minutes intervals starting at 4pm. Once again, to keep the police off the trail, we booked them saying we were going to see Enrique Inglesias at the CIA - I even had the event details sent to me and kept them in my back pocket. Our target was the Borough pub in the city centre which the Soul Crew frequented. If we could get in there undetected, it would be one hell of a result. We had fifty of our top boys, every one well game and sure to give Cardiff a stiff test. Cardiff had never attempted to break the ban, a ban that was unprecedented in British football. No other derby has been run under such strict regulations for such a long time as this game was the most violent per ratio of fan in the football league. They could police Rangers vs Celtic and Man U vs Liverpool but they couldn't police ten thousand Welshmen. I felt as if this was going to be my day and the plan was my 'Baby' so I was determined for it to work.

A few days before I bumped into Lyn Phillips, the football liaison officer and, as usual, he was fishing for information. He told me ...

"You'll never get to the city centre. It's impenetrable, surrounded by a ring of steel. There's no way past."
"We'll see," I replied. He gave me a wry smile which told me it was game on. I couldn't wait to see his face when we got there.

The day began with the boys meeting in the Railway Inn close to the site of the new Liberty Stadium. From the moment I woke up that morning, I had the feeling of anxiety in the pit of my stomach. Whatever happened, whether we got there or not, without any shadow of a doubt, we would be arrested but myself and fifty odd others would see this through no matter what. It was a 'shit or bust' situation and, fair play to our determined crew, they were going to do it for the 'Cause' and didn't give a fuck about the outcome. Whilst the boys downed their beers, I stayed sober hoping that everything would go to plan. I felt responsible to get everyone to Cardiff but, once there, the pressure would be off and I could

Chapter 1 - TOOZEY

enjoy myself. As long as we got there to show face was all that mattered. The boys were getting quite rowdy now and it was time to make our way up to the Marquis Arms in a fleet of taxis. The Marquis Arms was a family pub and 'Dull Martin' had warned me about the landlord who didn't like football boys so, instead of letting loose fifty hooligans in his joint, I sent half of the lads down to the Ivorites Arms, a hundred yards down the road. It was more of a drinking man's pub.

I was going through the full range of emotions now; anticipation of what awaited us, fear of arrest, anxiety in case the limo's didn't show, hope in that the boys could keep a lid on things until we got on our way but, most of all, anger and aggression, the hatred we all felt toward scum was like a volcano inside you ready to erupt. My relief at the sight of the first limousines turning up was overshadowed by the boys elation and surprise at their first class transport. Each one was equipped with a bottle of champagne for them to fight over. I had kept the limo's under wraps until they arrived and the look on the lads faces was priceless.

The lads were split up into groups of ten and eight and were set off on their way at fifteen minute intervals, ours being the last to go. Inside the limo, it was champagne all the way. At last the pressure was off and I could enjoy myself. In our car we had some of the top lads in Tracy, Stacko, Wallis, Alan, Dai, Wayne, Thomo, and Aggis and his boy. We were well up for it and confident of a result against any opposition.

When you had a tight group of fifty like this with no runners, you knew that someone would always watch your back. The closer we got to Cardiff, the less anxiety I felt. Every bridge we passed, the police ignored us. Every junction of the M4 was manned with a police car but still they failed to notice the hooligan filled limo's with us tucked away from sight behind tinted glass. But we knew we were in when we came off the M4 onto the roundabout which was swarming with police. So much for Lyn Phillips' ring of steel. Toozey's Trojan horse was in !

The only problem with leaving at staggered times was that we didn't have control over the individual limo's and communication was a problem. As we drove down the western approach to Cardiff, we could see Cardiff lads making their way to the game in small groups. It was very tempting to stop the limo and give them a pasting but the objective was clear. We were to hit their pub which meant no fucking about on the way there. Alas, without overall control of the limo's, George decided to get out of his at the Ninian Park pub, walking in and challenging the occupants. This act of indiscipline cost us dear as the landlord notified the police of a group of Jacks in a limousine. Until this point, we had been undetected. It was too late for the police to apprehend the first two limo's but, by the time we reached the city centre, they were on the lookout and were stopping all limousines. The first two were already on the streets of Cardiff and had made their way to the Borough pub only to find it empty. Cardiff knew we were on our

LUXURY LOUTS

Police at full stretch

Rioters left in lim(b)o

SUSPECTED hooligans from Swansea hired luxury stretch-limos in an attempt to outwit police trying to prevent trouble in Cardiff city centre.

Smartly dressed in collars and ties yesterday, the 32 fans had a cover story that they were on their way to attend an Enrico Iglesias concert at Cardiff International Arena.

They hired at least four vehicles in Pontypridd to try to throw police experts in soccer hooliganism off the track.

All knew they could not get in to the game because only fans on organised coaches had tickets.

They were held at police stations across the capital until after the Welsh Premier Cup Final between Swansea City and Cardiff City at Ninian Park was over.

None was charged but today Swansea City spokesman Peter Owen warned: "If police give us their names and addresses we will ban them all.

"We got £50,000 as runners-up in this match but if we got charged with bringing the game into disrepute we could lose it in fines and everybody knows in our situation it is money we could ill-afford."

There were scuffles in St Mary Street, Cardiff, before the match, and afterwards outside Ninian Park when

Swans fans returning to a fleet of 28 buses exchanged missiles with Cardiff supporters.

Chief Inspector Graham McCarthy, who was ground commander for the match, said: "We know the 32 left Swansea early and they were in Cardiff several hours before the match.

"They were identified and arrested and put them on the 10.40pm train back to Swansea."

At one stage after the match Swansea supporters broke down a barrier keeping the two groups apart and were forced back by a charge of police horses and riot clad officers.

Police are studying closed circuit television footage taken outside the ground, and troublemakers could face retrospective prosecution.

Horses and police with riot shields forced them back to the buses.

Police said after the game that two Cardiff followers were arrested in the course of the evening.

The Swansea people arrested before the game were aged 16 to 43.

Police were on high alert again today ahead of tonight's international between Wales and Germany at the Millennium Stadium.

AT A STRETCH: Type of limo used by yobs

Football thugs hire limos to dodge cops

SOCCER hooligans hired a fleet of luxury stretch limos in a bid to sneak past police and attack rival fans.

The yobs even donned smart shirts and ties and pretended to have tickets for an Enrique Iglesias concert to get past rigorous security checks.

Police anticipated violence between Cardiff City and Swansea fans as the teams met in the Welsh Cup final.

But at least six white limos managed to get into Cardiff city centre three hours before the match at Ninian Park.

Police swooped to arrest 32 Swansea fans two miles from the ground minutes after climbing from the limos.

The suspected thugs were put in cells until after the match ended under police powers that they "threatened to create disorder".

But the arrests failed to stem trouble as bricks and bottles were thrown between rival fans after Monday's match, which Cardiff won 1-0.

Police feared it could have been worse if they had not arrested the 32 limo-travelling fans.

The men – from Swansea and aged 16 to 43 – were arrested on suspicion of being about to cause trouble.

They had travelled in the hired limos knowing they could not get into the game without tickets.

Only the 1,500 fans on official coaches had tickets for the clash.

Controversial Cardiff

City chairman Sam Hammam even picked up the £5,000 bill for the 28 coaches for Swansea fans in a bid to stop trouble.

The hooligans told limo hire firms they were travelling to a concert.

But they asked to be dropped off in the city centre – and started looking for rival Cardiff fans.

But police say they were quickly picked up in Cardiff bars because of their distinctive accents.

A spokesman for Swansea City said: "We are aware that these limos were hired by some people to get to Cardiff.

"If these people are identified to us by police we will ban them for life."

Chief Inspector Graham McCarthy of South Wales Police said: "It just seems they were intent to get into the city centre to look for trouble. But they were quickly arrested.

"They were released after the game and taken to the railway station to get a train home."

way but, to our disappointment, apparently they had had a poor show and stayed down by the ground in Canton. The phones were buzzing in our limousine with the lads warning us that the police had rumbled the plan but we had just turned onto St Mary's Street only to see the fleet of limo's surrounded by hoards of police and wagons. A police officer was in the middle of the street waving us over. We urged the driver to ignore him and drive past but he bottled it. We were gutted. We had been felled at the last fence all because one of our own lads had let us down and not followed the plan.

The police pulled us over outside a pizza shop. The street was full of people wondering what the fuck was going on with all these limousines and legions of police. People peered out of the windows, forgetting about their pizzas as the bizarre scene unfolded. One by one, they pulled lads out of the limo's, searching them in shop doorways then lining them up along the street in handcuffs.

Our limo was a left hand drive and I sat next to the driver's seat on the right. The police peered through the smoked glass windows trying to make out who was inside. One of the doors was opened for us to be confronted by many police officers with telescopic truncheons drawn. Alan was the first to be dragged out but he wasn't going peacefully. The police rained down blows on him as he kicked and punched them back until the barrage became too much for him. Eventually, they emptied our limo but I was still sat in the passenger's seat whilst the driver was being questioned. A police sergeant noticed me, tapped the window and motioned for me to get out. I mouthed to him "I'm the driver". He said "Oh sorry mate" and walked away. For a split second, I thought I might get away with this until another officer with pips on his shoulder opened the door and said ...

"Get out, clever cunt" - it was worth a try !

"Not so fucking clever now, are you ? Bet you lost a fortune cause you certainly ain't going back in these !" The officer motioned towards the limo's.

Travel thugs taunt police from limos

POLICE knew there was a high probability of trouble in Cardiff city centre on Monday afternoon before the Welsh Premier Cup Final at Ninian Park.

What they were not prepared for was the means of transport to get there — stretch limousines normally used for weddings, business and other formal occasions.

The were caught by surprise but they were quickly on their trail after they were picked up on CCTV, or their Swansea accents gave them away. Pubs either refused to serve them or tipped off police where they were.

Thirty-two people from the Swansea area were arrested, kept in custody until after the match, and then escorted onto a late night train out of Cardiff.

Considering the history of trouble between the fans of the two clubs the attempt was no real surprise. What was more worrying was that people travelling on the official convoy of buses were prepared to cause trouble afterwards.

All those arrested in Cardiff city centre were well known to police as 'prominents', always likely to be at the heart of any aggro, or their hangers on.

Others on the buses were previously unknown faces, and many are adults not fitting the traditional image of a teenage tearaway.

For the people who travelled by limo the day was 'a result.' Being locked up and missing the game will have concerned them little.

In their eyes they had succeeded in getting into the heart of enemy territory with their Cardiff rivals unaware of their presence.

The incidents have dismayed the new management at The Vetch. Ultimately if the club was charged with bringing the game into disrepute a large part of their £50,000 runners up fee for taking part in the Welsh Premier Cup Final could be swallowed up in fines.

TELEVISION programmes have highlighted how football hooliganism has developed into a sophisticated battle between police spotters and the yobs. Swansea City thugs almost caught them on the hop this week by hiring stretch limos to throw them off the scent.

Peter Owen, spokesman for the club, said: "If the police pass on the names and addresses to us we will exclude them from The Vetch permanently. We do not need or want these type of people."

Not wanting or needing them goes without saying. What to do about stopping them is an entirely different manner.

The new Swans management intends to emphasise the community aspect of having a Football League club, and most experts agree having the city or town name read out with the results every week projects a positive image.

They will be visiting or writing to every Nationwide League club asking them about their links with the local community.

The Wales against Germany match at the Millennium Stadium last night was the seventh big football game in Cardiff this month.

Fans of the English clubs who have played there have been enthusiastic about their visits to Cardiff, and Swansea undoubtedly gets a spin-off in hotel bookings and other trade.

Sadly, and predictably, the Swansea v Cardiff match produced the largest number of arrests in connection with what was, ultimately, the worst attended match of them all.

The two clubs are not due to meet next season unless they are drawn together in one of the cup competitions.

Apart from a few diehards, and of course the thugs, not too many people will be sorry.

"Don't think so pal. I only booked them one fucking way," I replied, waving the booking form in his face.

"You knew full well that there was no way you were going to go to the game."

"We're not going to the game, we're gonna watch Enrique Inglesias at the CIA," I said, pulling the ticket info out of my back pocket.

"Put the cuffs on this clever cunt," said the angry copper.

As they led me away, I saw Lyn Phillips. He just smiled and shook his head in disbelief. They took it so personal that we had won the 'cat and mouse' game and got past all the efforts they had put in to stop us; they just don't understand us.

We were all disappointed but didn't give a fuck about what was to happen to us as we had made it outside their main pub with another twenty inside. Cardiff were nowhere to be seen but they knew we were here as Wallis had seen Dai Jones, one of the authors of the Soul Crew book, walk past as he was being searched in a doorway. Once again, we upped the ante in the South Wales derby. No matter how much shit they could write on the internet or in books, it took the Jacks to break the ban for the first time. In fact, they never seem to write about our results. The Scum had never had it toe to toe with the biggest mobs in England in the Eighties at the height of the hooligan scene like we had. Leeds, Man U, Liverpool, Tottenham and many others had been challenged. They had never smashed our ground to pieces like we had done to theirs. They had never run us into the sea like we had done to them. They had never run us right around our ground with a small mob of forty like we had to them. We had certainly never locked ourselves in our own pub with a mob waiting outside. And they had never been in our pub and knocked out our top boy and his son after letting us know they were coming ! The only thing they could write about was their result in the FA Cup in '91 and that would have been a different story if most of us hadn't gone chasing after the buses ! The truth was that we held the upper hand in the derby games and the truth fucking hurts.

I was sat in the front seat of one of the police wagons on our way to the cells as the rest were all full. To lighten the mood, I put on a coppers helmet and turned to the boys in the back and said "You're all fucking nicked." The boys roared out with laughter as the Old Bill drove us to several different police stations. There was no booking in and no questioning so it was clear that there was to be no charges. We were all relieved as we expected to be charged with some made-up bullshit but, in the end, they just used the Section 60 to hold us until the game was over. They released us at 10 o'clock and sent us home on a train from Cardiff Central under a heavily outnumbered escort. The game, an FAW Cup Final saw us losing to a strong Cardiff side but, even without their top boys, the rest of the Swansea lads at the game pulled down the eight foot security fencing in the car park outside the ground and chased the Cardiff fans across the car park. TV footage showed one of the lads, Duffy, bulldozering the fence as the bricks flew. Even though we had missed the game, we still felt that we had we made a point and the boys at the game hadn't disappointed either.

I was delighted at the write ups in the papers with the Sun, Star, Mirror and Daily Mail running stories of 'First class thugs' fooling the police in a fleet of limo's going to watch Enrique Inglesias dressed in suits ? Where they got the suits from, fuck knows, but it gave me a great feeling of ...

'Yes, I done that'

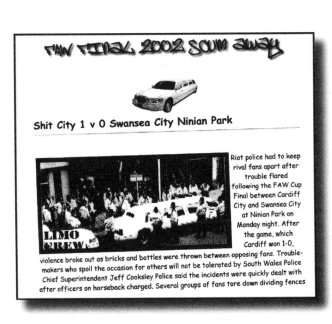

FAW FINAL 2002 SCUM AWAY

Shit City 1 v O Swansea City Ninian Park

Riot police had to keep rival fans apart after trouble flared following the FAW Cup Final between Cardiff City and Swansea City at Ninian Park on Monday night. After the game, which Cardiff won 1-0, violence broke out as bricks and bottles were thrown between opposing fans. Trouble-makers who spoil the occasion for others will not be tolerated by South Wales Police Chief Superintendent Jeff Cooksley Police said the incidents were quickly dealt with after officers on horseback charged. Several groups of fans tore down dividing fences

CHAPTER TWO
MICHAEL BULLER

I'm 51 years old now and I first started going to football when I was 14. The fashion then was skinheads. My first recollection of football violence was in 1971 when we played Aston Villa at home and I got thrown down the terraces. A lot of our boys in those days were teenagers, you know, 15 to 16. The Villa boys were in their 20s and had a few black faces as well. The majority of them were big bastards and arrogant with it. It was a third division game and they bought 8,000 fans down so you've got to give them credit. The thing in those days was to pinch other team's scarves. It was a sort of trophy thing - a sort of scalp. You'd slap someone and nick the scarf. It didn't matter if it was home-made and their Nan had knitted it. Portsmouth away in

WHO are the leaders of this gang?

The first person to spot himself in this picture dating back to September 1971 can have the original colour print.

The picture was snapped by Mr. Neville Jones, of Carmarthen Road, Swansea, as this gang of lads, probably Swansea City supporters,

basked in the sunshine on the perimeter wall at the Kingsway roundabout.

Mr. Jones takes up the story: "I used a 300mm. lens and thought they hadn't spotted me, until the boy in the white pullover ran over to me asked me what paper I was working for.

"I quickly said the Liverpool Mercury! Suitably impressed,

he ran back to tell the others, by which time I had discreetly disappeared.

"They are probably in their early thirties now. About the only thing that hasn't changed since those days in 1971 is that Swansea are back in the third division, as they were then.

"If any of the gang recognises themselves the first one to come forward can claim the print," said Mr. Jones.

'71 in the FA Cup was a shock to us. They were all dockers and off ships and our average age must have been about 16 whereas they were about 25 to 30 - and all huge big fuckers. And they all came together to get the Welsh. They kicked the fuck out of us.

Not blowing my own trumpet but over the years it seems I have built up a certain reputation at Swansea. Maybe I used to get stuck in where others would stand back and wait. I would never ask anyone to do something I wouldn't do myself. If we came face to face with another mob, I'd be the first in, no matter what the odds. The buzz and not knowing the outcome - I loved it. I loved pitting myself against people I knew nothing about. I've been arrested many times for trouble at football and I've even been to prison for it. My first offence was when I was 14. I've never been arrested at an away match, only at home - now how's that for a record ? That could even become a Trivial Pursuit question, couldn't it ? In those days there were no cameras or CCTV but I still managed to get caught. How daft was I ?

As for football intelligence - there was no such thing. I say that but, in 1975, we played Lincoln City away and we took 140 boys up there on two coaches. On the way up, we stopped in Birmingham. Man Utd were playing down at Southampton and a couple of coach loads of their fans had stopped. There were the usual jibes of "sheep shaggers" and "Welsh bastards" so we went at them and ended up giving a few of them a bit of a kicking. When we got back to our coaches, the Old Bill were waiting for us. "Right," they said. "Forty five on that coach, and 45 on that coach." And they loaded two coaches up but that still left 40 boys standing by the roadside. They couldn't work it out. So they piled the rest of us onto the two coaches. Everything was fine for about five miles as we made our way up the motorway then we were pulled over by the police who pulled us off the coaches and took our photos with a Polaroid camera, one at a time. I had a bit of a laugh with them because I had my picture taken and then got back in the queue and had it done again. I kept doing it until one of the coppers recognised me and tumbled what I was up to. They threatened to nick me for wasting police time. I kept my mouth shut but wanted to say "How about you wasting my time ?"

We get back on the bus and get to Lincoln where we lose 4 - 0, arrived late and missed the first goal - which wasn't a bad thing. At the end of the game, we come out and there's a river which has a few bridges over it. On the other side are about 20 Lincoln fans calling us names and goading us into a fight. Seven of us manage to get across one of the bridges but, before we get into them, a police van screeches to a halt and coppers jump out with truncheons drawn. The Lincoln boys run around a corner so we follow. As we turn the corner, there's hundreds of them waiting for us. We now have a choice - have it with the Lincoln or go back to the Old Bill and get arrested. There's only seven of us and they can now see that so they let out a big roar and come towards us. But, before they could reach us, there's a skip so we load up and let them have it. I had a lump of 3'x 2' in my hand and, at that time, Kung Fu films were all the rage. This geezer comes flying through the air at me, thinking he's Bruce Lee and I've crashed the bit of wood down straight on his head and down he went like a sack of potatoes. A couple of the boys actually climbed inside the skip and were digging for gear to throw. We gave them a right seeing to. They backed off and we went back towards the ground where, standing in lines, were rows of Old Bill. We were all thinking, "we're well nicked here." They've seen the lot, they've witnessed the whole fight but, as we walked up to them, they've parted like the Red Sea and let us through - not a word. We got on the coaches and off we went.

In the 80's, every team - town and city - had a mob of some sorts who were willing to have a go and make a bit of a show, especially against Swansea. They'd see it as an England v Wales thing. A lot of teams use the excuse that it's a long way down to Swansea for a game but, if the truth be known, any mob that came down here knew they were in for a rough time. Travelling's a piss poor excuse. We travel to away games, mostly in big numbers. In the early days we used to have a tight little crew of 50 boys whereas teams like Man Utd and Chelsea and West Ham had a mob of thousands, yet we'd still make a show and do well. We had a motto "We never run" and that was true.

We went to Southend for a game on a 52-seater coach and we'd only been there a short while when it kicked off with some locals and the Old Bill. We were now down to just 22 of us when we reached the ground. Out of that coach there was only 18 of us, the rest had been nicked for fighting. Mad, mad days.

Now playing Cardiff was different. It was fun and games and you didn't have to go looking for them - there was that many of them, they weren't hard to find. In the end, you'd get fed up whacking the thick fuckers. I went with a mate of mine to a Wales v Scotland game in Cardiff and we ended up in the Grange which was a Cardiff boys' pub. We had a pint and all these boys packed in there were singing Cardiff songs. Then the chant went up, "Swansea, where are you ? Swansea, where are you ?" My mate shouts out at the top of his voice. "Here we are !" and points at me and him. A circle of bodies opens up around us. "Get 'em," someone shouts and they piled into us. We got a right kicking but it could have been worse as there was that many of them they didn't have the room to get right into us.

Another sort of derby is when we play the Bristol teams, Rovers and City but I've always rated Rovers better than City. Rovers have always had a good crew, I've got to give them credit. We played them one time at Tiverton Park after they'd moved from their old ground. Four of us travelled over there as we'd just missed the bulk of our boys. Me, Rabbit, Miller and Dai Bevan found a pub near the ground so we ventured in. I ordered four pints and everything seemed to be cool. Next thing, this head's come through a window which led into the bar next door.

"You bastards !" he said in his Wurzel accent. "You can have it now."
I had a sip of my beer. "Come and get us" I said.

What I didn't know was that the pub was full of their boys who were outside drinking in the beer garden. I carried on drinking my pint when they all came piling in. One bloke had a newspaper rolled up and unwrapped it and pulled out a big carving knife. I punched one cunt and hit another over the head with a wooden stool. I had bottles raining down on me. Next minute, they've picked up the fruit machine and thrown it at us. The police came in and broke it up and we headed towards the ground.

Once inside I climbed up on a fence to have a look around. A copper came up on the other side and told me in his West Country drawl to get down.

"Get down off that fence !"

"Make me!"

"Do you know what I am ?"

"Well, you have a police uniform on, so I'd say a policeman, you thick cunt."

"Get down!"

"No, come in and get me, you English cunt." He left it at that and walked away.

Just for a bit of fun one weekend we decided to go up to Leeds to watch them play West Ham. There was no trouble as the East London boys failed to show. We caught the train back down south and it stopped at Crewe where on jumps a group of about 20 Man Utd fans. Me and Billy are sitting there minding our own business when these United fans enter our carriage. Next thing this huge, big geezer about 6' 6', who's obviously their leader, is standing in front of us. He turns to his gang standing behind him and sneers "Skinheads". Me and my mate have cropped hair and, for some reason, have our Swansea scarves on. I looked at Billy and we both laughed.

"He's got to have it, eh Bill ?" And he nodded.

"Have a look," sneered this giant shithouse. "He's got Dr Marten Bovver Boots on, he must be hard."

I'd had enough of this cunt now, so I said to Billy. "You take the one on the left and I'll take the cunt on the right."

"You was in the paper recently saying how hard you was," said Billy, taking the piss out of the big-headed giant.

He nodded and smiled with arrogance oozing from every pore. He was now giving it the right big one in front of his mates. Then Bill jumps up and cracks him on the jaw and knocks him clean out. The rest run but they can't go far as they've reached the end of the train. I've got a rolled up umbrella in my hands and as they cower from me, I'm lashing out and battering the fuck out of them as they plead for mercy. They're not so brave now old Billy Big Bollocks as been knocked out by my mate, Billy Little Bollocks. After a while I get bored of hitting this pack of bullies and leave them crying and snivelling in a heap. When I get back to where I'd been sitting, I can see a pair of legs being dragged towards an open door as the train is speeding along. Billy is trying to throw the geezer he's knocked out off the moving train. I have to intervene and persuade Billy otherwise and, thank fuck, he sees sense.

Me and bother have never been far apart when it comes to football. Another time, a few of the lads from Swansea went up to Elland Road to watch Leeds play Liverpool. Fourteen of us made the trip with seven of us following Leeds and the other seven supporting Liverpool. We went into a pub in Leeds which was chock-a-block with Leeds. I had a nosey around and came across a set of double doors.

"What's through there ?" I asked a geezer with a Leeds scarf draped around his neck.
"Oh, you can't go in there," he said, "It's full of the away supporters."

I pushed the doors open and, sure enough, all you could see was red and white.

"What the fuck's going on here ?" I asked.
"It happens every other week," said a couple of Leeds fans.
"It wouldn't happen in Swansea."
"What do you mean it wouldn't happen in Swansea ?"
"I'll fucking show you !"

So with that, I've dived through the air, hit this Scouser and sent him flying onto a table full of drinks which have gone everywhere. Tracy's come flying in behind me, followed by the rest of the Leeds fans. It's now going off big time. Within a minute the pub was wrecked and the police came and shut it down. I think I showed the Leeds fans that day how not to behave. This was well before the Leeds Service Crew was even thought of. I instilled a bit of Welsh fire and temperament into the Yorkshiremen that day.

I wonder if they still let away fans into the pub after that ?

CHAPTER THREE
TRACY NECREWS

I'm 49 years old and the first game I ever went to down at the Vetch was against Arsenal in front of a 32,000 crowd. I was only about nine - and what an atmosphere ! The old Vetch field was rocking that day, believe me. Billy Pridmore and Michael Buller were skinheads in those days and were a couple of our main faces. From that day on football hooliganism grew in my mind and I wanted to be part of it. As I grew older, I ran with the firm and most Saturday mornings it was a matter of getting up and putting the clobber on. Pull on the old Dr Martens' button up the Ben Sherman, do up the jeans hanging half way up my ankles and I was out the door ready for action. That Arsenal game was about 1969 and there was trouble inside and outside the ground. The local market got wrecked with stalls tipped up and smashed.

One Boxing Day, when I was about 12 years old, we had Aston Villa at home and they had convoy after convoy of coaches coming into Swansea - the Brummies were everywhere. Me, Pete and Doddy were hanging around town in the morning and it was just going off all over the place - the police just couldn't cope. We went up to the ground early as Villa were in our North Bank. A mob of them were standing at the back singing and chanting and were well pleased with themselves. Our boys were mobbing up outside the turnstiles and it was decided that half of us would go in one entrance and the rest would come at them from the other entrance into the ground. About 200 of us went in one way and the rest came at them from the opposite way. "Come on, we're here !" went up the shout and Villa were running down the terraces and out of our end. A few of their black geezers with shaved heads made a bit of a stand but, with no police there to protect them, they didn't have a chance. Villa ended up on the pitch and the police with dogs surrounded them. They were taken off into the West Bank with order restored. After the game, our boys filled the streets behind their end and Oxford Street and Western Street was just filled with boys waiting for the Villa to come out. They were held in for ages but, when they came out, it was bedlam. In those days, the Old Bill didn't have much of a clue. If they caught you fighting, they'd clip you around the ear. If they had a dog, they'd let it have a bit of you - that was your punishment. It was mental, not like nowadays.

Over the years, we've had some good firms come to Swansea but I'd have to say Chelsea have been the best. We played them in the league in '80/'81 and it was their last away game of that season. We heard they would be bringing five or six thousand fans down and they didn't disappoint. On the day of the game, we were all in a town centre boozer early and we were out in numbers. The Garibaldi Pub and the Park Pub were stacked out. Chelsea's boys steamed into Swansea from all angles - they had mobs everywhere. We started fighting with some of them and we ended up down near the Wyndham Pub. At this stage we had them on their toes heading towards the Garibaldi. We cut down a few back alleys and lanes and met them head on outside the pub. This time they stood and it went toe to toe. What we didn't know was that someone was taking photos that would later appear in the local paper.

This was only 12:30 - 1:00 and it was going off all over the place. A few of their boys got in the North Bank before the game but they got sussed by the coppers and were slung out. After the game, we had a massive mob out and we tried to steam the coppers with bricks and bottles but they wouldn't shift as we tried to get to the Chelsea fans. We continually tried to attack the escort with no luck. We tried on Western Street and were beaten back by the coppers. A mob tried again on Oxford Street with no luck and then again we charged them on St Helen's Road but were moved back by coppers with dogs. We decided another plan of attack - to let the bulk of our mob move off and the rest of us to head to the Queen's where there was a good chance we could cut them off. Near the YMCA, we saw a mob of Chelsea that had slipped out of the escort and away from the law. They came towards us and I remember thinking, 'this is it'. We had a good mob of 200 boys but this Chelsea mob meant business and came straight into us. They steamed us and were all over our boys. We just couldn't handle them - they were as rough as fuck and as game as fuck. They stuck together like glue and never once split up. That was like a lot of Cockney firms, they stuck together and were very well organised. I ended up walking up the road towards the train station in the middle of this Chelsea firm when a couple of them sussed me out. Just outside Stride's the Jewellers, one of them came running towards me and punched me in the side of the head. "You Welsh bastard !" I went down in the doorway and took a few kicks to the head. I got up, gathered my senses, rallied a few boys that had seen what had gone on and got my revenge on a couple of the Chelsea back stragglers. We arrived at the station and the Old Bill had it sealed off with dogs and vans so me and a few of the boys went back to the Swan pub for a drink. There must have been 20 or 30 of us sitting in the little bar. We were on our first pint when one of our boys, Noddy, came in and said they he'd just seen a mob of Chelsea up near the Kingsway, heading in this direction. We came out of the pub and there they were. It went off and they got the better of us and a few of the boys took a bit of a kicking and then we headed back to the pub.

Later on that evening, word was going round that Chelsea were still in town. We got a mob together and caught them near British Home Stores. This time, we were ready and better organised and got in amongst them and kicked the shit out of a few of them. We did outnumber them but we showed we were up for it. Before that game, Billy Pridmore and some of the boys were drinking in the Buccaneer and a Chelsea mob appeared. We came out and, at the time, Littlewood's Store was just being built so there was scaffolding and bricks lying about. Jeff Burns, the doorman, told us straight, "If you go out, you ain't coming back in. I ain't having trouble at my pub."

We squared up and a Chelsea geezer asked Billy who was the top boy. Billy replied "I am." So the two of them squared up. Crash ! Billy caught this geezer with a punch and it was all over as we backed them off up the road. Bobby Holland, one of ours, had been on the Littlewood's building site and was armed up to the teeth with poles and bricks. We ran them all over the shop a couple of times. They tried to make a stand but we just overran them. We booted them everywhere - but what a day ! Chelsea were as game as fuck.

That was the first time I ever saw someone wearing those green nylon flying jackets with the orange coloured lining. At the time, we were wearing tank tops and really baggy jeans and capped sleeved T-shirts. Music-wise I was into Tamla Motown and a bit of Northern Soul, then it was The Jam and a bit of punk - although not many punks ran with the football boys and sometimes the skinheads and the punks would clash on a Saturday night. If we had nobody to fight with after the football then the punks got it. We'd go into the Coach and Horses, get in amongst them as they were jumping up and down pogo'ing and spitting and we'd stick the head on them and it would kick-off.

When we got into the old Second Division, we went as a mob to every away game. So I took it upon myself to organise some coach travel to games. I'd run a 52-seater and, the week before the game, take a deposit off anyone that intended on travelling. Sometimes we'd end up with 70 boys squeezed on a coach. It isn't like today where, if the police spotted you, they'd send you back. You could take as much beer on board as you liked. They were mad, mad trips. We'd be on the piss all night before we left, more booze on the journey and we always planned to arrive at where we were playing at the latest by 11 o'clock in the morning. I always used Ken Hopkins' Coaches with Raymond, the driver, who was as mad as a March hare. If I weighed in with a few bob he'd do anything. We'd say "Ken, can you stop at such and such ?"

His reply would be "Weigh in."

I'd have a collection among the lads and weigh him in and he would be as sweet as a nut. He always gave us a good trip and took no notice of any instructions he'd received from his office about meeting up with the police for an escort off the motorway and towards the ground. If we were going to Manchester, he'd come off the motorway the exit before the back way in. He never did as he was told by his bosses. He was brilliant and loved a pound note. He'd always find us a little boozer out of the way in some little village and, by the time we'd get to the game, the whole bus would be steaming - we would be paralytic. That's why most of the time we arrived in a fair-sized mob and go on the home team's terraces.

Violence-wise we were always involved in something away from home. In '92 we played Brentford away and I ran two minibuses. We had a booze before the game, watched the match with no trouble and then boarded the buses after having a few pints a couple of miles away from the ground. Before we reached the buses parked up near the ground, I noticed a group of fellers running towards us waving baseball bats around. Now we're all strung out along the road, most of us pissed as farts with no idea of what was going on. I pointed to George who quickly realised what was going on and stood in the middle of the road . I stood to his right and a few of the lads stood to his left. The first boy into us is waving a snooker cue around and he catches me on top of my head with it. My head splits open as the cue snaps in half and the boys give him a kicking. As he got up, I thought to myself, "Right, you cunt, you're getting it now." I was in such a temper, he backed off trying to slip away and I steamed into him. He went down and he took another pounding. I ended up having 15 stitches in my head and still have the scars to this day. We left this mob on the floor in a heap but we first had to hide from the police on a sort of allotment. In the end, two of the boys drove the minibuses to where we were hiding, we all jumped on board and made it back to Swansea. I was covered in blood with a silly little plaster trying to stem the flow of blood.

When I was a youngster, Leeds Utd were a team I followed closely. They were my second team, so to speak. We played them one time down here and lots of Yorkshiremen arrived in Swansea. On the night before the game, the Leeds fans took over nearly every pub in town. Lots of their lads had suede sheepskin coats on and didn't give a fuck about walking around town. They had some right old heads in their firm. We were drinking in the Park and about 200 of them turned up outside and wanted us to come outside and mix it with them. A few of our lads were up for it but they had such huge numbers nothing happened. A few of the Leeds fans had slept down on the beach on the Friday night; they were everywhere. On the day of the game, they were all over the Mumbles Road and Stacko ended up knocking one of them out. They were the good old days with Liverpool, Man Utd, West Ham, Arsenal and Spurs all turning up down here. The Swans won that Leeds game 5 - 1 with the crowd around me singing ...

"Tracy, Tracy, what's the score ?"

CHAPTER FOUR
AGGIS

I've been going to Swansea games since about 1969. My first game at the Vetch was a Welsh Cup game against Cardiff and my old man took me. Lots of the Cardiff fans arrived on double-decker buses. I was only about 12 and the whole event was just amazing. There was trouble all through the game and I could feel the buzz. I looked at the old man and he was glued to the game. He wasn't the slightest bit interested in the fighting.

Even in those days I was very fashion conscious and used to wear a brown shiny jacket with different colours on the arms, with corduroy trousers and big hob-nailed boots. I thought I looked the bollocks. Then around 1970, the skinhead fashion of Crombies, Ben Shermans and Dr Martens appeared on the North Bank. Caffer, one of our lads, used to shop in London a lot and as far as I can remember he brought the skinhead look down to Swansea. Every Friday night, all the young skinheads would meet at the Canoldrun Youth Club and listen to Reggae music and early Slade. I used to look at a few of the older lads and clock what they were wearing and try to copy them. My favourite look was the Ben Shermans with the braces, turned-up jeans and the cherry red Dr. Martens. Later on I got a Harrington jacket. Before long, all of the Swansea North Bank were skinheads.

After the game, we used to meet up in College Street and attack the away fans. Sometimes there'd be two or three hundred of us ready for action. The top boys in those days were Ray Tilley, Parkins, Dude, Pixie, Michael Buller and Billy Pridmore who were all a couple of years older than me. Those boys were always up for it and our main rivals in those days were the two Bristol teams and Aston Villa who came down here twice in big numbers. I remember the first time we played Villa the newspaper ran the headline '500 Bother Boys Expected In the City Tomorrow'. So that alerted all our skinheads to turn out. On the day of the game, they came down on Football Specials and there were hundreds of them. They were more organised on the day and a lot of the Swansea fans got filled in. Keith Spooner, who was a big local skinhead, led a mob of Swansea across the pitch to attack the Villa fans. The second time we played them was a Boxing Day and we were better organised and caught a trainload of them early that day in the city centre. It went off before, during and after the game.

Arsenal was another big skinhead firm to come down here in the late 60's.

They brought hundreds of skins down and a few people have credited them with having and creating the original skinhead look. They went mental after the game and smashed the market to pieces. They went through it like a whirlwind.

Cardiff were another skinhead mob who came on our North Bank one game and walked towards all us youngsters gathered there and gave the **'CEEEEARRRDIFFFF'** chant. There was a bit of a rumble as our older boys came in from behind them and filled them in. I remember it was a dark, cold Tuesday night game and lots of the Cardiff were asking the police if they could be let out of the ground. That was in '72 and most of our boys were still skins.

My first away game was down at Portsmouth in the F.A. Cup. We lost 2 - 0 and took a bit of a battering by their skins. It was a baptism of fire, that was. We had a good shop in the Arcade which sold all the skinhead gear but by'73 the original skinheads were no more and the suedehead was born and the fashion was then Rupert the Bear check trousers, loud, big collared shirts and fringe and buckle loafers. Musically it was glam rock with Sweet, Slade, T Rex, Bowie and Roxy Music. Bob Dylan was right - 'the times were a changing'.

The Buccaneer and The Park became our pubs to meet in and us youngsters who were now growing up kept our mob going. My first arrest came in '76 against Cardiff. I was on my mate's shoulders, trying to get a look at the Cardiff mob who were packed under the double-decker stand when someone grabbed my shoulder from behind and pulled me off. I thumped this geezer and he turned out to be a copper. I was marched across the edge of the pitch and that was my lot. When we played them at their place that season we caught the train from Swansea early. We slapped a few of their boys at Port Talbot and, when the train pulled in at Bridgend, there were 20 or so of their boys on the platform dressed in big sheepskin coats. By the time the train pulled away, there was a pile of bodies lying there where they'd tried to escape up the steps to the street. Gary Walley, one of ours, walked into a cafe and sparked a Cardiff fan clean out. That was it. It was going off all the way down to the ground. We went straight into their Grange End singing 'Swansea' and they came in behind us and it was going mental. The Old Bill rounded us up and stuck us into the Bob Bank but the fighting still carried on all throughout the game. Afterwards, there was the odd scrap and scuffle but the Old Bill had it sorted. I think we caught Cardiff on the hop that day as they were a bit disorganised. I reckon they didn't believe we would show. After that game, they were always up for us. During the 70's and the Home International games, Swansea and Cardiff would even stick together.

That all changed in the 80's and now they'd go looking for us if we're about at a Wales game.

CHAPTER FIVE
STACKO

My name ? Paul Stack. But everyone knows me as Stacko, for obvious reasons. I'm 45 years old and I've been going to watch the Swans since I was 9. My first game was against Bristol Rovers and I went with my Dad and brother who's five years older than me. One of the first things I noticed was the dress code. Lots of the boys were dressed in Ben Shermans, had shaved heads and wore Dr Martens and braces.

As the years went by I followed the lads, started drinking in the pubs and, basically, got into the football scene. It was a huge adrenalin buzz. Wallis, Boxer, Ginger and Terry Davies were a few of the lads I knocked around with. My first recollections of seeing any violence was when we had Brentford down at the Vetch and the police were escorting a couple of hundred of them from the train station to the ground. Us youngsters were like moths to a flame and took everything on board.

When any visiting fans arrived in Swansea a buzz went round. There was an air of expectancy. The pubs in those days for the boys were The Park and The Prince of Wales but a lot of the boys used to hang around the side streets down near the ground. We were out defending our territory and, if invaders turned up, we were ready for them. That's how we saw them, as invaders. And we had the good name of Swansea to uphold. It was our patch and nobody was coming down here and taking the piss. We didn't win every battle but we didn't lose many either.

The biggest firms I've seen at Swansea over the years were teams like Man Utd, Leeds, Newcastle and Chelsea - that was when we were top of the old First Division. The Cockney Reds came down here with United and us youngsters couldn't believe the age of some of them. Lots of them were in their late 30s, early 40s - they were old enough to be our granddads. It was frightening. There were hundreds of them and it was a bit of a culture shock. Middlesbrough, Bristol Rovers, City and, of course, Cardiff, have all turned up in big numbers. But then, Cardiff have a big catchment area of fans. Their fans come from the Valleys, Barry, Merthyr, Bridgend, even Holyhead and Wrexham, right up into North Wales. It seems that everyone in Wales supports Cardiff and on the other hand everyone hates us Jacks. Most of the Welsh International games are held in

Cardiff so these little mining villages and towns seem to be blue-nosed bastards. We played them in '91 down here and Cardiff claim they came down here big time and ran the place ragged but that's not true. It did seem on the day that half of Wales had turned out against us but, to be honest, although they had a massive mob, we turned out in big numbers as well.

One mob of Cardiff were drinking in the King's Head down on the High Street. A couple of our youngsters went up and Cardiff wanted to know where our firm was. We were half a mile away in a boozer. As soon as it was confirmed that they were in the King's Head, 300 of us attacked the pub and they got annihilated. One of the boys actually filmed it and it's been doing the rounds for years. It was their main firm up against our main firm and they got battered. The thing was that all our firm know one another and we operate as one unit whereas their mob, as I say, come from all over Wales, so some of them haven't got a clue who they're standing fighting with. There's even some in-fighting among the Cardiff boys. The Barry boys and the Cardiff boys themselves don't get on.

But the days of having battles with visiting fans is now a thing of the past. Cameras and CCTV have put paid to that. The 70's and 80's days will never come back and to me that was when the fashion was in its heyday. We used to love our clothes and the music. I was even famous around town for my bright yellow Pringle jumper. In those days, a Pringle was expensive and I thought I looked the bollocks. As I say, those days are over - nowadays it's bans, fines or even prison. While we were doing it, it was great fun and all we can do now is sit back and laugh and joke about it and swap stories.

I do still run the odd away trip that takes my fancy. Tracy's stopped running his trips now so I've taken over from him and want to pay off my mortgage from the money, like he did. One game that springs to mind was a three minibus trip I ran up to Lincoln. The booze was flowing on the way up and the boys were in cracking form as the narcotics and lagers went down nicely. We were in Lincoln by midday so we parked up and had a stroll up the main street. Another mob from Swansea were already in the town so we were on the phone to them and arranged to meet them in the pub they were in. We passed a few pubs and a few of the locals gave us a bit of a look but nothing was said. A handful of us were ahead of the main group but we weren't bothered and we carried on walking. Then, in front of us, was a dozen or so skinheads standing at a bus stop. There was only three of us so these skinheads got right into us. The boys from the pub have seen what's going on and they've come steaming out. Lincoln's mob have appeared out of the pubs and our boys bringing up the rear have got involved. Within seconds there's a full scale battle going on in the middle of the street. These skinheads got smashed and it was only the Old Bill turning up that saved them. A few of the Lincoln boys even made a point of coming over to us when it had quietened down and shook our hands and told us "Well done, boys, you put on a good show." But, as I say, nowadays that sort of fight would be a one in a million. It just wouldn't happen without getting caught on camera.

Over the years, I've followed the Welsh football team and the thing with us Swansea boys is, we don't get organised for the International games. Recently we went out for the game in Ireland - 25 of us made the trip. We went across to Cork, spent the day there and then travelled up to Dublin. The Cardiff boys knew who we were and there was no real trouble. But previously we've had grief from them at away games. Five of us bumped into 300 of them on the ferry coming back from Holland and they sang all the Cardiff songs and anti-Jack songs. But they wouldn't take us on one to one - they're bullies. The same as in Milan for the Wales game. They outnumbered us but they came unstuck as we didn't buckle and bow down to them. I knocked one of them clean out and they were going down like flies.

To me, when the odds are in their favour,
they fancy it
but, one to one, they're nothing.

That's how bullies operate.

CHAPTER SIX
LITTLE DAI

I'm 40 years of age and I went to my first Swans game when I was three and a half years old. It was Arsenal at home in the FA Cup. My father took me to that game and I went to a lot of games with him. Me and him were at Cardiff in the two-legged semi-final Welsh cup. We were in the enclosure near the half way line and could see all the fighting in Cardiff's Grange End.

The return was on a Tuesday night and as we parked the car near the Vetch, there was fighting up and down the road with the Old Bill nowhere to be seen. The Welsh cup was a strange competition with not only Swansea, Cardiff, Newport and Wrexham but also the likes of Chester, Shrewsbury and Hereford. The old First Division days down at the Vetch were fantastic. The first year in the top flight we finished sixth and then the following year we were relegated. John Toshack did well for us and put us on the football map. We had a cracking side then as we were top of the league for a long time. If we'd had a decent keeper, I reckon we would have won the title the first year up.

I remember we played Portsmouth away and I was only 17 and all our boys were drinking in Portsmouth's main pub. The Old Bill came in and asked a few of us our age and who'd run the bus that brought us down. I just pointed at a crowd of blokes at the other end of the bar and the coppers fucked off. Afterwards, Pompey came along that little alley which runs along the back of the away end and it was very tight but we ran them back to the park behind the ground. To be fair, there wasn't many of them but they put on a bit of a show.

Millwall, though, was very different. We got there and the game had kicked off and we queued to get into Millwall's CBL. We paid to get in, walked up the concrete steps and made our way onto the covered terrace. We chased a few Millwall off and went and stood in the middle. There were about 70 of us and all was going well. We then noticed quite a chunk of the ground calmly strolling around the terraces towards us. In those days at Millwall, three sides of the ground was terracing and you could walk all the way round. Next thing, they came into us and ran us down to the front. Next minute we're standing on the edge of the pitch with the Old Bill leading us around the pitch to the other end of the ground. About 30 Millwall boys are in the seats and we gob off to them and give them the wanker sign. We think we're safe and get a bit brave but next minute there's a roar from behind us and 150 Millwall fans are running straight across the pitch heading in our direction. I remember one of them had a tool bag and he pulled out a hammer and was waving it about. They're definitely a different breed over there. It was the day before my 18th birthday and I remember it was the first game of the season. Simon, one of our boys, had made this speech on the coach about all sticking together. Only half of us had gone onto the pitch, the others were left in their end.

I couldn't believe how many black and half-caste geezers Millwall had in their firm. At Swansea, we don't have a single black face in the mob. We have a few boys who are into the BNP nowadays and have links with the Loyalists in Northern Ireland. I even keep a close eye on the Glasgow Rangers' results. We've had a few English follow the Swans - there's a lad from Millwall who comes to quite a few games and we used to have a lad from Basingstoke called Cockney Paul who was a Chelsea fan but followed Swansea.

For my stag do a few years ago, 86 of us football boys went up to Blackpool and we ended up fighting with the Jocks. I ended up having a drink with a few Rangers' boys and some of Airdrie's Section B boys. These boys are very much into the Loyalist side of things so I now go up there three or four times a year and join in the Parades. I've also been out to Belfast and now follow their politics very closely - the whole thing really interests me. I've even had the CID round the house asking me questions as to my reason for visiting Belfast. We even got a pull at Bristol Airport on the way out and the three of us were questioned about the Swansea flag we had with us.

I've only been there the once but was made really welcome and I'd love to go back again.

CHAPTER SEVEN
LEE'S STORY

INTRODUCTION

"C'mon Billy Bonds !" The voice cried out like it had been yelled in a library. I turned around to see a group of lads standing behind me. Time seemed as if it was stunned into silence. There was only a handful of them and none of them skinheads ! Dressed in faded jeans, white trainers and smart jackets, they stood out like sore thumbs among the local skinheads, punks and hooligans who usually frequented the back of the North Bank.

Then, in a split second, the deafening silence was smashed by that roar that every hooligan waits for - "Come on then !" The place erupted, the sound of rushing feet, which was to become all too familiar to me, blended into flurries of kicks and punches. Panic and confusion reigned for what seemed an age but was in reality just a few seconds then, all of a sudden, 'bang', I had been kicked straight in the nose as I crouched under the crush barrier to get away. The noise turned into echoes as my senses were knocked for six and, by the time I remembered where I was and came back to reality, the West Ham boys were gone, replaced by the might of the South Wales Constabulary.

Those few seconds changed me forever. Before, I had joined in with the songs 'We hate England' and 'You're gonna get your fucking head kicked in' just for bravado and posturing. Now I fucking meant it.

My journey into the world of the football hooligan would take me to the heights of full scale riots in a European tie in Greece to the depths of being hunted by what seemed every hooligan in London during a first round proper FA Cup tie at Lowly Hayes. Being a Swansea lad is a roller coaster ride but I loved every minute of it.

THE BEGINNING

I had flirted with football violence ever since that first encounter with the West Ham ICF in 1981. I had chucked bricks at Leeds fans sleeping on the beach front, dabbled with Everton's Mob on Oxford Street, and been chased by hundreds of Cardiff fans with my schoolmates after the Welsh Cup Final at the Vetch but it wasn't until I'd received a good hiding off Man Utd fans on Rodney Street that I realised how dodgy my thrill seeking habit was. It made me realise that I had to get to know the firm and to do that I would have to prove myself as one of the lads.

I had started hanging around with a younger lad from school called Jez who had an older brother called Nutty who was in with the Sandfields Hells Angels (SHA), a gang of hooligans from around the city centre. They, along with the Sketty Park Herberts, seemed to form the majority of Swansea's Mob.

Jez and I, along with a few others, had started going on the odd trip away together. We had a bit of a skirmish with Arsenal by the refreshment hut on the clock end at Highbury and one of our lads, Robbie Matthews, had stuck the head into a gang of Tottenham in the services on the way home from Brighton, causing a bit of a row which saw us being banned from travelling with the official away supporters club.

We had started drinking in a club called the Four J's on Northampton Lane, just off the Kingsway in the city centre. The Four J's was a strange looking place, dark and moody with 'Clockwork Orange' style murals on the walls - just the place for a gang of underage hooligans to get pissed up and fuck about in. The mob had grown considerably, a strange mix of tattooed skinheads and smartly dressed casuals. Farah slacks and cropped bleached jeans stood side by side at the bar and on the terraces. By this time, Swansea had slipped down from our brief stay at the top of the League back into the Second Division, which meant some tasty games against some top mobs like Sheffield Wednesday, Leeds, Portsmouth and, of course, Cardiff.

'83 - '84

First up was Sheffield Wednesday, who brought a huge following and finding some like-minded individuals was a simple task.

The Vetch Field ground is situated just off the sea front behind Swansea Jail. It is an old, antiquated ground - untidy, dark and moody. But to us it was home - a home we would fiercely protect. The ground is surrounded by residential houses and is a real rabbit warren - just the place for a good row away from the police. A big ruck could happen down one street with the Old Bill oblivious down the next and often it did. The day would start at eleven in the Four J's. Holsten Pils and vodka chasers were the order of the day, then off down the Sandfields to have a scout about. The older lads would be in The Badminton, a real rough house 200 yards from the ground in the Sandfields. We would scan the streets for lads but, if we came across a big mob, it was off down the 'Bad' to get the SHA.

Sheffield had pockets of lads here and there but we couldn't find a mob. We came across one lad who must have been in his late 30s - Nike windcheater, split and frayed jeans and trim trabs - a right lump of a lad.

Chapter 7 - LEE'S STORY

"What's the time mate ?" Phelps said.

"Fuck off you Taffy cunts !" he said as he jumped backwards, motioning as if he had a knife in his jacket pocket.

"Fucking slam him !" one of the lads shouted.

Pitson punched him as he swung out his arm just past Pitson's ear. "That was close," Pitson said as the lad sprinted away.

Now the blood was pumping and it was off to the match. Going up the tunnel into the North Bank always gave me a buzz. The bank was enormous, the full length of the pitch and, when in full voice, the noise would reverberate right through your chest. We would stand in the bottom corner of the North Bank, opposite the away fans in the lower tier of the double-decker West Stand where both sets of fans would hurl abuse at each other. The atmosphere would always have a little more needle about it than other teams I had been to see as it wasn't just Swansea versus whoever, it was Wales v England. We lost 1- 0 which made it worse. First game of the season lost 1- 0 at home and some leery Yorkshire cunt had tried to slice one of the boys ears off ! Time for some fun.

Rumour had it that the police had changed their normal routine of keeping the away fans' coaches in the Sandfields at the back of the West Stand and that they were going to march them across Mumbles Road into the County Hall car park. All the boys marched out of the ground at a quick pace down William Street. You could look behind you and all you could see was heads - the boys were chomping at the bit. It was always the same. You could feel the adrenalin pump up from your stomach into your chest; anticipation, anger and fear, all at once. There's nothing like it. As we spilled out of the narrow streets of the Sandfields onto the wide expanse of the Mumbles Road, you could hear the shouts going up.

"There they are !"

It was fever pitch now - everyone just started sprinting towards the Sheffield fans in the huge County Hall car park, dust spewing up from the gravel floor as the stampeding hooligans raced towards their foe. There's a split second, just before the first lads clash, everyone bouncing on the spot, then suddenly someone goes in. "Come on you English cunts !" The fists were flying. One lad falls over, the boots go in as he kicks out from the floor. Fights break out all over the place. The pain explodes in my shoulder as the police come wading in with those pathetically small truncheons they used to have, not like the telescopic steel batons they use today but fuck me they still hurt. The place was chaotic. The police had really fucked up and they wouldn't be parking the away coaches there again, that's for sure. Nobody had run, nobody had won and nobody had lost but our lust for the 'buzz' was satisfied and it was off to the pub to share stories.

Our breakthrough year was 1983. We hadn't been accepted by the older lads yet, especially by one called Boxer. He used to say "Get these fucking kids out of here !" every time we turned up but he would soon change his tune. By now, we could conjure up a fair mob. We had boys from all over Swansea. There was Bobby, Duffy, Nell and Hoppy from Trallwyn; Jez, Braino, Maylin, Lenny, Mojo and Sarsfield from town; Phelpsy, Newt, Tute and Nicky the Skin from Gorseinon, Lougher and Llanelli and me, Alan, Hywell and Phil Carter from the Mumbles. We weren't getting to many away matches as we couldn't get a driver for a rental van and didn't have enough for a 52-seater so most of the action would happen at home.

Apart from a dozen Cambridge fans coming on the North Bank and getting booted off, not much really happened in the beginning of the season until the arrival of Portsmouth in mid December. We didn't see many Portsmouth boys before the match but it soon became apparent that they were there when we got to the Vetch. Instead of going in the area allocated for away fans, their mob had gone in the upper tier of the new East Stand and were giving it the big one, especially as they were beating us 2 - 1. We all left before the final whistle and gathered by the bus garage on Clarence Terrace. It was a pitch black December evening and the tension was mounting as we waited for the Pompey boys to come out of the back of the East Stand. It was so dark you couldn't really make out who was who. Were they Swansea or were they Portsmouth ? We'd soon find out. They came bounding out of the stand and they were really up for it. We didn't stand a chance. There were far too many of them and they were men and they meant business - not 16 year old wannabees like us. They went through us like a dose of salts and then off up towards the Quadrant. I was absolutely gutted, ashamed and furious. How had they gone straight through us as if we weren't there ? I couldn't believe it.

I saw Stacko, one of the top boys, with his nose all over the place and blood soaking his Pringle jumper.

"What happened to you ?" I asked.
"Fucking had it right off with the cunts," he said.

Stacko was a big lad with hands like shovels - he wasn't going to run. He would stand and fight no matter what and that's why he was a top boy - something I wanted to be.

With the memories of the Portsmouth firm fresh in my mind, next up was the old enemy, Cardiff, away on Boxing Day. I had been to Ninian Park on several prior occasions and it was never a trip for the faint-hearted. Every previous trip had been by British Rails Football Special trains. Memories of these cramped Specials were always one of excitement and anticipation. You would board the train at Swansea Station and be herded into the oldest, mouldiest piece of rolling stock British Rail had in its fleet. It was like a car that hadn't passed its MOT and had been lying rotting in the garden for twenty years ! The train would be made up of compartments of eight seats facing each other with a sliding door to enter and an aisle with just enough room for two people to pass outside the compartment. The police would squeeze as many people as humanly possible onto the train, creating a 500 yard steel tube full of human sardines on wheels. How there was never a disaster was a miracle. On the journey, we would pull up at Neath and Port Talbot and then straight through to Ninian Park Halt. The train would be full of pissed up lads chanting all the terrace anthems dedicated to our hated cousins forty miles up the M4, "Cardiff City went to Rome to see the Pope" and "Chim chiminey, chim chiminey, chim chim cheroo, we hate those bastards in yellow and blue" and many more would blast out down the carriages until we reached the outskirts of the capital. Then the mood would change. Instead of laughing, joking and cheering there would be anger, shouting and jeering, you could feel the malevolence coming over the train like a dark cloud. Violence was in the air.

As you approach Ninian Park Halt, the track winds through the back gardens of the suburbs and over several bridges and it was at these bridges that there would be first contact. Just before reaching the bridges, the light bulbs in the compartments would be unscrewed and darkness would envelop the train. The boys would then squeeze out of the small sliding window, a feat of pure contortionism ! You could only get your head out by turning it sideways and putting one arm and shoulder out, just enough to aim and throw the glass projectiles. As the train passed over the bridges, you would hear "Cardiff cunts !" and then the unmistakable sound of the exploding light bulb as it missed its target and hit the street below Occasionally it would be a cheer as some poor sod would cop it. The fans were in a frenzied state by the time the train pulled up. The Halt was beside the bridge opposite the Ninian Park pub. As we made our way down the steep steps to the main road, the police would stop everyone as they tried to disperse the Cardiff fans on the street below. You could hear the stressed dog handlers screaming "Get fucking back !" as the boys behind would be pushing the throng.

"Get into them !" they would shout as the boys in the front would push back, trying not to get bitten by the snarling Alsatian police dogs. The atmosphere was electric, every nerve in your body would tingle and you could taste the aggression. Once the road was cleared, the police would let us go. The walk to the Grange End would only take five minutes but you would live every second of it. The Cardiff fans would try and steam into us at every side street. Opposite, in the park, they would lob stones and, at every break in the wall outside the Grandstand on

Sloper Road, skirmishes would break out. It would be chaos but everyone would stand firm.

The hatred between 'the big two' in South Wales has no rival in football. Never will you see the colours mix outside the ground like you do at all other derbies in Great Britain - even the 'scarfers' fucking hate each other. So much so, that after the Grandstand was demolished in '92, there has never been an unescorted trip since the complete banning of away fans at both fixtures for three seasons after. The two cities have a history of one-upmanship. In recent years, we have even seen local politicians goading each other in the local press. But the main grudge is that Cardiff was just a village in the 1700's whilst Swansea was the copper producing capital of the world and has been a large populated town since the Middle Ages. Yet, after the establishment of the coal mining industry, in just 200 years, Cardiff was named capital of Wales which has meant a jealous glare from West Wales ever since. While Swansea saw no investment for years, we had to endure seeing Cardiff getting the Millennium Stadium, the Assembly and all sorts of inward investment. Even on the football field, they got all the important Wales Internationals. Also, when we graced the top flight in '81, the television reports on the local news would top the Premier Division - not so surprising as the studios are based in Cardiff.

Why do they hate us so much ? I don't know. You'll have to ask them.

Walking up the slope of the open air Grange End you would be greeted by a cacophony of noise. The huge Bob Bank would be a sea of arms all pointing in unison. "Who the fucking hell are you ?" Welcome to the South Wales derby.

It was Boxing Day, 1983 and, instead of coming on the train, we had booked on the official club coaches as we were still too young to get a van and there were no trains on Boxing Day. The boys were wearing their Tachini's and Fila BJ's, all decked out in the latest terrace fashions that had gripped the smart new casual scene. We stood at the front, as close to the Bob Bank as possible and exchanged insults with the Cardiff mob in the opposite corner. Sporadic fights would break out with the police in the home end as both sets of fans scaled the fences. The Grange End had a walkway which went from the turnstiles on Sloper Road into the Bob Bank home end. After the game, as the Cardiff fans were leaving, the Swans fans climbed onto the wall to trade insults with them. As a result, the Cardiff fans started hurling lumps of loose mortar and stones over the high wall into the away end. You couldn't keep your eyes off the sky as the missiles would come in from a high trajectory. I remember one Swans fan, who was oblivious to what was happening, just stood there on his own as everybody moved out of the way and shouted to warn him to no avail as the lump of concrete hit him square on the head.

All in all the game passed off without any major incident, probably due to it being held on Boxing Day and the restriction on our travel options - but this would be the case for nearly a decade as the 'New Firm' were about to come of age. Slowly but surely we started to get to know the older lads. I had bumped into the Sketty Park Herberts one night in Cinderella's, a nightclub in Mumbles, after they had been in a big row with some local piss heads. The way they stuck together, not even taking shit off the police, impressed me. They seemed untouchable and above the Law. One of them, Carl Mac, was a smart casual lad and had been wearing the gear since '81, copying off the Scousers - seeing as he was a bit of an Everton fan too. We would acknowledge each other and often talk about all things terrace culture when we met on the North Bank. The boys had started taking umbrellas to the games to use as weapons. Myself, I preferred a small telescopic compact umbrella with a real hard wooden handle, just right to use to slam into the top of someone's head in a hammer punch style. Some of the boys would be tooled up with craft knifes from the Pound Store but this seemed a bit too extreme in my eyes.

We had Barry Town in the Welsh FA Cup but due to the ground having no floodlights the game was kicking off when I was still at work. Jez had got a seat on a minibus with his brother and a few older lads as there was a likelihood of Cardiff fans turning up because Barry was a Bluebird stronghold. Sure enough, the small ground was full of Cardiff lads and Jez and Co had a real rough ride. The game ended up as a one all draw and the replay was set for two weeks later at the Vetch. I was sure Cardiff would turn up.

The Welsh Cup was never a crowd puller and this was to be no different. A paltry crowd of 3,139 had turned up but to no surprise of my own, so had some Cardiff lads. They had gone on the North Bank before kick-off and given it large, dishing out a few slaps but eventually chucked off. This was the ultimate insult. They had been on our end and left virtually unscathed. The hooligan rumour network soon reached us as we rushed to the ground, hearts beating like thunder to see if it was true. We got to the North Bank to meet an animated Pitson telling us of his encounter with the Cardiff fans. I was gutted. Why weren't we in there? Hardly any Old Bill in the ground and the perfect opportunity to make a show and where were we ? In the fucking pub.

"Where the fucking hell have you lot been ?" shouted Boxer, the first time he had really spoken to me directly.
"In the pub," I replied.
"Fucking no use in there. Fucking kids !" He turned away. He was spot on, no matter how much he pissed off 'us kids' - we knew he was a top boy and we

respected him for it.

Just as Boxer walked away Pitson shouted "He was one of them !" pointing at some guy in a green combat jacket. The guy dived under the crush barrier and Jez gave him a boot in the leg. He stumbled and I cracked him over the head with my umbrella. Some satisfaction was gained, just out of the frustration of missing out earlier but deep down we were all gutted. Our deadliest enemy had walked all over our territory and left with a smug grin. Little did they know that we would have revenge before the season was out.

The season was becoming a nightmare. On the football field, Swansea City was in freefall. Crowds were down to five or six thousand but our little firm was growing rapidly. Our Saturday mornings in the Four J's were becoming more and more boisterous and our 'hunting trips' on the Mumbles Road after games were getting more organised. The Mumbles Road is a dual carriageway which runs from Blackpill, near Mumbles, to the bridge over the Tawe and out of Swansea. The majority of the traffic going to the Vetch Field would travel along it eastwards after the match had finished. Occasionally the police would take the official coaches out west bound to avoid any ambushes but if you wanted vans or cars, the way most boys who were up for a row would travel, you would head down the Mumbles Road. If you caught some fans on foot they would have hardly anywhere to go as the prison wall ran the length between the away end and the home end and, once across the junction of West Way, the gasworks wall ran the whole way to the footbridge at the leisure centre on the Marina side. So, if the police were patrolling outside the Swansea Jack pub, you could lay in wait for cars and vans by the multi-storey car park and footbridge and if you needed a quick getaway you could dart through the St David's Shopping Complex. All in all, an ideal a spot.

At every game, we would have a scout down the Mumbles Road and very often small scale rucks would happen. We loved the excitement of one of the lads spotting a car full of lads, normally given away by their clothing, especially a Burberry scarf. You could spot one of those a mile off in a stationary row of traffic and at 5pm on a Saturday afternoon the Mumbles Road was just that ! The tension would rise as you could see one of the boys signalling down the road to a car which was soon to be our target. The sight to other motorists must have been bizarre. A gang of teenagers in tracksuit tops, roll neck jumpers - some wearing deerstalker hats - all digging stones out of the ground by the side of the car park. We must have looked insane. Then wham ! The bricks and stones would go through the windscreen and side windows simultaneously. We would steam in and boot the car door panels in. This is not a good idea when wearing Adidas trim trabs as I often ended up with a sprained ankle or a bruised foot. Nine times out of ten, the car would mount the central reservation and fuck off down the opposite side of the road 'Sweeney' style with burning rubber and smoke. On the odd occasion, they would get out and have a go after seeing their precious car demolished. This normally ended up adding insult to injury with our mob dishing out a serious hiding.

We had a few offs after the Barry game but nothing special, though our regularity on the Mumbles Road had led to the police taking an interest in us when we would appear. "C'mon, move on lads, there's nothing about today," they would say. On some occasions they would refer to me personally. "Oi, Ginger ! Watch your step - we've got our eye on you, lad."

Although slightly unnerving, I was secretly happy I was being recognised. The bad thing is, it's hard not being recognised when your hair is bright ginger. In a crowd of fighting fans, you're the one who's going to get picked out by the police.

We had played Charlton Athletic a week after the Barry game and we were on our way to the Badminton for a few beers to celebrate the rare 1 - 0 win. There were only five or six of us and, as we turned the corner onto Fleet Street, we saw six Charlton fans coming the other way. How did we know ? Well, in those days, only hooligans wore Pringle jumpers with Lacoste roll necks underneath and carried golfing umbrellas on sunny days - also, we knew all Swansea dressers. For a few seconds it was silence, then the tall lad with jet black hair in a red Pringle jumper raised his umbrella like a sword and said in a broad Cockney accent, "Come on Taffies !" He swung his umbrella and I jumped back. I threw a kick but missed. "Oi, you lot !" a voice shouted from down the street. It was the police, running at full pelt, one hand on their hats and the other fumbling for their truncheons. As they sped towards us, every one of us split and we made off in all directions. The Sandfields, being a maze of streets and houses, is made for an easy getaway on most occasions but, this time, I just couldn't shake off the copper. Every time I went around one corner, he would appear as I got halfway down the street. I got around the corner of Western Street when I noticed a front door open but the inner door shut, so I dived in and shut the front door as quietly as I could.

"Joe, is that you ?" an elderly voice cried out from the living room. I just held my breath and stood as quietly as possible. I heard the copper running past but couldn't be sure if he had given up his pursuit and started walking back. So there I stayed for a minute or so. "Joe," the voice said again. "I'll put the kettle on."

That was it. Now I had the giggles. I had to get out before the old lady saw me and had a heart attack. I sneaked out of the front door and the coast was clear. I made my way back to the 'Bad' laughing to myself. Why the fuck do you get the giggles when you're hiding ? As I turned the corner, my laughing stopped. I bumped straight into the Charlton lads, all six of the fuckers. I was punched in the temple and went down to the floor. I felt the kick under my chin with my teeth biting into my tongue but from then on it was a blur. I knew I was kicked but it was as if I wasn't really there, next thing the Charlton lad with the red Pringle was lying on the floor too, practically facing me. I couldn't understand what was going on. I could hear shouting and running feet so as I got up onto my knees. I looked down the road and saw that the boys from the Badminton had seen off the Charlton lads. Some of the lads had gone to the 'Bad' after the police had chased them and alerted the SHA and, luckily for me, Nobsy, one of the older firm, had smacked the boy with the red Pringle over the head with a brick as they were laying into me. That's what it was all about. Even though I hardly knew Nobsy, he was willing to put his liberty at risk by smashing some stranger over the head with a brick. The sense of camaraderie was second to none.

After a couple of away trips to Carlisle and Newcastle, we had Manchester City at the Vetch. We were out in force early doors but our search for the opposition was bearing no fruit. Rumour had it that the Man City fans had mistakenly gone into Port Talbot after seeing the floodlights of Aberafan rugby ground and been pulled by the police after fucking about.

The away bank in the West Terrace was normally just for away fans but, if a large following wasn't expected, they had a fence which separated the terracing straight down the middle with the Swansea fans occupying the left hand side nearest the North Bank. During the first half, some of the Man City fans had gone into the East Terrace for home supporters. While they were being escorted around the pitch across the face of the North Bank, they pulled out a fluffy sheep and started taunting the fans with it.   The North Bank heaved forward as the Man City fans rattled on the fence. As we were on the West terrace, we stormed the gate at the side of the bank on to the pitch. It was manned as usual by a quiet middle-aged man. He didn't know what hit him as he was swept along when we broke onto the pitch side. We were within spitting distance of the Man City fans and could now see that they were big men and not young lads like us. Before we could reach each other, the police had anticipated what was about to happen. In they steamed with their truncheons and, before I knew it, I was in a headlock and on my way to the cells, being dragged backwards with the collar of my new Fila tracksuit top in shreds. I had only had it a week - what a gutter !

The Old Bill slung me in one of those large police lorries full of cells parked outside the ground and slammed the door shut. It's a strange feeling going from the noisy, chaotic scene of a football match to the complete silence of a holding cell in a police wagon. I was hoping, which seemed a selfish thing to wish on your own mates, that one of the other boys would join me to keep me company. Luckily for them, I was the lone detainee. While in the cold recess of a six by four cell you can't help but think the worst case scenario. What are they going to charge me with ? Will I go down ? Fuck me, I'm only seventeen - what are my parents going to say ? The worst thing was that I had only just been bound over for fighting outside a Mumbles Restaurant. This would be my second court appearance in two months. The door burst open and daylight flooded the cell. A robust police sergeant walked in.

"Mr Wallis," he said sternly.

"Yes," I replied sheepishly, wondering how he knew my name.

"Listen, boy, what are you doing hanging around with these idiots ?" I shrugged my shoulders, avoiding eye contact.

"You're not like this lot, boy, you're a good lad from the Mumbles." I looked at him inquisitively. How did he know me ?

"I'll tell you what I'm going to do. I'm going to let you go this once because I know your family - but this won't happen again, so wise up. OK ?"

"OK," I said.

He let me out of the wagon. As I walked down the street I pondered on my close shave. Was I going to heed the policeman's warning and feel happy he just saved me from a life of violence ? Was I fuck ! We had Cardiff at home next !

I'll never forget April 21st, 1984. It was my first South Wales derby with the firm and I can still taste the excitement today. It was a glorious, sunny day and I had parked my motorbike outside the Dolphin Hotel in Whitewalls, away from the Sandfields which was sure to be a war zone. I made my way to the Four J's which, at 11 o'clock, was already heaving with at least 100 lads. You could just tell it was going to be one of those days. I had just got my first bottle of Holsten Pils when someone ran in and said "It's going off down the Bad !" The place emptied in seconds, bottles and glasses left half-full as, en masse, we raced the five minutes jog down to the 'Bad' deep in the Sandfields. By the time we got there, the Cardiff boys were gone and the pub was in a state with some windows shattered and blood splashed on the pavement outside. I saw Nobsy and asked him what had happened. He told me that Lloyd the Landlord had invited a bus-full of lads down early doors for a pint as he was a Cardiff boy himself. Naturally, when the Sandfields boys came in, it kicked off with pool cues being brandished and a few lads getting a glassing.

We were gutted that we had missed it but we didn't have to wait long for some action. Within minutes, a gang of boys walked up the street and, as they approached us at the corner of the "Bad", one of them said in a broad Cardiff accent "All right, lads, seen any Jacks yet ?" This was not the last time we would hear this. It was if they thought we had no boys. Big fucking mistake ! We smashed into them fleeing down the road. I still had one of them by the sleeve but he flailed

DEAN DOUBLE LIFTS SWANS

SWANSEA CITY 3   CARDIFF CITY 2

TEENAGE STRIKER Dean Saunders struck a late match winner, his second goal, in an exciting match, as battling Swansea stormed back after trailing 2-0 to wind up a memorable Welsh derby

Swansea welcomed back striker Ian Walsh after a month's injury absence, while Yugoslav Ante Rajkovic was making his first home appearance since re-signing.

As expected, Cardiff recalled Gary Bennett in place of injured striker Jeff Hemmerman.

Rajkovic, a return for the day, made his presence felt during the first Cardiff attack, but the match was barely two minutes old before the pre-match violence, which produced 30 arrests for incidents in the city, erupted on the terraces.

The signs had been ominous from the moment Cardiff fans on the West terrace tried to pull down fencing preventing them from getting on to the pitch.

Police moved in swiftly to break up the running battles between rival supporters who had managed to penetrate the tightly screened North Bank and play was stopped briefly when Swansea fans on the East terrace invaded the pitch.

This time pitch with dogs drove them back and while many fans were led away, the resuming calm allowed Cardiff to take the game's first corner.

Swansea cleared their lines quickly and built several promising attacks, with Marustik and Robinson prominent, before Cardiff again surged forward in numbers.

Lee and Gibbins carved out a superb opening for top scorer Owen, but his first-time shot from 12 yards was brilliantly turned around the post by Hughes.

Cardiff, already assured of their place in the Second Division next season, continued to exercise the greater control and it came as little surprise when they snatched the lead after 17 minutes.

Swansea failed to clear a deep cross and Smith, running in at speed, hooked the ball beyond the stranded Hughes.

Cardiff's growing superiority was underlined by a succession of corners and their greater awareness up front.

Bennett came surging through to direct a Tong cross wide of the mark before Gibbins was narrowly wide with a shot from Lee's cross.

Swansea almost fell two goals behind in the 25th minute when an Owen shot swamped off Robinson's boot into the side netting.

Two minutes later, the Cardiff threat paid off handsomely when Owen raced clear down the right flank and was somewhat fortunate to see his intended cross for Bennett loop over the head of the unlucky Hughes.

Police, meanwhile, continued their vigilant operation and had to quell further trouble on the North Bank, while the action on the field continued at frantic pace.

Cardiff were still celebrating their second goal when Swansea caught their defence flat-footed to reduce the deficit with a superbly worked goal.

Walsh made the fullest possible use of the gaps in the Cardiff defence and raced clear down the right before crossing low to the near post, where Saunders side-footed the ball past the helpless Dibble to register his second League goal.

Bennett, clearly incensed by Swansea's swift reply, brought Saunders down outside the

referee's view the next time the young striker tried to break free and the battle between the pair continued before the referee separated them when tempers became frayed again and promptly booked Saunders.

Swansea could have been swamped out of sight in the 10 minutes immediately before the interval.

Marustik lost possession outside the area and it needed a smothering save from Hughes at the feet of Gibbins to keep Swansea in touch.

Gibbins continued to dominate in midfield and twice in the space of a minute his aggression took him to the Swansea penalty area only to direct his shots wide of the target on each occasion.

Just before the interval Swansea lost playmaker Wyndham Evans with a knee injury following a 50-50 tackle with Owen.

Evans was helped off and substitute Gary Richards hardly had time to take up his position in the re-organised Swansea defence before the

referee signalled a break in the action.

Half-time: Swansea City 1, Cardiff City 2

Swansea clearly had their work cut out against a determined side inspired by Gibbins in midfield and the aggression of the irrepressible Bennett.

But there seemed every hope as Swansea pushed forward immediately on the restart and should really have equalised from the first attack of the second half.

Richards, having his first touch of the match, beat off the challenge of Lee, cleverly kept the ball in play and produced a superb far-post cross only to find no-one there to meet it.

It was certainly a lot off for the Cardiff defence which had been caught momentarily flat footed.

Next, Owen tried to finish the job from 25 yards but his shot was again wide of the mark.

The match continued to be fought at a fast pace and referee Stevens was quick to punish the over-vigorous approach.

Lewis became the second Swansea player to be cautioned when he brought down Gibbins.

Play was held up briefly when the hard-working Saunders required treatment before

TURN to back page

TODAY'S LINE-UP

SWANSEA CITY		CARDIFF CITY
HUGHES	1	DIBBLE
EVANS	2	ELSEY
McQUILLAN	3	GRANT
LEWIS	4	DWYER
STEVENSON	5	SMITH
RAJKOVIC	6	TONG
SAUNDERS	7	OWEN
ROBINSON	8	GIBBINS
WALSH	9	VAUGHAN
MARUSTIK	10	BENNETT
PASCOE	11	LEE
RICHARDS	12	GOLDSMITH

REFEREE: MR. B. T. STEVENS, GLOUCESTER

FANS IN RETREAT ... supporters are chased off Vetch Field after a pitch invasion held up play.

GOAL CHART

SMITH	17mins
OWEN	27mins
SAUNDERS	29mins
WALSH	68mins
SAUNDERS	85mins

HOLD ON ... Swansea goalscorer Dean Saunders cannot make any progress this time.

his arms and spun out of his jacket falling onto the floor. One of the Morriston boys, 'Jaffa', kicked him as he tried to get underneath a Volkswagen Beetle. A lone policeman turned up with his truncheon at the ready. "Back off, you fucking animals!" he screamed. Everything seemed to stop for a split second until Mike Buller hit the copper square on the jaw with a haymaker and knocked him clean out. The Cardiff boy crawled as far as he could back under the car after seeing his

'BLOODY ANIMALS'

A Swansea fan is kicked after being attacked by rival fans.

Blood streams from a head wound to a Swansea fan.

A SWANSEA city centre shop manager told today of the terror that hit the Quadrant when marauding football fans went on the rampage during peak Easter shopping time.

Mr. Benny Corbisero, manager of Gilesports, had to have seven stitches inserted in a hand wound after Cardiff City supporters kicked in the plate glass door of his shop.

And a city licensee described the fans as "bloody mindless animals."

"It was a terrifying experience to be confronted by more than 200 fans rampaging

by Adrian Howells

through the centre," said Mr Cirbisero, who added that shopkeepers and shoppers were afraid throughout the day.

"The atmosphere was very tense, but I would like to praise the police. When this terrifying incident happened they expertly diffused what could have been an explosive situation," he added.

Off the field, the result of Saturday's derby match between Swansea and Cardiff was 68 arrests, mass violence in the streets and a trail of damage to shops and pubs.

Deplorable

Cardiff City football club today condemned a "certain element" of their fans.

"The behaviour of some of them was deplorable and we as a football club do not want to be associated with them. Unfortunately this small element gives the rest of Cardiff City's genuine fans a bad name," said the club's managing director Mr. Ron Jones.

"Drink is the root cause of all these troubles and an early kick-off would mean the match being played before they can get drunk," he added.

"Unfortunately, scenes like those witnessed in Swansea is the unacceptable face of soccer," Mr. Jones said.

Kicked

It was the worst outbreak of soccer hooliganism to hit Swansea this season as violence flared in and around the city centre throughout the day and continued on the terraces at Vetch Field during the match which Swansea won 3-2.

The Cornish Mount public

POLICE move the crowd from King's Lane, Swansea.

saviour flat out on the floor with his helmet rolling on the tarmac.

We continued to bump into small pockets of Cardiff lads in the Sandfields, always with the same infuriating question. "Seen any Jacks, boys ?" innocently thinking that they had the freedom of our city. I'm sure they would never make that mistake again.

We had heard that a big mob of lads had just come off the train at the station so we made our way up towards them. We were mob handed now - at least two hundred of us, maybe more. We got to Castle Gardens when 'Cardiff John', one of the Swansea skinheads, came towards us with a Cardiff scarf on. He told us they were just around the corner on the High Street on their way and that he had been mingling in with them as one of their own. Castle Gardens was a green park of flowerbeds, walkways and trees, frequented by the local drunks. It sloped down from the High Street to where we were at the end of Oxford Street. As the

'Bloody animals'

● From Page One

house in the Strand was attacked by more than 50 fans chanting, "We are Cardiff Boys," and hurling missiles at the building and regulars. Another customer was hit in the face with half a brick. A baby and its mother were also in danger," said Cornish Mount landlord Mr. Terry McDonnell.

Mr. McDonnell said: "I've never seen human beings behave so badly.

They were bloody mindless animals — they were worse than animals."

Three of these fans were involved in an accident with a car outside the public house as mass fight broke out. They were taken to Singleton Hospital for treatment, but were not detained.

In the city centre the fans rampaged through the Quadrant as both Cardiff and Swansea supporters marauded in large gangs looking for each other.

Mr. Corbisero was injured by flying glass and treated in hospital.

Missiles

Terrified customers cowered behind clothes rails as the glass shattered around them.

The violence continued inside the ground and the match itself was held up when a mass of Cardiff supporters invaded the pitch within two minutes of kick-off.

Police using dogs had to move in to restore order as fights broke out all over the ground. Missiles were thrown on to the pitch and a linesman was struck.

Of the 65 arrests, 46 were in and around the city centre and 22 inside the ground.

Almost two-thirds of the people arrested were Cardiff supporters, said a police spokesman.

Most of the arrests were in respect of public order offences, using threatening words and behaviour, drunkenness, assault, damage and theft.

All those arrested have been bailed to appear before Swansea magistrates at a later

BEHIND WIRE, but the "battle" goes on inside the Vetch Field ground.

THE STRONG arm of the law grapples with fans.

Cardiff fans came round the corner, they had higher ground. They came steaming down the gardens full of confidence at the sight of us but I don't think they realised we had the numerical advantage. As we streamed out of Oxford Street and fanned out like beer spilling from a bottle neck, we covered the whole street at the bottom of the Gardens. After the initial clash, they turned and made a clean pair of heels up past the David Evans store and back up the High Street. We were jubilant. The thrill of seeing them take flight had the boys in a state of euphoria but you had to give it to them, they were everywhere. There were rumours of them in all parts of the city - they had turned out in massive numbers and we hadn't met their main mob yet.

By now it was near kick-off so we made our way to the Vetch. The atmosphere in the ground was supercharged by the clashes that had happened all morning. The sun was still beating down and I was cooking in my Pringle jumper after all the fighting and running about. I was drinking some Olde English cider to quench my thirst with Roger Holland, one of the Sketty Park Herberts, this was still a time when you could drink and watch football. Then, all of a sudden, a large mob of boys came spilling onto the pitch from the East Stand Terrace, directly on our right as we stood on the North Bank. At first, I thought they were Swans fans just trying to get on the North Bank because they came from a terrace allocated for home supporters. But as they got to the fence right on the halfway line, you could see they were calling it on. Most of them were dressers so it was plain to see this

56

was their main mob. What an insult - they were on our pitch shouting the odds. By the time we got to the front where they were, the Old Bill had started clearing them away. In all hooligans' eyes, this was no doubt a result for them - in the full gaze of the national media, this one incident was bound to fill the column inches. I was gutted. After all the results we had before the match, this one act of bravado would no doubt seem a big result for the Cardiff fans in the newspapers. To add insult to injury, by half time we were 2 - 0 down and all the talk amongst the boys was about the "cheeky cunts" who had invaded the pitch.

Our mood was lifted in the second half with a comeback on the pitch. A player, who we would give away for nothing the next season, netted two goals. His name, Dean Saunders. A third goal by Ian Walsh gave us victory to send us home happy. But, before that, we had a score to settle with the enemy. As we exited the back of the North Bank, to our disbelief, the Cardiff mob had come round on a suicide mission. Fair play, it took some bottle but they got murdered. The shout went up and we charged into them, laying them to waste. As well as our mob, who were determined to seek them out and have a go, they faced everyone, literally thousands of fans. I chased one lad, after booting a few of the many who laid out on the floor, caught hold of him and kneed him in the back as we both fell into the open porch of someone's house on Western Street. I straddled him and punched him repeatedly in the face until I split my knuckles on his teeth. It was rage and satisfaction in a strange blood-rushing high. We had them on the run now.

Our mob was now massive as we chased the Cardiff fans back towards the train station. The police had gained some sense of order and were escorting the Cardiff fans who had made the journey by train. As the Cardiff mob were herded up the High Street, we made our way up Orchard Street parallel to them. At every adjoining lane between both roads we would hit them, at one stage splitting them in two at Kings Lane. The lane was jammed from top to bottom, full of lads and, as we steamed through the police lines, we saw them run both up and down the High Street. They had lost their fight and the police had lost control - it was absolute chaos.

As the police got them on the trains, the Swansea boys sauntered back into town, all with their own individual tales. Cardiff had come, called the odds and in true Western fashion had run the fuck out of town. What a day, 2 - 0 down, then 2 up and victory off the pitch. But, best of all, we had recognition off the main lads for a job well done.

Our season was drawing to an end and, with the finale of an away trip to Portsmouth looming, we had the pleasure of entertaining Leeds Utd at the Vetch. Just a couple of seasons earlier our first game in the top flight was against Leeds and we dispatched their football team 5 - 1 with ease. But, off the pitch, it was a different proposition. Their famous Service Crew had turned out in huge numbers; certainly the biggest firm of lads ever to visit the Vetch field. This year, Leeds were a different outfit altogether. Since relegation to Division Two, they had lost the massive numbers that had visited the Vetch just under three years ago. With memories of Leeds fans invading the city and setting fire to the double-decker stand fresh in our minds, we were out for a bit of retribution but alas they brought nothing. As we watched the match, one of the lads came up to us excitedly and said "There's some dressers down the front and they ain't ours." We filed down to the front section of terracing on the North Bank and slowly filtered through the crowd to stand secretly around the unknown casuals. We listened attentively to try and make out their accents until one of the boys just walked up and confronted them. Sure enough, it kicked off. The hidden crowd of Swansea dressers enveloped them like a wave crashing over rocks. A few ran the length of the bank and out to the police at the corner gate while one lad climbed up the fence to escape to the pitch. He was quite a lump but he cleared the fence like an Olympic high jumper. We thought we had seen the last of them but, sure enough, as fate has a way of doing these things, our paths would cross once again later in the day.

Why a mere handful of boys would go on a Home End seems a foolish and pointless thing to do. But, looking back, I have done it myself on many occasions. It's normally because someone mentions it in the van or car on the way to the game and nobody has the bottle to bottle out ! The thing is, if there's not a mob with you, it's a way of getting a buzz and a bit of one-upmanship on what could have been a quiet day out. Strange thing, football culture; risking life and liberty for no financial gain. If you share a cell with a con and tell him what you're in for, they'll be bemused as to why you risk everything for just a thrill and no financial gain. "Go skydiving, for fuck's sake !" would be their recommendation.

The match finished 2 - 2 and our encounter on the North Bank was enough to convince the lads that some sport was to be had on the Mumbles Road. The final match of the season always brings out a good mob of lads and, even though we had been relegated, today was no different. Probably because it was Leeds United. Our sorties on the Mumbles Road would normally consist of twenty youth lads but today it was buzzing. There were lads lining both sides of the dual carriageway all eager for a bit of action. The tension rose as someone spotted a white transit van coming up the road in the slow traffic. Sure enough, the lads in the front seat were the same boys who had been on the North Bank earlier. The shout went up and the mob swarmed in from all sides. The driver and passenger doors were pulled at but locked as the terrified Leeds boys sat in the front seats, faces like rabbits caught in the headlights, waiting for the windows to go through. We pulled the back doors open but, to everyone's surprise, the lad who had done the high jump out of the North Bank earlier was waiting with a shovel in his hands. Everyone jumped back as he lashed out with it. That's when the bricks came in, smashing into the windows and panels of the transit from all directions. In total panic, the van crossed the central reservation and up the wrong way on the opposite side of the dual carriageway. In the melee, the boys had been throwing bricks from both sides of the road with some of them missing the van and hitting lads on the other side. Hence there were a few bloody heads on our side but nobody seemed to mind. We were all just a bit gutted that Leeds hadn't turned out.

Back in the 'Bad' later on, the youth were mixing with the older lads. We were now as one, especially as Terry Dustbin had invited us to come on their bus to Portsmouth the next Saturday. A breakthrough had been made and we eagerly awaited our first outing with the main firm.

Another sunny day awaited us when we met outside the Badminton at eight in the morning and the boys were already on their way because Lloyd had opened up early. The bus was a 52-seater coach and the driver was sure to be in for a rough ride with the passengers he was carrying that day. This was no family day outing to the seaside. We knew Pompey were going to be a major force on their home turf because they were certainly no mugs at the Vetch earlier in the year. They had also been active at Cardiff and we read all the reports in the local papers. The beer flowed on the bus with some lads swigging straight out of brandy bottles or whatever they could get their hands on. The lads were a mixture of ages and they came from all parts of the city. There were boys from the Sandfields, Townhill, Brynmill, Sketty Park, Plasmarl, Morriston and Clase - also from outside the city from Neath and Port Talbot - all with a main face from each area. A lot of reputation from different areas always meant a fair amount of banter and rivalry on the bus journey with quite rough mock fights between the Herberts, the Angels and the Morriston Monkeys. Being the youngest, our little mob was in for some stick, but, as Lloyd the landlord was coming, he would get the brunt of the abuse as he was a Cardiff fan. We set off as soon as everyone was there, already pissed up and with various illegal substances consumed.

The experience of travelling with the boys was very far removed from journeys with the club's official coaches. Even the driver of the coach seemed to be up for it until one of the boys, called Donald, set fire to Lloyd the landlord after Big Roger had stuffed his jumper and jeans with newspaper while he was sleeping. Up jumped Lloyd in a panic, patting his feet, legs and head. One of the boys said "Put him out !" Another voice replied "I wouldn't piss on the Cardiff cunt if he was on fire !" Laughter filled the bus as poor Lloyd danced around trying to put himself out. Big Rog then gestured to douse him with his bottle of Napoleon Brandy. "No !" came the shouts from everyone as it would have fuelled the fire. To Lloyd's relief, he was put out with about three pints of lager as the boys simultaneously emptied their cans over him.

These pranks seemed to be a feature of most trips. The golden rule was no sleeping on tour or you faced possible burning, shaving of hair and eyebrows, Hitler moustaches applied with permanent pen and many more punishments.

By the time we arrived in Portsmouth, everyone was supercharged on drink and drugs but nobody seemed to give a fuck that we were going into Portsmouth - a town of some considerable repute - just forty-handed !

When you're 17, you just have blind admiration for the main boys and you would follow them anywhere without question. To me, they were like supermen and they surely could never be beaten, could they ? Well today we wouldn't find out as we had been in the Lord Nelson pub for just ten minutes when the police arrived en masse. The landlord had tipped them off to avoid trouble as we had arrived early before the locals were out. I was really pissed off. Our first chance to impress and the Old Bill had spoilt our fun. When you have only a coach-full, there is no way you can beat the police. I was to learn that you need at least a couple of hundred to turn the tables and boss them around.

Unfortunately for us, our team was in freefall with a second consecutive relegation and so was our firm. The police took our coach to a car park by the ground and we were kept guard by the police until kick-off. A couple of lads from Port Talbot decided to sneak out of the fire exit of the coach, so I joined them. Only three of us managed to escape, me, Alan Roberts and a man called Tony Jackal, known to everyone as Betty. Betty had a reputation of some repute. He was a man who would never run no matter how outnumbered he was. To look at him, you would never think so. His hair was bedraggled, he wore a brown pin-striped suit and black-rimmed, thick glasses. His voice was so rough it sounded as if he was gargling gravel. We got into a pub full of Pompey boys and got to the bar. As soon as we walked in, I noticed they had clocked us straight away. The drinks were ordered at the bar in Betty's finest Port Talbot growl. By this time, a few lads had come within earshot just to confirm that we were truly indeed Welsh bastards. Nervously I whispered to Alan and Betty that we had better leave, hoping they would just let us go with a bit of an ear bashing. To which Betty replied with a growling voice loud enough for everyone to hear "Don't worry, Ginge, the first cunt will get this in his fucking neck," motioning to his old-style, chunky pint pot. Why did I have to open my mouth ? Surely we would now die ! But people were turning away from his stare. His wild looks and gnarly voice had put out all the signals that this man did not give a fuck and would slit your throat and think nothing of it. He had fronted them and they had thought, "fuck it, it's not worth it", carried on drinking and ignored the fact that we were there.

We got back to the coach where the boys were now steaming after downing their bottles of brandy and cans of lager. Big Rog was stripped down to his pants, pushing a plastic penguin on a stick with a wheel and two flippers. "Anyone touches the penguin, fucking gets it !" he would shout, giving everyone the evil eye. We were all in hysterics at the bizarre sight - even the Old Bill were well wary of him.

Once in the ground, we were greeted with a chorus of "Sheep, sheep, sheep shaggers !" To which we replied "Rule Britannia, Britannia rules the waves. How many English fans got stabbed in Spain ?"

The banter had begun but there didn't seem to be the tension I had hoped for - no Pompey lads baying for our blood. It all seemed to be a bit of a stroll in the park which was not what we expected after the rows that had gone on with Cardiff and Chelsea. The results of the latter still evident in the stand; the rows of seats had been ripped out and were strewn all over the upper tier to our right, like the twisted wreck of a train crash. Why couldn't we turn out a mob like that ? A mob willing to smash everyone and everything in its path. The game and day in general turned out to be a damp squib. We lost 5 - 0 and apart from seeing Jaffa climb the floodlights and us chasing some spotty Pompey herbert after the game, it was a real let down. Let's hope next season gets better.

'84 - '85

As soon as the fixtures were out, a fervent buzz was going around the hooligan circle. It was Millwall away, first game of the season, who could have asked for more ? During the summer I had spent my time down the Mumbles, a posh seaside resort a mile away from my home, famous for its long stretch of pubs. One Saturday afternoon, I was chatting with some local lads on the promenade, when a car pulled up with a gang of casuals in it. It screeched to a halt and five lads bailed out and made a beeline towards me.

"Hello, mate. We're the Caewern firm." A few slaps were thrown my way and, as I pulled away, the collar of my tachini was ripped.
"Fucking Jack bastard !" they taunted as I pulled away.

'Who the fuck are the Caewern firm ?' I thought as I caught my breath across the road. The white car sped off down the road with the occupants laughing at my expense. Little did I know but we would meet on many more occasions to come.

Apart from the Mumbles Carnival when the boys would come down from town to cause havoc with the locals, I hadn't seen them all until today and today it was Millwall away. Filling the bus for this fixture was no problem. By the time we pulled off from the Badminton there were 75 of us on a 52-seater coach. All the usual suspects were in evidence - the Angels, the Herberts, the Fowler boys from Clase, the Morriston Monkeys, the Gendros G-Force and us, the newly-christened Baby Squad. We eagerly made our way up the M4 with the lads all fuelling up on beer and downing wraps of speed.

As we made our way past Bristol, a coach full of boys passed us with a yellow and black barrel with 'Newport County Booze Crew' written on it. They were bouncing, giving it the big one and gesturing for us to pull over. In reaction, our boys pulled out their Day-glo plastic Stanley knives which one of the lads had lifted from Hyper Value the day before. Sure enough the Newport firm weren't so eager to pull over at the sight of a crammed, three to a seat coach full of tooled-up Jacks.

We stopped off in Slough to have a few beers. Chaos ensued, with the lads pouring their own beer and terrorising the bar staff while some of the others looted a local Paki shop and smashed it up. We decided to move on before the police arrived. The tension on the coach was high as we made our way into South London. An eerie calm had descended, probably because we were in the territory of the most feared firm in the country. We all knew Millwall didn't take any prisoners. The environment didn't help either - rows of ramshackle houses with corrugated iron in place of windows and doors. This was true bandit country long before the yuppies had arrived south of the river. Our bus driver was lost and 3 o'clock was fast approaching. We stopped outside a pub where a man was enjoying a pint and the Racing Post. Stacko got off to ask directions.

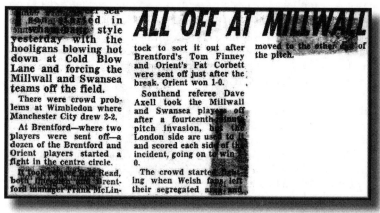

ALL OFF AT MILLWALL

...again started in ...style yesterday with the hooligans blowing hot down at Cold Blow Lane and forcing the Millwall and Swansea teams off the field.

There were crowd problems at Wimbledon where Manchester City drew 2-2.

At Brentford—where two players were sent off—a dozen of the Brentford and Orient players started a fight in the centre circle.

It took ... Read, both ... Brentford manager Frank McLin-

tock to sort it out after Brentford's Tom Finney and Orient's Pat Corbett were sent off just after the break. Orient won 1-0.

Southend referee Dave Axell took the Millwall and Swansea players off after a fourteenth minute pitch invasion, but the London side are used to it and scored each side of the incident, going on to win 2-0.

The crowd started ... ing when Welsh fans left their segregated area and

moved to the other side of the pitch.

"Where's Cold Blow Lane, mate ?" Stacko enquired.
"Fuck off , you Taffy cunt !" he replied.

That was the wrong answer. Stacko released one of his legendary right hooks, lifting him off the ground and knocking him out stone cold. The bus sped off and we looked back at the cheeky Londoner sleeping on the pavement next to his smashed pint with his Racing Post blowing away in the wind. 'Wrong answer, mate,' I thought.

As we made our way to the ground, the boys were buzzing. Everyone was up for it after the little taste of violence we had just witnessed. The blood was pumping - surely nothing would stop us now. As we pulled up at the aptly named Cold Blow Lane, one of the Eastside lads, Simon Ivey, stood up to rally the troops. "Right then, this is where we make our mark! We're going in their fucking end and nobody fucking runs. We stand together and any of you youngsters run, don't forget you have to walk the same streets as we do. OK ? Let's fucking go !" Off the bus we charged. The game had already started, so there were no police or Millwall fans around - only the turnstile operators, who were shaking their heads and grinning to themselves as we filed through the rusty antiquated turnstiles. They knew full well the reception we would get. Once through the turnstiles, we were directly faced by steep steps up towards the entrances which entered the bank from the topmost section of terracing. We filed into the vast bank behind the goal with the Swans fans facing us from the opposite side of the ground. Nobody seemed to notice us coming in as we came from behind everyone. The atmosphere was quiet until Jez shouted at the top of his voice ...

"SAAWANSEEE !"

and we all steamed forward, spilling onto the terrace. All 75 of us felt like Trojan warriors but we were soon to be lambs to the slaughter.

To my great surprise, Millwall ran. The bank split open as the Millwall fans fled at the surprise attack. All of a sudden we seemed very alone on this big open space as the Millwall fans came to a halt and turned to see the small band of Welshmen who had caused them to flee at their own end. It was payback time! Instead of charging back at us, they seemed to stroll with a swagger, some of them smiling menacingly. You could see the Millwall boys steaming from the far end next to the Swansea fans. The terracing was without a barrier from there to us and it seemed as if everyone in the whole ground was heading our way. As they hit us, the whole "sticking together" mindset went straight out of the window. It was only a few seconds of rucking until everyone realised we were well out of our depth and then the "every man for himself" attitude kicked in. In the chaos, one of the lads, Mojo, had fallen over. I fell over him and so did a few others. As I managed to get up from the weight of everyone piled up on the floor of the terrace, I could see most of the older boys had made it onto the pitch. Our top boy, Tracy, was astride the fence, his face bleeding, giving it the big one to the Millwall fans to join them on the pitch. We had been pushed to the fence at the side of the grandstand and the only thing that had held the Millwall boys back had been Dulais, one of our lads, waving them back with his Stanley knife. We dragged one of the boys, who had received a severe kicking, to the fence.

I shouted at a copper "Get us out of here !" He replied "You got in, you get out." What did I expect ?

We got over the fence into the grandstand. By this time, the players had been taken off the pitch. This was a real football row. We had kicked the new season off in style by going on the most feared end in the whole football league and it wasn't over yet. We ran the length of the grandstand with the Millwall fans in hot pursuit. I could see the fence into the Swansea end in sight and I thought we were going to make it. We charged towards the fence, dodging kicks and punches, until I leapt onto the railings and climbed up towards the safety of our end. One of the lads, Craig, gave Millwall the finger as he got to the top of the fence only to find out, to his horror, that there was chicken wire - invisible to our eyes as we went towards it - from the top of the fence to the roof. We were fucked ! I got battered out of the grandstand and managed to get out of the ground and onto the concourse behind the stand. Once outside I thought 'I don't want to be caught out here, anything could happen'.

"Oi, Wallis !" a voice called out. It was Phil Carter, one of the lads who had managed to get out after being trapped at the back of the bank.

"Fucking hell, Wall, that was a bit naughty !"

"It's not over yet, mate. We'd better get in our end," I said.

The atmosphere in the ground was now on fire. The Millwall mob had made its way round to our end and were scaling the fences chanting "War! War! War!" The game had been restarted but seemed to pale into insignificance compared to the game going on off the pitch. The barracking continued relentlessly throughout the game. "You cheeky Taffy cunts - you can't come here on our end and take liberties. Who the fuck do you think you are ?" a particularly leery individual blurted out.

Some of the lads were giving it back but I was fucking exhausted. I had taken a fair few boots after falling over in the Millwall end, then an even worse beating in the grandstand. I had fucking great lumps all over my legs and back and the adrenalin rush of it all had sapped all my energy. The game finished with us on the losing side once again, going down 2 - 0. I wondered what our new manager, Colin Appleton, thought about his first game in charge. With the game over, the police were letting us go nowhere. The Millwall fans were attacking the huge blue doors at the back of our end. Fuck knows what awaited us outside but, by the sound of the bricks and bottles hitting the back of the bank, I didn't think they wanted to have a friendly chat. Finally the police opened the doors and we were let out to our coach where one solitary Millwall skinhead abused us as we got on. We left

4J's, 1983, Lee bottom right

4J's, 1983

Millwall, 1984

Just left the Swan Pub in Slough en route to Millwall, 1984

Millwall fans, 1984

In the Services on the way home from Millwall, 1984

Scum home, 1984

Jacks on the Swansea North Bank (Scum at home, 1984)

Cardiff fan battered in Swansea, 1984

Fighting with Manchester City on the North Bank, 1984

Phelps & Newt

Torquay away, 1986 ...
and later on, in the cells !

Cardiff & Swansea confront each other

Scum head for safety of Swansea Bay

Cardiff invade the pitch

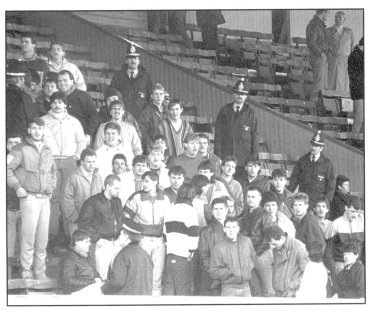

Swansea fans in the stand at Cardiff, 1988

*Tenko & John The Clog in Greece for the Cup Winners Cup
Game against Panathinaikos*

"Ees a big problem - the relatives want to pay to keep them HERE"

Swans fans break the world record on how many pissheads you can get in the back of a Greek minicab !

Jacks on Tour, Olympic Stadium, Athens, 1989

The boys take their weekly bath in Greece

Enjoying the Greek sunshine

Borat, bottom right - "I like you, we make sexy time ?"

Swansea fans outside The Queen's Pub, 1991 FA Cup Game

Jacks on Tour in Monaco, 1991

Pinto, Bozo & Little Dai in Monaco, 1991

On the way to Wembley, 1997

Crazy Dan, The Mad Doctor, George & Mike in Hull

George in Hull

The lads on the way to Hull's ground

Swansea & Hull trying to get to each other

"Hands up if you've got an Aquascutum Hat"
Aggis, Bazzy & Watsy have !

Whitey & Carl know the answer in the Pub Quiz

with the police on the coach but the Millwall mob had moved on to the train station thinking we had come late by train, luckily for us.

The mood on the bus on the way home was jubilant. Even though we'd had a bit of a kicking, we had gone on Millwall's end and called it on. That took some bottle and it was bound to hit the papers the next day. The journey home saw us getting initiated into the firm with a bit of a roughing up at the back of the coach. Each one of the new recruits being called to the back of the bus to get a slapping. The lads were getting more and

Millwall 2 Swansea 0

A FIERCE battle between Swansea and Millwall supporters spilled onto the pitch and Southend referee Roger Axcell ordered the players off ...

The match was only 15 minutes old and the police restored order, for play to resume after a two-minute stoppage.

By then Millwall were already well in control, and had taken the lead when Bremner scored after Lovell had hit a post.

Millwall had numerous chances, but it was not until the extra two minutes added on for the stoppage that Roffey rocketed in a second.

more boisterous and, after the frustrated driver refused to put the radio on, they collected the seat cushions and made a bonfire at the back of the bus. The driver pulled the bus over and said we should all get off or he would go to the police. Stacko went over to him, pulled the keys out of the ignition and said "Get off then, cunt. I'll drive us home." Not surprisingly, the driver had a change of heart. By the time we got back to Swansea, the bus was an absolute wreck and Boxer, who had hired it, was not best pleased. He had a good right to be because a few days later Swansea CID paid him a visit.

We were all 'landed' with the Millwall trip. It had made all the main Sunday papers and was also mentioned on the final scores on television. Sadly our jubilation soon turned sour. One of our boys, Robbie Matthews - a real game lad from Penclawdd - had received a kicking on the Millwall bank and died a few days later from a brain haemorrhage. We were devastated - he was only 18. I was quite close to Robbie as we had been in a row in the Carlisle grandstand the season before. There had just been a handful of us and nothing bonds you when your backs are against the wall against all the odds - and Robbie would never let you down. RIP, Rob !

Next up was Bristol City at Ashton Gate. The word was out that we were all going on the 11 o'clock train. But, to my surprise, when we arrived at the station we found out that the older lads had gone early, on the 10 o'clock. I was gutted and a bit pissed off that they had just ditched us like that even though we had all done our bit at Millwall.

On arrival at Bristol Temple Meads, the rumour mill was in full flow. Stories were coming back to us that the boys had been ambushed and a few had been hospitalised. Judging by the police presence at the station, it seemed as if something had gone down. One copper told us that it had gone off in the Black Horse Pub, that the Bristol boys had used ammonia on our lads and that six were in hospital. The police escorted about 150 of us to the ground. On the way there was no sign of the Bristol firm. It seemed all too quiet. We passed the Black Horse Pub and, sure enough, there was an acrid smell of ammonia in the air. It burnt our eyes and stung our throats as we walked by. There obviously had been an altercation as there were also broken bottles and bricks in the road.

As we made our way into the open end behind the goals, I could see the boys - a few of them bruised and bloody. I spoke to Craig who told me that they had been ambushed by the Bristol firm. Ammonia had been squirted in their eyes and a few had gone to hospital but the majority were OK. It had been a violent clash, with weapons used on both sides. There had been a building site close by, so iron spikes had been pulled from the ground and house bricks and planks of wood used. One of our lads, Vince, had been about to be thrown off the Bedminster Bridge - and most probably would have been, if Boxer had not intervened by smashing the Bristol boys with a piece of 4' x 2'. I was really gutted that I had missed it and hoped we would have some more action later on. I had been to Bristol before and many times since and you've got to give it to them. They are always up for it - a real game firm. The ammonia trick was a bit below the belt but, hey, all's fair in love and war, they say !

During the game, the banter flew between us on the bank and their firm in the top tier of the grandstand directly on our left. They were giving it the big one, waving the local paper with a report of the morning's event on the front page. This spurred us on, like a red rag to a bull, to steam the fence and the boys broke the gate open. On seeing us attempt to get at them, Bristol came streaming down from the grandstand while the police battled to hold back both sets of fans. Order was restored for the time being but we couldn't wait to get out at the end of the match. By now the police presence was massive and they kept us in for ten minutes before opening the gates. Outside, the riot police were waiting, lined up like storm troopers with a mass of dog handlers with Alsatians drooling, snarling and chomping at the bit. A ridiculous over-reaction, I thought. It was like a scene from Nazi Germany. As we moved out of the stadium it became apparent why the riot police were there. As we moved opposite the park, an enormous mob came streaming over the hill through the trees like fucking madmen. At the time, this was the biggest mob I had ever seen en masse - and mostly dressers too - it was a truly impressive sight. I must admit my bottle was going. I was still only seventeen and after what happened to Robbie, I didn't fancy being the next one in the hospital.

Fair play to the boys, though, they tried to break the police lines but the police would baton us back and ward us off with the dogs. Not once did they try to stop the Bristol boys, though and by now everything they could get their hands on was being pelted at us. They threw coins, bricks, bottles, lighters - even clumps of mud from the park. It became so relentless that the police had now backed us against the wall, shielding us and themselves with their riot shields. We were edged slowly up the road until we came across a junction directly behind us and the police. As we crossed it, another mob of Bristol lay in wait and charged as we came into view. We were in no mood to take any more shit and the sight of a team of wurzels without any riot police in between us was our opportunity to dish out some retribution. We steamed into them without any hesitation or bouncing up and down on the spot. We had had enough - and it showed. The Bristol mob had it on their toes - admittedly we outnumbered them, as their main mob was still behind us in the park. But our fear had turned into frustration and the frustration into pure anger. It was what I call 'fuck the police time' - the time of fear of arrest going straight out of the window. We got back to Temple Meads Station without seeing any more City boys. At the station some of the boys from the hospital were waiting for us, all bandaged up with eye patches from the ammonia attack but in good humour.

Another day out was nearly over but we had one last stop. We had to change trains in Cardiff - and their team had been playing at home. As the train pulled into Cardiff Central, I opened the door before the train stopped and jumped off the still-moving train. Greggers and I were walking down the platform when a lad came out from behind one of the advertising hoardings. He was dressed in a light blue Tachini with a red collar. The blonde haired lad said "Hello boys, we're the Neath Blues."

Greggers replied "Take a look behind us, mush !"

What the Cardiff lad hadn't seen was 200 Jacks coming off the train we had got off earlier. Punches were thrown and we chased them down the platform stairs. Once again, the police came steaming in, batons drawn. I had recognised the blonde lad and suddenly, it clicked. I had heard his voice before when I had been jumped by the car full of casuals down the Mumbles in the summer.

The season had started off as bad as the last two and the team was still in freefall. Crowds were down and, if it carried on, we would make it a third consecutive relegation. The football was so bad that our concentration on the off-field activities was magnified ten fold.

The casual look had turned into a whole new football culture. You would know who was up for a ruck just by the way they dressed and the police still hadn't cottoned on to it. This showed at our next home game against Bradford City. A few of us were on the prowl after the match in the car park on the Mumbles

Road when we came across a few game Bradford boys. Phelpsy, Hoppy and I got into them. I had smacked the fuck out of one with my golf umbrella which had attracted a few of the lads who were still skinheads. One of them, Dai Smutto, a right fucking header, came steaming in with his boots flying, complete with a fucking Hitler moustache ! It was a bizarre sight that had us in stitches laughing in the pub afterwards. Fuck knows what the Bradford boys thought ! But when the Old Bill turned up we just walked away nonchalantly as the police chased after the 'nasty' skinheads.

Our next fixture was Bolton Wanderers at home. We had started drinking in a pub at the edge of the Sandfields called The Queens. It was a perfect location for our firm as it was situated on a crossroads with one road coming down from the Kingsway where anyone who came by train was sure to come; another road came along Oxford Street, straight from the bus station and the main city centre; the other routes ran to the Mumbles Road and the exit of the city and the other from the Sandfields and the Vetch itself. This was the most strategic place to be for any possible situation. We fully expected Bolton to bring a firm and all the time they played us in the lower divisions not once did they disappoint us. With us now drinking in the Queens, it had brought all the small firms together as one which made us a considerable force at home. But we still didn't travel well.

One of the lads come by from the Pant-y-gwydr pub to tell us that a mob of Bolton were in the lounge. It was only a two minute walk from the Queens so we left immediately - the pub emptying in a second, pints left where they were standing. Walking down Oxford Street we were an awesome sight - well over a hundred of us. There's no feeling like it as we marched towards our impending clash. This was the feeling we all craved like a drug, the feeling of power. It enlivened every nerve like the best buzz you could possibly achieve. This was it. This was football. One of our main lads, Simon Ivey, was first in, steaming into the lounge, fists flying. To be first in when entering a pub, was always the most dangerous position because you didn't know what you would be facing and a glass in the face wouldn't be a surprise. So it took a lot of bottle - something Ivey certainly wasn't short of. The Bolton boys didn't stand a chance and they soon made off out of the emergency exit which, unfortunately for them, led to a fenced-off courtyard. Their only escape was up the fire exit towards the landlord's quarters up on the flat roof outside. As we followed them up the fire escape, they threw down plant pots and all sorts of stuff. One of them picked up a pitch fork and was trying to fend us off as we chased them over the terraced series of flat roofs. Luckily for them, the police arrived pretty sharpish otherwise a few of them would have had a right pasting. They might have thought they would have had an easy ride in the lower divisions but not here. Welcome to Swansea !

After our relegation to Division Three, the South Wales derby switched from our bitter rivals, Cardiff, to Newport County. Now, not many people would think that Newport was a place you would have a battle but believe me it could be a nasty place to go. They might not have the numbers but they would always have a welcoming committee ! The season before we had played them in a pre-season friendly and, while we had been drinking in the Trout pub, the Newport mob had steamed in. Unfortunately for one of their firm, he had been glassed in the neck, cutting his jugular vein and had nearly died with blood gushing from the gaping wound. This was the first time we had played them since that incident and they were sure to be out for revenge. We had travelled up by train and around hundred of us had made the journey. It was not long before we met the opposition. We had just left the train station and were making our way down the road when the shout went up.

"Here they are !"

Fans caused terror in pub battle

TERROR was created by a violent distrubance involving rival soccer fans from Swansea and Newport in a town-centre public house in Newport in August last year, a jury at Newport Crown Court was told yesterday.

Mr. Patrick Eccles, prosecuting, told the jury that there was a "battle of considerable violence" in the Trout Vaults public house in Market Street, Newport, at lunch time on Saturday, August 13. He told the jury that the fight which broke up "fairly quickly" caused terror in the pub. Women were screaming

with fear. Rival fans were involved in throwing beer glasses at each other. Chairs were knocked over and stools were also thrown.

CHANTING

He said ten to15 supporters were also involved in fighting and wrestling. And one of the 13 defendants in the case, John Waters, fromNewport, was taken out with blood pumping from a wound in his neck.

Mr. Eccles said that afterwards about 60 or so were milling around in the street and

a stallholder from the nearby market disarmed one young man who was still carrying a beer glass.

Mr. Eccles was opening the trial of 13 young men — three of them from Newport and the rest from Swansea — who all denied unlawfully fighting and making an affray in the pub.

At the end of the prosecution's opening statement, the three Swansea defendants changed their pleas to guilty yesterday afternoon, Paul Ronald Thomas, aged 20, unemployed, of Llangyfelach

Estate, Swansea, 19-year-old Simon Anthony Ivey, a labourer, of Grenfell Park Road, St. Thomas, Swansea, and Mark Brian Drew, aged 18, unemployed, of Carno Place, Morriston, Swansea, were all released on bail and will be sentenced later. The trial of the ten Newport defendants continues.

Mr. Eccles said the incident in the Trout Vaults started with "a calculated act of hooliganism" by the Newport youths. He said they burst into the pub at 1.30 p.m. About 25 or more came in and against immediately confronted the Swansea supporters, shouting and chanting at them and provoking a confrontation.

DELIBERATE

The prosecution accepted that the battle may not have lasted very long but Mr. Eccles said it was "very frightening and violent."

The defendants had blamed each other for starting to throw beer glasses. Apart from the neck wound to the Newport supporter, another defendant was hit on the head by a glass and two others were cut. Another was seen later with cuts around his ear.

The landlord's fiancee was struck by a flying glass, another woman was hit on the chest and yet another woman was cut on the hand.

Mr. Eccles said it was the prosecution's case that the Newport youths had "engineered a deliberate confrontation which they must have known would involve a number of fights innocent bystanding."

10 fans held after affray

TEN soccer fans, three of them from Swansea, were detained by police after a town centre affray involving rival supporters Saturday's Somerton Park friendly match between Newport County and Swansea City.

Police say that a Newport lan 35-year-old John Waters, of Ballug Street, sustained a serious wound to his neck during disturbances where there was a confrontation when the two, in which chairs and tables were thrown. Waters was taken to the Royal Gwent Hospital where he was said to be comfortable. Today he was said to be comfortable. Police say it is believed his injuries are

on holiday in the Tenby area, the According to the police, the disturbances took place around 1.30 pm. Swansea fans were drinking in the public house in Market Street after they were public house in Market Street after they occurred after the match began by Newport fans.

It is also understood that these clashes at about the same time in the High Street.

* See match report, Page 19.

We rushed forward as one in anticipation of a set to, only to be disappointed because they were just a handful and they had made off when they saw they were heavily outnumbered. Boxer, one of the lads who was at the front, had been nicked as the police swiftly moved in. However, to our surprise, our greeting party was not the Newport boys, they were fucking Cardiff ! The Old Bill now had a tricky situation on their hands. Not only did they have to separate us and Newport but also had Swansea and Cardiff and Cardiff and Newport to keep apart. And there was no love lost between those two, either. We were heavily policed all the way to the ground by riot vans and dog handlers. Our bit of fun was over for the day, though some had a little 'off' with some Cardiff outside the ground. The Newport boys weren't to be denied their revenge, though. They stabbed a Swansea fan at the bus station - a fucking cowardly act, as he was just a 'scarfer' and not a hooligan. Well done you mugs !

On the pitch, the season was turning into another disaster with six losses out of ten games - just three won and one draw. We were looking like a good candidate for a rapid return to Division Four only two years after topping the whole football league and six years after leaving Division Four. That was the Swansea experience - up one minute, down the next.

Things had died down a bit on the hooligan front after the mad start against Millwall, Bristol City and then Newport. There seemed to be a bit of a lull with some games against teams without much form. One such game was against Reading so we were fucking surprised when a couple of Reading lads came on the North Bank, shouting the odds. We shifted through the crowd at speed towards them - a couple of old heads in denim jackets, probably old school hooligans from the 60's and 70's. I smashed one right on the nose and he went down, out cold. Once the boys had smelt blood there was no stopping them. He had a real fucking stomping in the tunnel entrance into the North Bank and there was blood splattered all up the bright white walls of the entrance. I must admit I felt it was a bit out of order, even though the cheeky twat had given it the big one on our end, to see him carted off in an ambulance driven right up on to the North Bank. It wasn't what it was all about. It was supposed to be firm against firm, not ten against two. This incident would hold me to the so-called 'hooligan code' in future rows. Nobody likes it to happen to them and it had to me in the past and would again in the future.

The FA Cup always gets the blood flowing in every football fan's veins - and the hooligans are no different. But this year our first round draw was a home tie against non-league Bognor Regis. Obviously, we expected a quiet day at the Vetch Field. Oh how wrong could we have been ! Reports had been coming into us all morning of a large following for Bognor. We just put it down to us being recently relegated from the top flight so we were quite a big draw for lowly Bognor. It wasn't until we started to queue to get into the North Bank that we found out the truth. As we queued up, Phelpsy noticed a gang of casuals in the front of the line. He approached a tall lad with black curly hair dressed in a Pringle and split, frayed, faded jeans. Out came the oldest trick in the books - a way to hear someone's accent to determine where they came from.

"What's the time, mate ?" The lad turned round and just handed Phelpsy a card with the inscription 'You've just met the 657 Crew'.
"They're fucking Pompey !"

It kicked off. Maylin grabbed one and dragged his face down the wall and Braino slammed one over the head with a brick. We chased them off towards the away supporters section where the police were waiting. We didn't expect that - in fact nobody did - the police were caught out and we certainly didn't have a firm organized. Once in the ground, the Pompey boys battled with the police on the West Bank, at one point physically chucking a police dog out of the crowd after the handler had let him go. After the match, we couldn't really muster up a good mob and, as the 657 Crew had called it on with the Old Bill, they had called up the heavy mob with robo cops all over the away fan section. There was no way of getting at each other.

Things were getting worse in the league but off the pitch we were getting stronger with all the small mobs joining together and drinking together. We were starting to be able to put a good mob of 100 or maybe more together which would rise to 300 or more for big matches but still we didn't travel well - only to derby matches or trips just over the bridge to Bristol. I was doing a coach building apprenticeship at the time which gave me free travel on all coaches and buses throughout the country. So I would often travel to away games on my own. I saw us play at Bolton, Derby, Burnley, Lincoln, Hull and Gillingham. We could have had a row at every one of those games but we had nobody there. It would bug me no end but travel was too expensive because Swansea was out on a limb in football circles - it was an hour on the train before you got to Cardiff, let alone fucking England. We couldn't get coaches because no bus company would touch us after the routine wrecking of coaches every other week when were in Division One. And even if we did get a coach booked, the police would lean on the company like the fucking Mafia. We would all be waiting for our bus and the fucker wouldn't turn up.

It was now March and our next big one was Newport at home. We all anticipated a big turn-out from our Welsh cousins from just up the M4 but alas it was a poor showing - so poor, in fact, that they herded them in the left hand section of the West Bank and they didn't come anywhere near to filling that.

It was a glorious sunny March day, perfect for football violence and we had a good mob out too. We were well disappointed about the Newport turn-out until halfway through the second half when more came into the ground - and these were casuals, unmistakable in their pre-faded jeans, Benetton jumpers and an assortment of tracksuit tops. The strange thing was that they were being let into the right hand section of the West Bank nearest us on the North Bank, segregated from the rest of the Newport fans. The reason became apparent as soon as they started to sing. "CARDIFF !" sang the new arrivals, knowing full well the reaction they would get.

The North Bank heaved forward . "Who the fuck, who the fuck, who the fucking hell are you ?"

One minute we were 3 - 0 down and silent, the next the noise was deafening as the football paled into insignificance. These 30 fucking herberts had sneaked in three quarters of the way through the game and really put the cat amongst the pigeons. Just as the game was finishing, some of the lads went out of the bank to the big earthen mounds which supported the terrace up the concrete steps behind the North Bank. There, they tore out the rocks and stones and armed themselves and others as they came back in. A steady hail of stones and rocks was being hurled over at the cheeky intruders as the referee called a halt to the game. The police came wading in with their truncheons but were forced back by the amount of rubble coming their way. The Cardiff boys had really wound us up and if the Old Bill wanted to stop us, they would have a real fight on their hands. The police had ushered the Cardiff lads to the exits so we made our way out to get at them. I can still remember the rush, 23 years on, as we armed ourselves with rocks from the bank which now resembled an abandoned quarry. As we came out, we turned left onto Madoc Street and, as usual, the police had the street barriers in operation. Normally the police would stop the boys and there would be a lot of pushing and shoving, shouting and screaming. Not today. Today was different. Today was not about posturing and posing. Today was about action. The police didn't know what hit them. The bricks went through the police car windows and the sound of smashing glass filled the air. This was the sound of riot. The sound seemed to spur on the crowd as bricks rained down on the police who were trying to hide in the doorways of the small terraced houses. One copper was laid out and a police woman was punched to the ground as she tried to stop the wild mob. The street barriers, which for so long had been effective at keeping the opposing fans apart, were now being used as battering rams. The onslaught went on for what seemed an age until re-enforcements arrived on the scene to restore order. But even though we got through to the away section, the small Cardiff mob had ghosted out as quick as they had ghosted in. The next day, the incident was front page headlines "THE BATTLE OF MADOC STREET" in big bold letters in the South Wales Evening Post - another cutting for the ever-increasing scrapbook.

The season was drawing to an end. We had both the Bristol clubs at home and Millwall to look forward to but for some reason, even though we had we had taken it to them, not one of them turned up. The biggest disappointment was Millwall. We knew it was an evening kick-off which would affect their travelling support but seeing we were one of only a couple of clubs who had ever gone on their end, we thought they would have returned the favour. The boys were gagging for revenge over Millwall not just for the kicking we had but to avenge Robbie's death. Even though he died a couple of days after the match, we knew the hiding he'd received must have been the reason for his brain haemorrhage. We even had a plan. One of the lads had welded six inch nails together as stars and bent the sharp ends over at right angles so that they would sit upright. These were to be placed under the wheels of the coaches so that as they pulled off, the tyres would burst and we would ambush them with bricks which we had stashed around the Sandfields. The plan was a winner and would have worked - if only the fuckers had turned up.

The season came to an end at home to Bristol City. We had a massive firm out in a crowd of eleven thousand. The atmosphere was electric - like a cup final. We needed a point to stay up and a thrilling 0 - 0 draw saw us do exactly that. It was a real night to remember.

'85 - '86

The mid 80's saw the arrival on the scene of a new gang of Swansea hooligans. Whereas we had grown up during the punk and skinhead era, this new breed grew up out of the hip hop and dance music scene, bringing in different styles and tastes. They had grown up with BMX and break-dancing while we had been reared on pogo'ing and 'fuck the system'. Their emergence was announced by the 'tagging' graffiti all around the Sandfields. Everywhere you looked it was there - The TMA. The Sandfields' Boys had evolved from the Bridge Boys in the early 70's, the Sandfields' Hells Angels in the 80's and now in the late 80's and 90's, there were The Mini Angels. The Mini Angels were a game bunch even though they were still very young. They had good numbers and if opposing firms thought nothing of them because of their age they would be making a big mistake.

As we grew older it was easier for us to hire vans which we were doing in ever increasing frequency. At last we were starting to travel on a regular basis. One such trip was to Wolverhampton Wanderers. A transit was hired and 20 of us had piled in the back. Usually we would use milk crates for seats or just lie on the floor. The front seats normally held the top boys and, in the back, the wheel arches were the prime spot. Tesco carrier bags full of Carling were the order of the day and Townsley, one of the Gorseinon boys, brought along his bong. It was a long journey up to the Midlands as we were stuck in a traffic jam on the M5. We arrived at the ground just after kick-off but, as usual, at Wolves they had a mob waiting. As we pulled up to the roundabout near the ground, a shout went up from the front of the van "Here we go !" The windowless back doors were kicked open and sunlight came flooding in as we scrambled out, not knowing what to expect. We ran up towards the small mob of Wolves boys. Rabbi had the car jack lever in his hand and Phelpsy threw his half-full bottle of Smirnoff at a half-caste lad in the front. They were on their toes at the sight of us tearing towards them tooled-up with all we could get our hands on. As they fled, I heard Phelpsy say "Fucking hell - my bottle of vodka !" He raced up the road after it because it had just skimmed across the tarmac without smashing. He came sauntering back down the road with his vodka cradled in his arms and said in his unmistakable Gorseinon accent "I wasn't fucking wasting this !" Fair play, he liked a drink.

Once in the ground, you could tell the once-great Wolves had hit rock bottom in recent times. With just over four thousand in the vast arena, the atmosphere was terrible. They hardly supported their team and the biggest cheer of the day came when four lads staged a sit down protest on the centre circle to delay the start of the second half. We thrashed them 5 - 1 and I hadn't seen Swansea win away for what seemed like years. No wonder Wolves weren't happy. When we left the ground, they battled with police in the subway outside the away end to get to us but the Old Bill had it sussed. On our arrival back at the van, we were greeted by what was becoming a familiar sight - a van full of tiny fragments of glass and a brick in the back. Cue the freezing cold, fume-filled drive back home to Wales.

Apart from our 5 - 1 victory at Wolves, the season was once again turning into the disaster; we were becoming accustomed to. My father had recently died and I needed an away trip with the boys to get some anger out of my system. This came in the form of a Milk Cup tie versus West Ham. After beating Cardiff in the first round in a two-round affair which saw hardly any trouble (one of the only times until the fan ban in the 90's) we drew West Ham away in the first leg. We were eager for a trip like this and it would be our first visit to Upton Park since the incident where the boys kicked the toilet wall down and invaded the West Ham end. This was sure to be a good one and Terry Dustbin had ordered a 52-seater, deposit paid and leaving the Swan Inn at 1 o'clock. The only problem was that the boys were getting a name for themselves with the South Wales police and either we had an informer or they were very good at always being one step ahead of us. 1 o'clock came and went. Frantic phone calls were made to the coach company with them stalling us with bullshit. It wasn't until 3 o'clock that they told us the truth - that the police had paid them a visit, threatening all sorts of retribution if they took us. We were gutted. It was too late to get a replacement and none of the boys were willing to hire a fleet of minibuses.

I scanned the papers for night cup fixtures and saw that Bristol Rovers were at home to Birmingham City. Only a handful of us were up for it so one of the lads, Millsy, took us up. I was well pissed off at the no show of the coach and even more angry about the death of my father. I needed an off and, as usual, Rovers didn't let me down. It soon became apparent that the Birmingham mob were up for it as, when we took our seats in the grandstand, they were in there with the Rovers fans. All through the game the Brummies were making sure that everyone knew they were there but Rovers didn't make a move - probably because their boys stood on the tote end, to our right.

At the end of the game, as we made our way out of the stand to the area behind, there was suddenly a roar of "Zulus! Zulus!" The Rovers fans came running back down the steps. We rushed towards the front where a mob of Rovers boys had pushed their way through the crowd. There I saw this massive, bald Rovers fan - he was fucking huge. "Like a boat upturned," Millsy recalled later. The Zulus were giving it large and it was dark as fuck behind the stand so, as you can imagine, they weren't a pretty sight. The Rovers boys were hesitant so I put my hand on the big guy's shoulder and shouted "Come on, lets get into them !" It was all he needed to hear. He charged forward, screaming at the mob of Zulus in front of him. The whole contingent of Rovers fans coming out of the stand seemed to steam forward as one with this giant of a man in front. The Birmingham mob scattered; they had taken the piss in the stand all night but not now. Even though it hadn't made up for the disappointment of not getting to West Ham, at least we had a little taste of the buzz we thrived for and, ironically, we played Bristol Rovers on the following Saturday at the Vetch. Guess who got nicked for fighting with them one day, nicked against them four days later ? It's a funny old game !

Cardiff had been relegated from Division Two the season after us which meant a return to the real South Wales derby. The people at the Football League headquarters had a nasty habit of putting our away fixture up there on Boxing Day when there were no trains, no buses and a three day hire on minibuses - making it practically impossible to get there as a firm. And Cardiff's fixture at the Vetch was normally an Easter Bank Holiday giving them an easy chance to come down en masse to enjoy the extra curricular activities. It was no wonder they used to taunt us with the fact that they used to come down mob handed but we didn't return the favour. The real truth was that in the days of the Football Specials in the 70's and early 80's, we would take thousands there but now, in the more organized mob days of the mid 80's, we always played them on Boxing Day.

Without transport as usual, a mob of about 40 of us booked on the organized 'pop and crisps' supporters' coach. All was going swimmingly for the Old Bill as they escorted us down to Ninian Park but just past the playing fields the bus came to a halt by the lights at Sloper Road. We opened the emergency exit and we were off into the territory of our most hated enemies. Anyone who has been to Ninian Park will know how intimidating the place can be but when we're in town you can magnify that tenfold. As we got off the coach, the police came from all angles but there was no chance we were getting back on. Our heads were held high, chests puffed out and the nerves were now gone as the adrenalin was kicking in and we were walking the rest of the 300 yards to the ground. The Cardiff fans came from all directions; you could see them running through the park getting to the railings in front of the lush green playing fields. They were streaming through the gravelled car park, dashing in between the rows of parked cars and we could see them being pushed back by the police up ahead on Sloper Road. The sound of insults filled the air, mixing with the snarling police Alsatians. "You fucking Jack bastards !", "Jack scum !" "Die Jack wankers !"

Of course we gave as good as we got which just enraged them more. They didn't like the fact that we didn't give a fuck for them even though we were heavily outnumbered albeit surrounded by police. But the police had made a mistake. They had formed a line to our right with our left side flanked by the houses just before the entrance to the Bob Bank. But at the point where the high, white wall in front of the grandstand had a break in it, there was no-one. This was where the break was and you didn't have to ask the Cardiff boys twice to take advantage of it. We could see them following us on the concourse between the stand and the wall and as soon as we passed the gap, the roar went up and in they steamed. The roar was enough to have some of our lads on their toes but a group of us stood firm against incredible odds. I was at the front and screamed at them "Come on then !" One of them swung at me but missed as I threw one back. Then they stopped. I couldn't believe it. They were just bouncing on the spot, not one of them wanted to be first in. There were hundreds of them and maybe 20 of us left but still they wouldn't get into us. I was walking forward, gesturing for them to get in, when suddenly I was taken down from behind. But it wasn't Cardiff - it was the police. I was nicked and dragged into a police cell underneath the Grandstand. Once there, they took my details and put me in a cell which resembled an old toilet with grey wooden doors. The game was underway and I could hear the crowd above me in the Grandstand gasping at missed chances and berating the ref until a huge roar went up and we were 1 - 0 down. I was gutted we were losing and I was missing the atmosphere. But at the same time I was elated that I had shown my worth to the older boys - that I would stay in face of adversity - and that we had stopped a big mob of the enemy in its tracks on its own ground and made them think about who they were facing.

Later on the cell door opened and in came another detainee. He had a familiar face with a gap in his front teeth and a large beauty spot. I thought I knew him but wasn't quite sure. When he was giving his details he said he was from Neath so I assumed he was a Jack. It wasn't until the next week I found out that not only was he one of the Caewern firm but also that he was one of those who had jumped me down in the Mumbles previously.

They let me out first which was lucky for me as I'm sure my cell mate would have announced his colours as soon as I set foot out of the door. The game was just coming to an end and I nervously made my way around to the Swansea end, catching the curious glances of many a passer-by. It must have been the longest hundred yards and two minutes of my life but I was made welcome by the big up from the lads on my return.

We didn't have to wait long for a return to Ninian Park because we had drawn them in the Freight Rover Trophy.

One of the lads, a smart dresser called Neil Cooney, had just left the army and was back on the scene. Out of all the lads we had (and we had some real game boys in my time), I had never met anyone as game and just plain crazy as Cooney. He had a look and an air of violence about him, someone you didn't have to know to know not to fuck with. He had brought a more stoic attitude to the firm; people would follow him, a born leader of men as such. This showed when we took a full coach to Cardiff for the game in this new competition. It was regarded as a 'Mickey Mouse Cup' that fans didn't show up to and show up they didn't at Ninian Park, just a pathetic crowd of 1006. As we walked about unopposed, some of the lads, through sheer boredom, decided to leave our end where, unusually, they had put us below the Grandstand and go in the Bob Bank. They kicked the turnstile doors in and went in the sparsely populated home end. From our vantage point, directly opposite, we could see the boys coming in and it wasn't long before it kicked off. We cheered in delight as the boys fought off the home fans. Fair play to them, they had gone on only six of them and it was the police who had to get them off, though Terry Davies did say to me later that it might not have looked many from where we were standing but on there it was a little bit tricky. On the way home, the bus broke down in Bridgend, a staunch Cardiff stronghold. We searched for some action to no avail and ended up getting steaming in a pub which was, as usual, trashed and looted. I had lost a lot of respect for Cardiff that day. I can't speak for the rest of our boys but I did think they had the bigger and better firm. But the more and more I was facing them, the less and less respect I held for them. They may have had massive numbers but when it came to the nitty gritty of it all they just weren't lining up to their reputation.

My best mate at this time was a lad named Alan from the Mumbles. Like me, he was a dresser and liked the culture but he was more of a lover than a fighter. He had suffered from a hole in the heart as a youngster and had nearly died so I tended to be protective towards him which got me in front of the Magistrates and in a few scrapes. His dad was originally from Hartlepool so, when we were playing Darlington, he decided to go up and see some family. Meanwhile Alan, another mate, Simon and I went to Darlo to see the match. We stopped in a pub near the ground after a long walk from the train station. The pub was quite full of Jacks - Tenko and a few of the Manselton boys were in there. While we were in the pub, a shaven-headed Darlo fan came in, a bit of a dresser but scruffy with it - I'm sure all football boys will know what I mean. He was boasting about how he had a life ban and was always in the thick of the action against Hartlepool. He said we would have trouble in the ground as there was no segregation but I don't think anyone believed him. On arrival at the ground, I couldn't believe what a shit hole it was. I know the Vetch wasn't the best of grounds but compared to this it was a palace. True to the Darlington fan's word, there was no segregation. In all my six years following the Swans away, I had never come across a situation where you just stood with the home fans. Sure enough, with just ten minutes gone, it went off - but to our surprise the fans on the official coaches just stood together and took no shit, fighting off the Darlo boys.

After we conceded the sixth goal without reply, we decided to make our way back to the train station. While we were walking through the Saturday afternoon shoppers, I noticed we were being followed by about 20 lads. There were only three of us so the odds were insurmountable . I said to Alan and Simon, "Don't look now but we're being followed by a team of dressers !" Problem is, when you ask someone not to look, they inevitably always fucking look ! That was all it took. They charged through the shoppers, sending them in all directions. The chase was on. We could see the British Rail logo up ahead on the street; maybe there would be somewhere to lose them in there. We sprinted down into the station concourse, hearts beating in our ears but there was no sanctuary, just rows of platforms with a couple of waiting rooms. As usual there wasn't a copper when you needed one. When you don't want them there's fucking thousands of 'em! The Darlo boys came running in the station and spotted us at the end of the platform. It was either jump onto the tracks and let the chase continue or stand and fight. It's a strange feeling how the 'fight or flight' reaction kicks in. One minute you're out of breath from running and every sinew in your body feels fucked, the next it's like you've taken some wonder drug and your body is running on optimum performance levels. The Darlo boys had now stopped running and were walking towards us, arms outstretched in the 'come on' position. A lad in front, wearing a Hugo Boss sweatshirt, came forward, arms open wide. He was a sitting duck so I just cracked him on the jaw and he went down. Another jumped forward and I caught him a beauty right on the nose and he went down too. With this, the rest just stopped in their tracks, not knowing what to do, just looking at each other. A voice came out of the blue.

"Oi, you lot !" A gang of men came running over from one of the waiting rooms. The Darlo boys made off.

"Are you's alreet ?" one of the men asked.

"We're OK, mate," I said.

"Looks like ya didn't need our help but you was outnumbered, like."

"Cheers !" I replied.

What had looked like a good kicking on the cards turned into an embarrassing situation for those two Darlo boys in front of their firm.

It was May again and time for the visit from our rivals up the M4. We had been planning this one for weeks and a meet was set for the amphitheatre behind Swansea Leisure Centre at 10am. It was another traditional sunny day as it always was at home to Cardiff. On arriving at the amphitheatre, we were greeted by a magnificent sight of hundreds of boys, all sitting on the terracing as though they were waiting for a gladiator fight in ancient Rome. It was one hell of a turnout for so early in the morning. They would never catch us out as they had before in the 'Bad'. We set off towards the Sandfields in search of our foe. In a time before the internet and mobile phones, pot luck and rumours on the grapevine were the only means of a possible meet. As luck would have it, Tenko had been driving up past the recreation ground and had seen a mob of Cardiff heading our way. I was up ahead of everyone with Cooney as we spotted two casuals walking across the Mumbles Road. Cooney sprinted towards them, grabbing the first one.

"Where you from, mate ?" ,

"Its OK, we're Cardiff," he replied. Even after the running we gave them a couple of seasons back, they still hadn't learnt their lesson. Cooney smashed him down instantly as I tackled the other. By the time the one I had smacked had run off, Cooney was stamping relentlessly on the other's head.

"Leave him, he's fucked," I said.

"Fuck him, he's having it !" Cooney screamed back at me. I then had to grab him with all my might and drag him off. "You're gonna kill him, Neil !" I shouted.

"Fuck him !" he retorted. I could see a copper running towards us at full pelt, helmet under his arm.

"Come on, lets go !"

As usual, Cooney was oblivious to the Old Bill - the reason why he would eventually be nicked on so many occasions. We made our way off the Mumbles Road and, as we looked back for the police, we could see the rest of the mob reaching the unconscious Bluebird just as one of the local kids was bunny hopping on his head on his BMX. The hatred certainly ran deep in these parts, right down to the kid. Hating Cardiff was a tradition passed down from father to son, generation to generation.

We joined up with the rest and moved down Oxford Street towards the direction of the incoming mob. As the clock tower of the Guild Hall came into sight, the pace hotted up and, by the time we had come into the wide open space of the Guild Hall Green, it was a full-on charge with the enemy in sight. We fanned out as the Cardiff mob did the same. It must have been an awesome sight to them as there was 200-300 of us to their 50. To be fair to them, they stood their ground and, believe me, it took some bottle to do so against so many. As you do in gang warfare, I picked out a sparring partner and made my way to him but he turned to run as I clipped his heels. He stumbled as if to fall but, after some deft footwork, he regained his stride and managed to leap up onto a fence and over into someone's house. By the time I turned to look for someone else, they were all gone. As if by magic, they had scattered in all directions. One lad had stood and traded punches until he had been knocked unconscious. He had taken a right kicking but you've got to give him the utmost respect for standing. I'm sure many wouldn't have, faced with such odds.

The mob we had faced were from nearby Neath and Port Talbot. The Port Talbot boys, named the PVM, were Jacks until they were given some stick from some of the more far right members of the firm as some of them were half caste. Swansea had no black or ethnic areas apart from Indian and Pakistani so, seeing lads not from Swansea who were coloured, some of the lads found it hard to take. This turned them towards Cardiff which had a traditional ethnic society. In my opinion, this was a shame as the PVM would always turn up for a row even if they were on a hiding to nothing. Our loss was Cardiff's gain. I later found out that the Cardiff lad who had stood alone was Bully Fulman, one of the Neath Caewern Firm and the same boy I had been locked up with in Cardiff.

After we had obliterated the mob who had come in from the west to try and catch us out, we moved back up towards the Queens. Although delighted at giving the Cardiff mob a slapping, I was a little concerned about the lad Cooney had battered unconscious on the Mumbles Road. Rumours were rife about his demise and both Cooney and I had been spotted at the scene by one of the regular match day Old Bill. Nevertheless, it wouldn't stop us going to the game. The pull of a derby game outweighed the risk of getting nicked so a few shirts were swapped and we were in. The match was won 2 - 0 and although a few slaps were given out, we didn't come across another big mob. They hadn't shown in the massive numbers that they had previously, even the crowd of seven thousand was very disappointing.

For a few weeks afterwards, I was a little nervous, especially after reading the report of the attack on the Mumbles Road, how a lad ended up in hospital and the police were concentrating on identifying his attackers. The feeling you get when you're anticipating a knock on the door throws your mind and body out of sorts and is not a nice feeling. I would come to experience this state on a regular basis, especially after the installation of CCTV in the 90's. But, would it make me give it up ? Would it, fuck. The firm was now my family and I felt I was right at the heart of it.

Our last away game of the season was at York and Cooney and I had ordered a 52-seater which had cost us a fucking fortune. And to our despair, only thirty of us turned up. As usual, many had said they were going to give a couple of quid deposit but obviously had no intention of doing so and were too scared to say so. The journey cost us over £20 each which was a lot of money in 1986 but was well worth it as we had a right 'jolly boys outing !' It was not always about a row - a good piss-up and a day out with the boys was enough. A row would be a bonus !

After the club had been wound up as insolvent at Christmas time, this trip was seen as a piss-up, a bit of a celebration of our survival as a Football League Club. We had thought about the idea of fancy dress as a lot of club's lads had seemed to enjoy a day out rowing dressed as Hitler or a gorilla but we ended up agreeing on a type of uniform. We decided to paint our faces black and white and wear black sweatshirts emblazoned with our firm's name. The problem was that we didn't really have a name. The youth were the 'Baby Squad' and the older lads had come from many smaller local mobs. We needed a name but were reluctant to use the pubs name as the 'Queen's Crew' sounded camper than a row of pink tents ! I can't be totally sure but I think the name was coined by Cooney and one of the older lads, Craig Chapple. And so the Jack Army was born on May 3rd, 1986. The jumpers were printed with the word 'Jack' emblazoned horizontally, with the word 'Army' printed vertically from the 'A' in 'Jack'. We must have looked a right state as we got off the bus at Strensham Services in the Midlands, all pissed up with painted faces. As was the norm, the Services were looted and on our way back to the bus four coach-loads of Plymouth fans pulled in, all giving it big through the windows at the sight of us all painted up. Some of the boys wearing strips, some half and half and Little Chris from Neath with a black and white Union Jack - what a sight ! As their coaches came to a halt, we ran over to them, beckoning them to get off but they weren't budging. One of the lads from Penlan, Mike Hadley, jumped on the first bus and called them off. The driver stood up and put his arm out. Mike was a stocky lad with a massive neck, thick as a tree trunk. He didn't take too kindly to the drivers intervention and knocked him clean out with one punch. This made a clear statement to the Plymouth fans that there might only be 30 of us but we weren't to be fucked with or abused by a bunch of wurzel 'scarfers', no matter how many of them there were. One of the other drivers called the police so we were off sharpish up the M5.

York produced no-one and the game was a non event with Swansea losing 3 - 1 and being relegated to the lowest tier of the Football League just eight years after leaving and topping the whole league. That must be some record.

'86 - '87

Our return to Division Four, depressing as it was, had some positives for us. The best being that the derbies would continue because Cardiff had also been relegated and Wolves had come down too - two definite offs. Our first away trip of the season was against Preston North End and a weekender in Blackpool had been organised. We travelled up in two minibuses. We had a cracking mob of 50 top quality lads arriving on the Friday night. After a night of trawling the seedy pubs and clubs of Blackpool, we set off for Preston early doors. We had a good mix of youth and older lads with Tracy, our main face, leading the mob. After a good few bevies were downed, we made our way up the hill towards Deepdale. As the ground came into sight so did a good mob of Preston. It was even numbers and you could tell that both mobs were up for it. My heart was thumping in my ears as we made our way towards them. The speed we had taken earlier was doing its job. I was rushing like fuck as they came closer, grinding my teeth, practically snorting with aggression. Tracy, always cool in a confrontation, was preparing the boys all the way with his commands. "Walk !" "Walk !" he barked. As they were practically on top of us, he screamed "Now !" All hell broke loose as the lads clashed all across the tree-lined car park outside the home end. A lad came towards me with a tree branch in his hands. As I steamed into him, he smashed me over the shoulder and the timber exploded into dust because it was rotten. I smacked him straight in the jaw just as Dull Martin volleyed him in the head with one of his karate kicks. He dropped unconscious on the floor. As we won the initial first blows, the main body of lads turned and ran. I pursued one lad into the car park as he was ripping a car aerial off to use as a weapon. He frantically wrenched it from side to side to get it off but we were on him as he did. Fair play to him, he tried to stand but was overwhelmed by our numbers. We set after them through the car park and were still punching them as they hurdled the turnstiles into their own end. The job was done - we had humiliated them on their own patch.

After the game, they rounded up a good mob but we were wrapped up by the Old Bill by then and escorted out of town. It was hell of a buzz to do this to a mob on their own turf and it was an impressive performance by the lads. But what impressed me the most was the way Tracy had led the boys. He was the oldest (in his thirties) but a very slight lad - though you shouldn't judge a book by its cover because this man had so much bottle it had to be seen to be believed. He had proved it many times before and would many times again. He was a true terrace legend.

Football violence was now everything to me and the boys were truly my family. My mother had died only a few months after my Dad and, even though I was just a fledgling in the firm, many of the main faces turned up for her funeral. This showed great respect and helped me cope with my grief and confusion at being left alone at such a young age. There is no stronger bond than putting your own safety on the line for the sake of another and I felt that we were a real band of brothers.

Our next game of note to come around was Wolves at home. I was out early doors with my best mate, Alan, in the conservatory of a bar called Martha's Vineyard. We were just scanning the Kingsway, looking at the vans going by and trying to spot some Midlands hire companies. I nearly spat my beer out as a van full of Wolves lads went by. I put my bottle down and said to Alan ...

"I'm off down the Queens to see the lads. You coming ?"
"Nah," he replied, "I'm staying put."

I sensed something wasn't right with him but the lure of an off was too much to resist. On arriving at the Queens, Cooney said that one of the lads had passed the Quadrant Gate pub by the shopping precinct and it was full of Wolves. We didn't have a big mob at the time but decided to go anyway. The Quadrant Gate had a five metre bay window of small eight inch square panes and a perfect viewpoint for anyone in there. As we got closer you could see the heads bobbing up and down frantically. I said to Cooney ...

"They're fucking there, all right !"
"C'mon then, Wall, we'll show the lads what the Squad can do."

When I was with Cooney I felt indestructible. He had that effect on you as you knew he would die before he'd let you down. He even had "Death Before Dishonour" tattooed on his forearm. Words I'm sure he meant. The Wolves boys spilled out of the doors armed with bottles and glasses.

"Here we go !" said Dustbin, as he pulled his leather fighting gloves on.

Pieces of glass rained down on us, one of them smashing near my leg and cutting me on the hip. Once their weapons were spent, we were on them. I smashed one in the mouth and pain stung my knuckles. Cooney had pulled down the main lad at the front who was wearing dungarees and a day-glo blue waffle jumper. He kicked him relentlessly against a litter bin which was secured by paving slabs. Cooney just kicked him and kicked him until the slabs were torn out of the ground. Once again Neil had his blinkers on and never saw the Old Bill as they arrived. I grabbed him and said "Run !" A copper grabbed Cooney but he brushed him aside as he was a real big lad. The copper gave him a look but had second thoughts as Cooney squared him up to him. We made off back to the Queens. My hand was bleeding as I had two neat holes in my knuckles where I had caught the Wolves lad's teeth. Cooney and I had been first in and enhanced the reputation of the Squad up a notch or two and once again Cooney had shown his lust for ultra violence by not being content with just giving someone a kicking.

In the ground I found Alan and watched the game. Near the end, Alan felt ill and collapsed. I ran to a copper to get help but the Old Bill said ...

"What's wrong ? Fucking pissed is he ?"
"He's got a fucking bad heart, you cunt !" we shouted at him.

An ambulance arrived at the back of the North Bank and by then Alan seemed OK. I asked him if he wanted me to come with him he and he said "No, I'll be fine," and gave me a smile. As soon as I left him, I felt bad. I was his best mate, I should have gone with him. I battled with myself; one half of me was saying 'Go with him' while the other half was saying 'We'll have a row after with Wolves'. Once again the hooligan lust consumed me. The chance of a ruck was too overwhelming and anyway he said he'd be OK ! Those turned out to be the last words Alan spoke to me. I phoned his Mum on Sunday morning, fully expecting to talk to him, only to find out that he had gone. I was devastated. First my parents, then my best mate. It was an impossible moment in my life, compounded by my immense guilt of not being there for Alan because of my addiction to football violence. Ditching your best mate in his greatest time of need just for the possibility of a ruck. What a cunt I felt. The lowest of the low.

Everyone likes a weekend in a quaint seaside town and we were no different. So when we were paired against Torquay with an evening kick-off on a Saturday, who could say no ? We set off on Friday afternoon with a fleet of minibuses and it seemed as if everyone had turned out. The night had passed off quite peacefully with the boys up to their usual antics of generally fucking about and making a nuisance of themselves. On our way back to the digs, Cooney, a couple of other lads and I stopped off in a fast food joint called 'Griddles' on the hill up from the seafront. Food outlets are generally a flash point for violence at the weekend so when a gang of "foreigners" is in town it's no surprise when it all kicks off. As we queued for food, some lairy locals spouted off about how us Welsh cunts were going to get a kicking on Saturday night. A standoff occurred with us at the bottom of a couple of steps in front of the counter and the locals up on top. This one cunt was mouthing off on one so I dived up the steps towards him. Before I could get to him, one of the others kicked

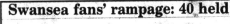

Swansea fans' rampage: 40 held

SOCCER INSANITY!

MORE THAN 40 SWANSEA City soccer fans were arrested at the weekend after they went on the rampage in Torquay which police today described as football insanity.

The fans, called hard-core violent hooligans by the police, smashed shop windows in the town centre and looted the premises.

They fought in pubs and restaurants both before and after Swansea's Saturday night match with Torquay.

Torquay police press officer, Mr. Mike Arthur said today: "It was a typical weekend of football passivity. The fans were hard-core violent hooligan."

Most of the arrests were for drunkenness and disorder and nine Swansea fans were appearing before Torquay magistrates today.

Terrified

Another six fans were bailed by police to appear in court at a later date.

One Swansea supporter, ho asked not to be named, went to the match with his wife.

He said: "The so-called fans just seemed to go beserk. I've never seen anything as bad at away games before. My wife was terrified.

"It was a frightening spectacle. About 200-300 so-called supporters charged through the centre of Torquay. They smashed shop windows

and looted them. They weren't the true fans. These were hooligans just looking for trouble," he added.

Police claim Swansea fans threw sharpened coins, fireworks and home-made metal 'Kung Fu stars' on to the pitch.

'Obscenities'

Fights broke out twice in Griddles Restaurant, and a youngster needed stitches over his eye and other treatment after he had four teeth knocked out during an attack by a mob of about 20 Swansea youths, police added.

Police were given advance information from Swansea that 200 fans, including the "hard-core", were heading for Torbay on Friday and shifts were altered so that more men were on duty.

Shopper Caroline Hearn watched as about 30 fans made their way down Union Street on Saturday afternoon.

"They were drunk, shouting obscenities and throwing empty beer cans into the road," she said.

About 30 fans terrorised staff at the Spectra Leatherware shop in Fleet. An attempt was made to smash one of the

windows and manager Mr. Christopher Morgan was hit on the back of the head.

Ridiculous

"Clothes rails were knocked over and we managed to get two jackets worth £300 back which were being taken," he said.

Swans chairman Mr. Doug Sharpe said today: "I spent the whole weekend in Torquay and had no bad reports of any violence.

"Our supporters have been ● To page 3

Torquay rowdyism: seven fined

Swans fan sentenced

A SWANSEA CITY FOOTBALL Club fan was sent to a detention centre for four months yesterday after causing trouble inside the Torquay United ground during last Saturday's match.

Alan Haydn Roberts, aged 20, was one of nine Swansea supporters who appeared at Torbay magistrates court yesterday on charges ranging from drunk and disorderly behaviour to threatening behaviour.

The magistrates heard that rowdy fans caused disturbances in the town centre in the afternoon, before the match and afterwards.

Roberts, of Protretteherne Road, Landore, Swansea, admitted using threatening words or behaviour.

The prosecution alleged that he punched and kicked a policeman but his solicitor, Mr. Laid Garrard, said he denied this.

Penalty

"He admits holding on to the officer for too long, but he denies punching and kicking," Mr. Garrard said.

Miss Carol Ann Lynch, prosecuting, said police were on duty at the Babbacombe Road end of the pitch. There was an incident on the pitch — Torquay were awarded a penalty — and the Swansea fans were roused. One was seen to

jump on the fencing and spit on the police.

Two police officers moved forward to arrest a youth and they were jostled, punched and kicked. One policeman saw Roberts punching and kicking. They had to let the other youth go.

Roberts was located in another part of the ground and put in a police van until the end of the game.

Mr. Garrard said that Roberts said he was pushed over by people behind him.

Seven other young men were also dealt with by the court.

Congregated

Three supporters who all pleaded guilty to being drunk and disorderly in Abbey Road, Torquay, in the afternoon were each fined £100 with costs. Craig Chapple, aged 23, of Lon Irfon, Cockett, Swansea; William Neil Holohan, aged 20, of the Victoria Inn, Westbourne Place, Mumbles, Swansea; and Andrew Raymond Fail, 21, of Western Street, Sandfields, Swansea, were among a group of about 100 men causing a disturbance in Abbey Road, said Miss Lynch.

Outside The Falcon public house after being barred because of their drunken state. Chapple was told to stop inciting the crowd. He walked away from the police and began singing. He was arrested and put in a van.

Fail was a member of a group which tried to open the door of the van. He started shouting 'Sieg', inciting others to shout 'Heil'. Because of the presence of a dog handler and dog, the potentially serious situation was defused, Miss Lynch said. Fail was arrested.

Holohan was also a member of the same group, he went into a nearby garden, picked up a stick and threw it at the police dog, narrowly missing the officers.

Mr. Garrard said they were all Swansea City supporters.

Two supporters were fined £150 each with £25 costs for being drunk and disorderly in Fleet Street, Torquay.

Sorry

David Alan Wassell, aged 21, of Clydach Road, Craigcefnparc, and Andrew Llewellyn, 18, of Lon Heddch, Craigcefnparc, admitted the offences. Miss Lynch said they were seen in Fleet Street drinking. They were singing and chanting: "Swansea boys we are here." In court they both said they were sorry.

Two men were fined £100 each with £25 costs. Peter Tunguy Geoux, 21, of Western

me in the throat. The shock of not being able to breathe for a couple of seconds turned into panic as I struggled to gasp for air. It was as if my throat had been clamped together. Even though it had only been a few seconds, it felt like an age before I suddenly gasped for air, coughing and spluttering.

Cooney dragged my assailant down the steps, smashed him with such immense force in the mouth that his teeth flew out and pinged against the glass. I had recovered from the initial shock of the kick so I grabbed him by the back of his head and rammed him into the corner of the laminated food counter splitting his face open. All hell broke loose as the locals ganged up on us but we more than held our own as not many of them fancied getting more of the same treatment the 'Karate Kid' had got. The Old Bill arrived and split up the melee, sending us down the road and the English lads up it. The only problem was that our digs were up the hill ! The restaurant was at a fork in the road so we doubled back on ourselves on the road parallel to the mob of locals further up the street. We made our way back on the same road as them and watched them re-enacting the row as their silhouettes danced back and forth under the yellow street lights. We jogged up behind them, running stealthily on the balls of our feet, not uttering a sound. One of them spotted us and screamed "Fucking hell !" The chase was on as they darted off in unison. There was no way we were going to catch them as they dashed off like startled animals but we weren't giving up the chase as the adrenalin was at full flow. They sprinted up past a churchyard with tall green railings until 'bang', one of them suddenly went flying sideways like a car hit at a junction. Big Laddie came out of the churchyard entrance swinging like a giant heavyweight, followed by a few more of the lads. The Torquay boys fled in all directions in sheer panic. It was a delightful sight to see one of them smashed off at right angles just as we thought they had got away. First blood had been drawn and we had the taste fresh in our mouths. Roll on Saturday !

The morning started off with us all in a pub called the Spread Eagle in the town centre. The lads were right off it early doors and some hadn't been to bed, just drinking through the night. All morning, more and more turned up until there was a big mob of over a hundred of us. By 1 o'clock the boys were dancing on the tables, swinging on the light fittings, robbing the juke box and pool table of their money boxes and stealing beer and spirits. It was a scene of anarchy with a strong undercurrent of potential violence in the atmosphere. As the police inevitably moved us on from the Spread Eagle and its petrified landlord, it all spilled over into chaos. The Saturday shoppers cowered in doorways as the lads went on the rampage, looting and smashing up a leather coat shop where a rail of coats was wheeled out with the alarm chords snapping off each one as it trolled out the door. They were like piranhas on a corpse, stripping the rail clean in seconds. The police had lost control and as they tried to recover the goods, fights broke out all over the street with a few lads nicked as boys traded punches with the Old Bill. At one point one of the boys, aptly named Hooly, dropped a block on a police dog's head. It was all-out war against the filth. There's nothing like the buzz of a full scale ruck at the football but a chance to settle the score with the Old Bill comes close. Every kicking in the back of a van, every hiding off the fuckers while outnumbered in a cell, every painful smash of a truncheon can be avenged. It doesn't happen too often because the potential for arrest is so high but, when the boys have had enough and the helmets start flying off, there's no sight like it. As the police brought in reinforcements, they regained control of the situation and marched us off up the hill on a long walk to the ground. Unfortunately for them, the kick-off wasn't till the evening so there was still a full three hours till the start of the match. With the threat of putting us straight in the ground the lads filtered off until there was fuck all left.

We all met up in a big bar near Plainmoor where more beer was downed with wraps of speed and giant spliffs sparked up. Torquay didn't seem to have any lads. If they did, they certainly weren't showing their faces tonight. Once, on the small open end bank, it was evident that not only had Torquay's boys stayed away but so had most of the town. The day's violence had affected the crowd badly as barely 2,000 had turned up and we had half the crowd. The Old Bill still had a bee in their bonnet about the day's events and were being heavy handed. There was jostling and pushing as the police moved in when the crowd started coming the Torquay players after an on the field incident. Fireworks were lit and hurled at the Old Bill. The smell of gunpowder filled the air as the sun set over a beautiful red night sky - it was a surreal scene. As Little Dai, Cooney, Alan Roberts and I were berating the police about their heavy handed behaviour, out of the blue, a copper made a beeline for Alan. As he did, Alan caught him square on the jaw and knocked him out. The crowd surged forward but the police had dived on him and he was carted off unceremoniously. We were gutted for Alan as he had already done a stretch and was a good candidate for another.

All the boys who were arrested were bailed for a special court on Monday morning. So, after a few beers on Sunday, we bode farewell to them and wished them good luck. All the boys pleaded not guilty and were bailed for a later date when all the fuss had died down and they were fined. Alan, however, was advised by his brief to plead guilty because of the seriousness of his offence and his previous record. The brief told him that if he pleaded guilty, the judge would go easy on him. It was six months before he walked back in the Queens one Friday night, fresh from the nick. So much for good advice !

There was a big fuss in the papers after the violence in Torquay. We were labelled 'Hardcore Hooligans', a new breed willing to attack the police and loot shops. Various police chiefs appeared on television talking about how they would hunt us down and arrest us. It was all sound bites. They didn't lift a finger to do anything. They knew who we were and half the lads had been locked up on Sunday after raiding the Services on the way home so they had their names and addresses. As usual they would talk shit and try to appease the 'outraged' public.

The South Wales derbies were always a hot spot for trouble but there's a real hatred from the people of North Wales towards South Walians. They believe that they are the true Welsh and that we in the South are too anglicised. They're not far off the truth, in my opinion. But this hatred hadn't often shown when we played Wrexham. Most games had passed off peacefully and the only real trouble we had experienced up there was at a Wales v Spain game where we had fought with Cardiff on the big Kop end. Wrexham weren't really interested that night so it took us a little by surprise when we took up a small crew of 20 on a cold late November afternoon. We had only just parked the minibus and were making our way down the hill into town when that all too familiar shout went up.

"Here they are !" Dustbin pulled on his leather gloves and with a steely glint in his eye said "Come on, Wall here we go !"

Fair do's to Terry, I had a real respect for him. He always got in and wasn't afraid to push the limits. If you didn't defend yourself, Terry was going to hurt you real bad. As they came up the hill, they were led by a fucking incredibly tall lad who was screaming "C'mon ! We're the front line !" Terry steamed into him as we all paired off. Their mob was split as some were forced into a shoe shop where a shoe chucking contest erupted. It was quite a comical sight and had us in stitches as we relived the encounter on the bus journey home. The police arrived as if from nowhere catching both mobs off guard. The first I knew they were there was when I felt a searing pain in my back as I was beaten with a truncheon. The Wrexham boys ran off from the Old Bill down the hill as some of the boys gave chase. Fair play to them, they were well game and made a boring 0 - 0 draw a little lively on the terraces as the banter flew from stand to stand. I, for one, wouldn't think Wrexham was a stroll in the park after this encounter.

December 26th was fast approaching and once again our Boxing Day fixture was against our deadliest enemies. Once again, with no buses or trains running, transport was our main problem. Just for once I wished the fixture would come out on a normal Saturday afternoon so we could get into the city undetected but, once again, the bigwigs at Lancaster Gate had spoilt our fun. The only choice we had was the official coaches. We booked our places separately but were delighted when we turned up at the Vetch and realised there were no seating reservations. All the lads piled on the first two double-decker buses in the fleet and a long rowdy trip began. The double-deckers snaked their way up the M4 at a snail's pace. Every time a car went past with a Cardiff scarf trailing out of the window, gestures were exchanged along with small change. The chanting and abuse continued the whole 40 miles until it reached a peak as we turned off the slip road at Leckwerth. The excitement had hit a peak and we had worked ourselves into a frenzy. It only took one shout. Who gave the command, I have no idea but, when it came, everyone moved instantly as if ordered by God ! "ALL OFF !" The doors were almost ripped off as they were forced open. Everyone spilled out onto the road, exhilarated by our escape, into the cold December air. One by one, each double-decker emptied as if it was some sort of chain reaction. A huge mob formed and started to make its way down to Ninian Park.

The walk to the ground was about five minutes and the police were frantically trying to reorganise their tactics. About 20 of us had made our way out in front as we reached the junction of Sloper Road. The police were still organising a road block as we slipped through the net and made our way past the Ninian Park pub towards the Canton Cross. So far, we were unopposed by the usual lack of a Cardiff mob until a team was spotted running towards us. One of their lads in front of their firm produced a gas canister and let if off, consuming both sets of boys in tear gas. We held our breath and regrouped away from the gas as the police waded in to separate us. The gas had just stopped us having a row and had backfired on their lads as well as us. But at least we had made an effort to thwart the heavy police operations and for a moment we had broken free from their grasp. It was just a pity that the majority of the Cardiff boys weren't about.

Once in the ground the atmosphere was pulsating with both sets of fans scaling the fences and hurling coins at each other. The Bob Bank heaved back and forth as they battled against the Old Bill in the corner of the large home end. It was a pity that a football match broke out amongst all the craziness to dampen all our spirits with a 0 - 0 draw.

It was time for the FA Cup third round and the draw had thrown out a home tie with West Brom. Not many teams come down this far as we are out on a limb here in West Wales. So when the draw had us against West Brom, only two hours away, we were sure they would bring a mob. After a morning of drinking in the Queens, we rallied the troops and set off down the Sandfields in search of some West Brom lads. One of the Mini Angels had been in after scouting around and told us that a mob of lads had set up stall in the Badminton. So off we set. There was no hesitation as we approached the Bad. Cooney was first through the door - it was like a Western ! The pub just went silent as we steamed in. The place was full of them. To our left in the bar were about fifteen big men, a few in shirts, with a big flag of St George draped over the window. And to our right, in the pool room was a gang of mostly lads. One stood out as a big, huge skinhead; your typical England hooligan stereotype. I was sure I had seen him before with a tall black boy back when they had come in 1982 on the North Bank in the First Division. The silence seemed to last an age until Cooney stepped forward without a word and just smashed his head into one of them standing by the pool table with a cue in his hand. The pool cue rack on the pillar in the games room was emptied in a split second by our lads and the sound of splitting wood reverberated in the smoke-filled air.

They were beaten into the corner of the pub but they never fought back. Not a glass was thrown, no chairs brandished, just a strange, passive retreat. "C'mon, you're fucking shit !" Cooney yelled at them, giving them a wide-eyed evil stare, veins popping in his forehead as he beckoned them on. There was no response. We turned and left, finding it hard to understand why they wouldn't fight. As we left, the Mini's started bricking in the windows with the flags in, just for good measure. We walked the length of the Mumbles Road looking for a firm but to no avail. There were some slaps dished out but no real mob on which to vent our anger.

The game was a cracker with us turning them over 3 - 2 in front of nearly 9,000. We left the Vetch happy at the result but still determined to kick it off. So we headed for the train station up on the High Street. We darted in and out of the January sales shoppers on a dark, dingy evening as we made our way to the station. I used to love the Saturday games in the middle of winter. There was always something sinister about the dark, early evenings which made ambush and escaping without detection a great deal easier. You could slip in and out of the shoppers with your scarf right up across your nose . It made you feel a little more comfortable than broad daylight and, as I had ginger hair, it made me less conspicuous. We stopped at the Pullman pub opposite the station and could see a few West Brom lads across the way but we would have to get past the police first to reach them. I crossed the road a little further down and walked up behind the police towards the Baggies boys. A shout went up but, before I could go any further, I hit the floor, felled from behind with an ankle tap. Before I could attempt to get up, I was pounced on by the Old Bill and thrown in the back of a van. Nicked again for the fourth time and, just to add insult to injury, a nice big hole in my Armani jumper. The copper who nicked me was Martyn Morris, a Welsh International Rugby player from Neath. He was a huge, athletic man with a big moustache and a massive hooked nose - a right fucking, ugly cunt with an attitude to match. He had a sidekick called Phil Williams, a slight man with blonde hair. They were like the Little and Large double act and were always together. I had played football for Mumbles Rangers against the Police team in which Williams played and had given him a bit of stick on how he and Morris would make my life a misery for the next few years. While being processed, I heard a familiar voice coming from the hallway; Cooney was in as well. At least I now had a bit of company with a few hours to spend before rushing down the Queen's to catch last orders.

March arrived and we had organised a coach for Wolves. We had a good turnout and the Baby Squad was now outnumbering the older lads as we grew from strength to strength. It's not often that you can get a 52-seater into the city without being picked up by the police but, in the Midlands, with so many routes in and out, it's a lot easier. We disembarked right in the heart of Wolverhampton City centre. We searched round the pubs but didn't come across anybody so we settled down in a bar. We were a little early so we waited for them to come to us - hopeful that the hooligan grapevine would do its job. That day the police grapevine was working quicker as the Old Bill turned up to swamp us,. As I've already explained, things were different back in the old days before mobile phones and Lady Luck would deal the cards.

In the stadium we were getting a hammering on the pitch 4 - 0. Meanwhile the boys took it out on the bar at the back of the bank after it had been shut on police orders. The cast iron drainpipes were ripped off and used as battering rams against the shutters until the robo cops stepped in. The police kept us in for ages while they cleared the streets and, once we were back on the coach, they were so confident they just let us go. Unbeknown to us, there was a massive police shortage due to some riots in the city a few days previously. As our coach made its way down from Molineux, a big firm of Wolves came over the grass banking out of an estate of high rise flats. Before we had a chance to react, the windows were bursting into a million fragments from both sides. The bus was full of flying glass as the deafening noise of multiple exploding windows had us diving in the aisles for cover. One of our boys, Jeff Batchelor, a big rugby playing lad, lost the plot and started kicking the windows out from the inside screaming "What you doing, fucking hiding ! C'mon - let's fucking do 'em !" He was spot on. The shock of so many windows going through had us on the back foot straight away and a result was on the cards for the Wolves lads but Jeff's cry had spurred us into action and we all jumped down the seven foot drop through the broken windows. I've seen buses stoned so many times before and sometimes the occupants would come out of the fire exit and sometimes from the front doors so it must have been hell of a sight for the Wolves mob to see the windows being kicked from the inside out and people pouring out like rats from a sinking ship. We chased them over the grass banking and into the high rise estate but they were gone - disappearing into the maze of walkways and tunnels.

The police were quickly on the scene, nicking Cooney and Cheesy, but they were reluctant to go in the flats area, telling us we must have been mad to go in there as it was a no go area. They obviously hadn't been to Townhill or Blaen-Y-Maes. After rounding us up, they sent us once more on our way home; with no fucking windows. It was freezing cold and the fumes were intolerable. Being so pissed off, one of the lads, Eddie Eyes (so called because of his mad staring eyes), took it upon himself to fill a black bin liner full of broken triplex glass and smack it over joggers' heads as we drove past at speed. It was an out of order act of madness that saw us pulled in once again. All 50 of us were nicked and taken to Wednesbury Police Station. Without enough cells for us, they handcuffed us all together in the main corridor, interviewing us one by one. After asking for a piss while threatening to do it on the corridor floor, we were even handcuffed to a copper while having a slash. The copper was a skinny cunt with small round wire glasses who looked like Herr Flick from the television comedy show "Allo, 'Allo'. He was staring over my shoulder, unnerving me, so I asked him "What are you staring at, you fucking homo ?"

"You couldn't shag a sheep with that !" he said.

"You wouldn't like it as a wart on the end of your fucking nose ,you bent cunt !" I replied.

The cunt kicked me in the back so I pissed over him. A struggle ensued and I was onto a hiding but the other coppers just separated us. They dragged me back down the corridor towards the rest of the lads and told me to sit down and shut up. Luckily for me, Herr Flick was not the most popular officer in the Midlands and they were a little nervous with so many of us littering the corridor of the station. It had been "no comment" from everyone in the interview room and it looked like a long night ahead for us all until Eddie owned up to clubbing the jogger with the bag of glass. Fair play to him, he knew he was out of order and took the rap, even though none of the boys would drop him in it. Eddie was nicked and the rest of us were sent on our way.

The police stayed on the fume-filled, windowless bus until we reached the county boundaries. Then, at every border, we would be met by another police vehicle with all slip roads blocked by a police van for the whole journey home. It must have cost an absolute fortune, involving forces from every county from Wolverhampton to Swansea. Who did they think they were escorting - a bus full of mass murderers ? The amount of tax payers money wasted on pointless tasks like that never ceased to amaze me.

Easter was upon us once more and the Friday nights before the big derbies were becoming a ritual. The Queens would be packed out with the lads downing the lager in a party atmosphere - chanting and singing the night away with the DJ 'Crazy Harry' often playing the Cockney Rejects just to wind the boys up to the hilt. The small space in front of the DJ would be a mass of lads pogo'ing, glasses smashing and lager flying through the air, all to the tune of 'War On The Terraces'.

We had prepared ourselves for this match, one we had been so eager to have for a long time. In the few years we had broken through as a new young firm. The Baby Squad was starting to call the shots. We were organising trips away and planning our tactics at home and, since the arrival of Cooney on the scene, we now had the muscle to front bigger, older firms. With or without the help of Tracy and the older lads, we could stand on our own feet and this game against Cardiff would be our coming of age. Before our Friday night out we had prepared a table with an arsenal of weapons at one of the boy's flats on the edge of the Sandfields. Thinking back to that day now is a sobering thought. But when you're 18, you don't think twice about the consequences. We had no mortgages and no commitments. All we could think of was smashing the fuck out of Cardiff. The table was a frightening sight with hammer handles, Stanley blades with masking tape over one end to make a handle - so small they could be hidden in the waistband of your boxers - and 50 timber connecters, flattened out to make throwing stars. I had etched SCFC KILL CCFC on each one.

The morning couldn't come quickly enough and to everyone's delight we woke to a sunny, beautiful day - just perfect for another tear-up with Cardiff. The butterflies in the pit of my stomach were there from the moment I woke up. They never seemed to go away until our first confrontation so hopefully that wouldn't be too long to wait. We loaded up with tools and made our way to the Queens, a short five minute walk away. The Queens was opening early for us as was usual on special games. Rose, the landlady, was firm but fair and ran one of the most violent pubs in the city centre. She had lots of practice at keeping the lads from going over the top but, in return, she had a loyal firm of lads who would protect the pub at all costs.

We handed out the Stanley blades and home-made throwing stars into the eager hands of the boys. We were ready and prepared for anything that would come our way. The lager was flowing; settling the nerves and fuelling our anticipation. Hooliganism had become more personal over the last few years with the firms knowing the locations of their opposition's pubs and recognising individuals. We knew where Cardiff drank and I'm sure they knew where we did. It didn't take long to confirm this as Divy came bursting through the door. "They're here !"

The pub emptied with the small exit creating a bottleneck and everyone fighting to get out of it at the same time. Once out into the bright sunlight from the dark, dingy bar, it took a couple of seconds for my eyes to adjust and to witness a truly incredible sight. The Cardiff mob were stretched out across the four lanes of the dual carriageway and they outnumbered us easily as it was still early and not everyone had yet arrived. In the middle of them was Laddie, standing alone, a full fifty yards from us, swinging punches like a man possessed. He was an awesome sight and I could understand why the Cardiff mob were reluctant to steam into him. He stood a good six foot four and had a large, athletic build like a heavyweight boxer. His long hair made him look even wilder. We sprinted towards them, glasses flying along with the throwing stars. As we clashed, you could tell within seconds that there would only be one outcome. Cooney had smashed one over the head with a hammer handle and a few were laid out on the floor already, getting a kicking. They turned and fled and the chase was on. They ran up past the Grand Theatre which was clad in scaffolding due to its renovation. As the Cardiff mob scattered in and out of the scaffolding poles, the workers were shouting "Get into them !" and chucking us all sorts of objects. When it came to Swansea versus Cardiff, the whole city was in it together, not just us.

Most of the mob fled up past the shopping centre and off in the direction of the High Street but a few dived into the sanctuary of the Quadrant Gate pub and locked the door. This was a big mistake as the landlord was a really strict man with two nasty Dobermans which he then released into the bar. The Cardiff boys made their way into the raised level by the huge bay window just as we got outside. We walked up to the window and peered through the small square Georgian panes. They started giving it the big one, taunting us in their bravado, happy in the knowledge that there was no way to get to them with the locked doors and the Dobermans. One of their lads pressed his face to the window in defiance to wind us up. Little did he know that Cooney had the answer up his sleeve and, with a flick of his forearm, the hidden hammer handle slid down into his hand and he thrust it through the glass pane and into the lad's face. That was the cue for the rest of the boys as we began smashing out all the panes and wooden rails. The Cardiff boys retreated from the window, preferring the company of the Dobermans to ours. The sound of sirens was now abundant in the air as police came from all angles but they were too late. The damage had been done and the 150 strong Cardiff mob had been scattered across the city. How that many could disappear was beyond me.

We made our way back to the Queen's where an unconscious Cardiff fan still lay outside the sex shop. Some of the Mini's began beating him again but were warned off to leave him. We were ecstatic. It was the third time we had routed them at home in three years - not that you would get them to admit it. But it wasn't over yet. We knew all too well that Cardiff had such a huge active firm of hooligans that we could face two or three more firms like our early visitors and we would have to be on guard all morning, right up until kick-off.

Rumours were rife all morning and all sorts of dubious reports were coming in of various impending firms but none were taken seriously until one of the boys from the Number 10 pub came rushing down with the news that another mob was on its way down from the High Street station. Once again the pub emptied. This time we were 200 strong with another 40 joining us at the Number 10. As we prepared to make our way up to meet them, they started to appear around the corner of Castle Street near Castle Gardens, a full 500 yards away. We charged through the deserted Bank Holiday streets towards our foe who were still streaming around the corner. The shouts of battle echoed through the deserted city centre. It was just us and them with no police in sight. As we got closer, we could see the ones at the back starting to filter off, disappearing back around the corner. The ones in front were beckoning their lads foreword to no avail. As the gaps started to appear in their ranks, they were breaking up and the boys knew it as the charge became a full out sprint. We could smell blood and the Cardiff mob knew that we weren't going to stop. There was a full 50 yards between us when they broke ranks and ran. You could see the frustration on the faces of the front men as they gave up the ghost.

We had outnumbered them but not by many so I don't know why they ran. There were no police, just the two mobs. Maybe some of the earlier mob was with them and had told the rest we were tooled up or maybe they had too much time to hold their nerve as we were so far apart at the beginning. I suppose we'll never know but the fact remains that they had the perfect opportunity - no Old Bill, no shoppers and no excuses. The result was ours.

We searched around for more mobs but most of our searches were in vain. Apart from a few scuffles, there didn't seem to be another big mob in town. We made our way back to the Queens and settled in for a quick pint before kick-off. Most of the boys had gone in the Vetch as 3 o'clock was upon us. As we left, right outside making their way to the ground, was a mob of about eight lads in total. As soon as we set eyes on each other, we just knew we were enemies. It was almost psychic. Maybe it was body language or slight movements but no one had said a word and we were already squaring up to each other. Being so close to the ground, the police were in between us before a punch was thrown. The insults began to fly and we could tell these guys were no mugs as we were deep in home territory and they seemed game for it and totally unnerved even though they were in a precarious position. Mike Hadley dived forward and a grey haired policeman drew his truncheon to ward him off. With that, Mike landed one square on the copper's chin and his helmet flew off as he was sprawled across the floor outside the entrance to the Queens. One of the Cardiff lads came running at us from the side, getting around the police and aimed a punch at Tracy. I swung a kick at him, catching his leg firmly in the thigh. To avoid all the punches and kicks aimed his way, he ran off in an arc around us and off the pavement right into the path of a double-decker bus. It clipped him on the shoulder and spun him around but, miraculously, he kept on his feet and made his escape behind the now reinforced police line. The lad had come a hair's breadth from being killed by the bus but was still up for it when repatriated with his mates. It never ceases to amaze me that how ever many times you have a close shave, the hooligan inside always gets you coming back for more even when you are close to copping it big time. The police now swamped the two small mobs and escorted the Cardiff lads to their enclosure. Respect had to be given to these lads; they were different from the rest we had come up against. You could tell they would not back down and were battle hardened. They must have been real top boys.

The crowd in the Vetch was frantic. There was scuffling both ends as police lined both the North Bank on our side and the West Bank on theirs. The players had to take corners with police dogs snapping at their heels. Players were being coined at every opportunity and golf balls, snooker balls and the home made stars were hurled the 50 yards between the two sets of supporters. The police would later talk of the "Mindless Minority" but in a crowd of just under 7,000, I think 6,000 were up for a ruck !

We won the game 2 - 0 and, apart from a few individual fights on the Mumbles Road after the game, the police had gained control of what had become a riotous situation beforehand. The papers the next day recounted the encounters outside the Queens and Quadrant Gate. There were pictures of detectives holding my home-made stars with the inscriptions on them and a report on one of the boys, 'Duffy', who had been caught with one of our Stanley blades. They talked of how it was a new breed of armed, organised, hooligan gangs. The Squad had made its mark in black and white and we had been at the forefront of all the clashes. But best of all, we had done Cardiff once more.

'87 - '88

After the unremarkable season back in Division Four, we embarked on another term with a bit more hope on the pitch. Off the pitch, we had an early season visit to Cardiff to look forward to. At last the fixture list had thrown us a chance to go to Cardiff on an ordinary Saturday afternoon. One of the Winch Wen boys, Mansel, had hired a transit van and, unbelievably, 35 of us squeezed in like fucking sardines in a can. At least another ten had to get out because the wheels were dragging on the wheel arches and the vehicle couldn't get going. Once we had managed to get a couple of cars for the others, we set off in earnest. It must have been the most uncomfortable 40 minutes of my life, being jammed in like one of those Guinness Book Of Records attempts, but it was well worth it as we got into Cardiff undetected by the police who had set up a military style operation with vans on all exit slip roads off the M4 and spotters on all the bridges.

I had dyed my hair black for this game because I was increasingly getting spotted and nicked in a crowd due to my ginger mop especially by my two admirers, Morris and Williams.

We stopped off for a livener in Ely where the boys dismantled a skittle alley, robbing the wooden skittles to use as weapons later on and then made our way to Ninian Park. We parked the van and cars in a back street around the corner from the Ninian Park pub and set off in search of some action, still undetected by the Old Bill. We walked down past the Ninian Park pub where one of the lads, Harold, who was on crutches, smashed the pub sign up with his sticks. No one moved from the pub which was frequented by 'scarfers' but at least they would spread the word that we were there. We set off up Ninian Park Road towards the city centre, heading for their pub, the Philharmonic. There were 45 of us in total - all good boys - so we were brimming with confidence. As we came opposite a pub called Whyndam, bricks came raining down on us from a side street. "Here we go !" Harold shouted as he tried to bat the flying stones away with his crutches. The ruck was on as we charged towards each other. The windows of a nearby Post Office went crashing through as the bricks kept coming but we weren't stopping. We got within a few feet of them when one came out with half a breeze block raised above his head. He hurled it in my direction and it came spinning through the air towards me. At the pace I was running towards them, there was no way I could avoid it. It hit me in the stomach, winding me instantly. I fell to the floor as if hit by a truck, gasping for air and awaiting the impending kicking. But Mansel was on them in a flash, slugging my assailant into a daze. Tony Buller then smashed his head down on the tail light of an old American car parked next to us. I was back up on my feet as the boys were laying into the rest of the brick-wielding mob. They must have thought that we would back off because they had so much ammunition from a nearby building skip but we were going nowhere - in fact it was the Cardiff mob who were backing off down the road, their numbers diminishing as we hammered into them. The sound of police sirens grew ever nearer as we saw off the Cardiff lads. The police came charging out of their vans as a dog handler lost control of his Alsatian. The dog came pouncing into the boys, biting one of the lads right in the nuts. I could see my two favourite policemen, batons drawn, searching the crowd looking for me. However, without my ginger locks and with the help of some sunglasses and a new haircut, they failed to noticed me.

The police presence around us now was massive. Many vans with flashing lights and dog handlers flanked us, along with a massive line of police down both sides. We began the escort to the stadium in a defiant mood. We had beaten the major police operations, walked the streets in search of a row and succeeded in seeing off a fair mob of Cardiff who had the advantage of a skip full of bricks. Not bad for a morning's work !

We could see the activity bustling about in the streets ahead as our conspicuous escort made its way closer and closer to Ninian Park. The closer we got, the more Cardiff lads would walk the other side of the police, drawing their fingers across their throats in a slicing action and gesturing as if they had a knife in their coat pockets. It's just a pity they weren't so eager earlier. As the Ninian Park pub came into view, the police were becoming more and more stretched as they tried to control the mobs of Cardiff ahead, behind and to the side of us. We could see the police were panicking and starting to lose control of the situation which made us prepare for the inevitable penetration of the police lines.

I become aware that we now had Cardiff lads in escort with us. Cooney said "These aren't Jacks !" about three lads to our right by the low stone garden walls of terraced houses. "Are they fuck !" I said. He launched into one of them knocking him clean off his feet and over the wall. Little Dai and I grabbed the other two and, as we were forced over the wall and into the garden by the weight of the mob, they heaved as one towards the cheeky intruders. For a moment the police lost control as the scuffle saw attacks begin from all sides but the boys stood firm as kicks and punches lashed out.

More reinforcements joined us on the corner of Sloper Road to calm the situation a little. We could see how riled the Bluebirds were that we had come and given it the big one on their own turf. For years they had said Swansea never go to Cardiff unprotected by the Old Bill but, here we were, right in their faces and they fucking hated it ! But they had to get used to it because we would be back again and again.

Once again we were placed on the open-air Grange End. No matter how many fans we would take there, the noise of our crowd would dissipate in the open air and, no matter how hard we would try to make a noise, it was always in vain and was drowned out by the massive home Bob Bank. I loved the animosity that emanated from the huge bank that ran the full length of the pitch. Their arms would all point in unison as they screamed out "You Jack bastards !", their faces contorted in pure hatred. And that day it seemed as if they meant it a little more because we had given some of their boys a good slap earlier. The crowd erupted into a wall of sound as the back of our net bulged with the impact of the ball. The Cardiff players ran behind the goal, right in front of us, joyous in celebration. The banked heaved forward in an outpouring of abuse. The fences were scaled as arms lashed out through the fencing towards the celebrating footballers. Somehow, despite his broken leg, Harold had scaled the fence and hurled his crutch down on them. This started an attempted pitch invasion from the home end in disgust at the attack on their celebrating heroes. Fair play to Harold, it took some nuts to come to Cardiff 40-handed and give it the big one, let alone to do it on crutches with a broken leg. But that was the pull of derby day, you wouldn't miss it for the world.

Disappointed at the 1 - 0 defeat, we were finally let out of the ground twenty minutes after the final whistle. The police marched us down the road, barking orders all the time. I felt a sharp smack on the back of my head "You dyed your hair, you ginger cunt !" came the rasping, heavily accented voice. It was Martyn Morris, the copper.

"I was looking for you earlier, you twat !"
"Unlucky," I replied smugly, happy in the thought that he would have nicked me for sure if he had seen me at the row earlier.

When we arrived at the van, the police were not a bit happy about 35 of us clambering into a solitary transit and we were ordered back out. A head count was taken and ten of the lads were separated from the rest of us.

"Right then, this lot back in the van and this lot to the train station," said the Sergeant.

After a heated protest they forcibly separated us. We knew the ten would have a rough time at the station and we were determined not to leave it at that. The police began escorting us out towards the M4, driving past the ten lads who you could tell weren't relishing the walk to the station. As we drove onto the slip road onto the M4, westbound back to Swansea, we could see the police van escorting us go round the roundabout and back into Cardiff. Once they were out of sight, Mansel slammed on the brakes and rammed the van onto reverse.

"Right lads, train station here we come !"

A roar of approval came from the back of the van as Mansel drove the transit back down the slip road in a dangerous manoeuvre and back into Cardiff. As we pulled up outside the train station, it was apparent that the police had taken the boys there in a wagon and they were already safely on the platform. But outside there was a small mob of Cardiff giving it some towards the lads inside. The van screeched to a halt and the back doors flew open. We steamed out, screaming at the Cardiff lads. They scattered instantly, the shock and surprise on their faces was a picture. The sergeant who had separated us all earlier was berating another officer.

"I thought you had escorted this lot onto the motorway,"
"We did, sir," he replied.
"Well, what the fuck are they doing back here then ?"

We laughed at them arguing over our failed expulsion but they wouldn't make the same mistake twice. They escorted us the whole 40 miles back home.

Once back in the Queens, the boys who came back on the train recounted their stories of a bit of a set to on the platform with a dodgy 20 minutes until the train arrived. All in all, it was a successful trip for us. We had taken it to them on their own turf and been successful in all our encounters with their lads even though I had a painful reminder on my stomach that we didn't get it all our way. More and more, our feeling was getting stronger that Cardiff's reputation was misplaced. Despite meeting people on holiday or around the country who all thought their firm was the dog's bollocks, we certainly didn't think so.

There were always teams with a bit of a reputation in the lower leagues, one in particular was Hereford United. I had heard stories from the older boys of battles with them and they would say you were always guaranteed a row against them. It was the Saturday morning after the wedding of one of our main boys, Craig. We had a good drink the night before and I was still a little groggy and suffering with a hangover. As I hadn't been home I was a still dressed in a suit from the night before. We had been told that a good mob of Hereford had come off the train earlier and we set off in search of them in the pubs on the High Street. After visiting all the likely venues, we gave up the hunt and made our way back to the Queens. I stopped off on the way back to chat to Laddie who told me he had been around the pubs in town but had seen nothing. We got some cigarettes and made our way down to the Queens. As we reached the entrance, Laddie said "Look at this lot !" Coming across the road to the pub was a team of Hereford dressers. My heart skipped a beat as they called the odds. There were only two of us but there was no way I was going to do a runner right on our own doorstep. I thought for a second about opening the door of the pub to call out the boys but I knew I wouldn't make it and they would be on my back before I got there. There was only one choice and that was to stand and fight and, if need be, take a kicking. I bawled at them ...

"Come on then !"

Laddie and I both took up a fighting stance as they came in without hesitation. I had hardly thrown a punch when I was dragged down by the sheer weight of them all. I covered my face as the kicks and punches came fast and furious. All I could think of was that the boys would be out any minute now - but they never came. I pulled back, wrenching myself from their grasp in a sudden burst of hidden energy and looked over to see Laddie still standing tall, lashing out at all comers. This gave me the time to open the door of the Queens but, to my horror, the door was slammed shut in my face. I couldn't understand what the fuck was going on - now we were sure to take a right hiding. Just as I was resigning myself to a hospital visit, the Hereford mob was hit from behind and split in two. Coming through them were the welcome, familiar faces of Big Bob from Port Talbot along with Coombsy, Tom, Bishy, Johnny Oi and Alan. The boot was instantly on the other foot as the Hereford boys searched for an escape route. They made their way off down the West Way just as the boys came charging up the road from the Garibaldi. All the time I thought they had been in the Queens, they were down the Gari ! The boys steamed into them and, with no escape, they took a good beating. The boots were flying in from everyone. I dealt out some revenge of my own and a couple of their lads had been glassed before the police separated us. Laddie and I had escaped without any significant injuries but one of our other lads hadn't fared so well. Dull Martin had been caught by the back of the Queens and had a good kicking, losing a few of his teeth in the process. Hereford had lived up to their reputation. They had brought it straight to us, coming to our main pub and kicking it right off. Only pure luck had saved the day. Too bad it never saved my suit.

That year, the home fixture with Cardiff was on New Year's Day and we had a good mob out early doors, up and around the train station. It was an atrocious day with persistent rain. We were sure that Cardiff would be out for some retribution after our venture into Cardiff the previous August but it wasn't to be. Maybe they had travelling problems like we'd encountered on Christmas holidays or maybe the police had them all wrapped up. One thing was for sure though, they hadn't turned up and certainly made no effort like we used to when the date of the fixture made things difficult. It takes two to tango but there would be no dancing that day. The general view among the boys was that Cardiff were shit; a spent force with no stomach for life in the Fourth Division. Their massive numbers had dwindled and even we were getting better attendance figures. As far as we were concerned, we held the number one spot in Wales and they had a lot of catching up to do.

Frustrated by the Cardiff no show, we didn't have to wait too long for our next adventure. In a rare situation, we played Hereford United away the very next day after the Cardiff game. After the hostilities at the home fixture, we thought it would be only right to return the favour. A good mob of 80 of us made the short trip to Hereford and, seeing it was only a small market town, it wouldn't take long for our presence to be noticed. We had settled into a quaint, old pub in the town centre. Half the boys had 'gone for a walk'; a term that referred to hunting down the opposition. They were gone about 20 minutes when Eddie Eyes came through

the door shouting "They're down the road. We've just had it off with them - look
!" He raised his hand to show us a bad split. The boys downed their pints and
we made our way down to where the clash had happened. Eddie pointed out
the bar where they had come from; a wine bar with a huge blacked out window
with a 'Chasers' sign in gold fancy writing across its length. The door opened and
a lad in a leather coat came out wielding a baseball bat "Come on, you Welsh
cunts !" he shouted at us. With that, at least ten stones flew in his direction. The
fancy window exploded into the bar. The lad with the bat took cover as more and
more bricks flew into the interior of the wine bar. The occupants were now taking
cover under tables and behind chairs as the stoning continued. The police were
quick on the scene to find the bar smashed up with the Hereford lads cowering
in the back. The police rounded us all up and escorted us to the small shabby
ground. We didn't encounter any more lads on our way to the ground but it
wasn't surprising as we were numbering up to nearly 100 now and, in Division
Four, that was a formidable force.

Though disappointed about the lack of real action, we were more than
happy with the turnout and there was still a good buzz as we marched chanting
anti-English abuse through this anti-Welsh border town as the locals looked on
angrily. We were now travelling well and in good numbers. The firm grew from
strength to strength.

That year's FA Cup draw had seen us drawn against non-league Hayes on
the outskirts of London. I loved the FA Cup but this match had failed to grab
the boys' imagination and none of our mob could be bothered to make the trip.
Little Dai and I decided to go so we hitched a lift off Tenko and his boys. Not for
one minute did I think that there would be any trouble at this fixture but, once
in Hayes, the atmosphere was all too familiar. The tell tale signs were apparent
in the pubs dotted around the ground; every one of them seemed to be full of
lairy Londoners. As we entered the ground, it become apparent that there was no
segregation whatsoever and we would share the terraces with the locals. Dai and
I stood by a few familiar faces on the bank behind the goals. A few of the Port
Talbot boys were there, along with Jeff Warren from Bridgend and Probert from
Bishopston. Because Dai and I were well known faces, Jeff and Proby came up,
pointing out a few lads who'd had a pop at them earlier. I thought 'We're not
fucking having that - we'll give them a slap'. We walked up to one of them and I
said "You got a problem, cunt ?" Before he could answer, I punched him, sending
him back across the terrace. I certainly hadn't bargained for what happened next -
the whole terrace erupted and they came from all sides. What had been a sparsely
occupied bank became a heaving mass of lads in the space of a couple of minutes
and Dai and I were the main faces of their attention. I could hear cries of "Get
the ginger cunt in the Aquascutum coat ! I stood out like a sore thumb and was

starting to fear the worst. We had been backed into the corner of the terrace, our backs against the fence like a pair of cornered rats. A big geezer came rushing towards me. I had noticed a big litter bin oddly placed on the banking behind us and, as he made his move, I turned and grabbed it with the full intention of smashing him over the head with it, only to find it was bolted into the floor. He smashed me one, right on the jaw, as I pulled at the bin. I dropped to my knees and a few kicks came my way but the mob's attention had switched from us to Big Bob from Port Talbot who had been laying into them from the top of the bank. This was the second occasion he had made a timely appearance and to this day I am eternally grateful for it.

The police had finally turned up and brought in the dog handlers as they battled to restore order. The mob of Londoners had turned on the Old Bill, giving us a bit of breathing space. The violence dished out to the police took my breath away. I had never witnessed anything like it before. There were Old Bill being knocked out all over the place and these boys certainly didn't give a fuck for them. The police called in reinforcements and, by half time, the bank was crawling with them. By this time Dai and I had been separated from the rest of the Swansea fans and been cornered against the fence. The police had regained control of the situation but we were by no means safe. We could see that there were different mobs of lads all around us and most of them were men, not fucking teenagers. Lots of different tattoos could be made out, showing different allegiances to various London clubs. I couldn't believe the amount of different firms. What the fuck did they want with lowly Swansea City ?

I felt a poke in my back and a threatening Cockney voice spoke into my ear from behind. "Right, you Taffy cunts, you ain't so fucking big now are you ?" I looked at Dai as another one pushed into him, gesturing that he had a knife in his jacket pocket. I looked around but the nearest copper was 20 feet away with a mass of lads between us. I took a big breath to steady my nerves as I was starting to panic, my heart beating irregularly in my chest. The voice spoke out again "You've been coming up here taking fucking liberties but now you ain't so tough. We got West Ham, Millwall, Chelsea, QPR and Tottenham here to give you a slap, you Welsh cunts."

A roar went up behind us which caused the whole bank to turn around to see what was happening. That was our only chance so Dai and I both took it without hesitation. We cleared the perimeter fence in the blink of an eye and made our way across the pitch, darting in between the players as the match continued. I looked back to see the mob scaling the fences in hot pursuit. Dai shouted "Down here, Wall !" pointing to the tunnel on the halfway line. I dived down, only to see a black security guard standing with his hands out as if to ward us off. I just put my shoulder down and slammed him out of the way. The strong smell of liniment oil filled the air as we entered the changing room area. There was no way out as every door seemed to be locked. Footsteps could be heard coming down the tunnel, echoing ever closer until they burst into the changing room. Panic turned to relief as we saw it was more security guards and not the baying mob we had expected. The guards dragged Dai and me back up the tunnel onto the pitch side and walked us along the front of the grandstand on the way to eject us from the ground. Suddenly there was a shout from the grandstand. I looked up into the Directors' Box to see our chairman, Doug Share, beckoning the security men to let us up in the stand with him. Fair play to Doug, we had given him plenty of stick in the past for keeping a tight grip on the purse strings but he was a Swansea Jack through and through and wouldn't see a fellow fan in a sticky situation. "Come and sit by us," he said. We didn't have to be asked twice.

The ordeal was far from over. The roar that had given us our opportunity for escape was the London mob jeering at Tenko and his boys as they left in the van from the car park behind the bank. The cunts had just upped and left after it had become a little too dodgy for them and had left us behind without a second thought. We had been stranded and now faced the unenviable task of getting out of the ground through the mob who occupied our only exit through the car park. The match ended in a slight 1 - 0 victory to us but during all the trouble I had no idea of the score whatsoever and hadn't even realised we had scored at all.

It was time to go but you could see the mob of lads hanging around in the car park which was our only exit. We made our way sheepishly to the edge of the car park and could see the official coaches parked behind the large gang of Londoners. I said to Dai "Let's make a run for it." I didn't fancy the walk to the train station, especially as I was so conspicuous in my Aquascutum coat. This damn fashion could really get you up shit creek sometimes ! Just as we were going to make a run for it, the crowd kicked off when the different gangs decided there was more chance of an off between each other than against us. Dai and I skirted around them as they scrapped it out in the dimly lit car park. We jumped onto one of the official coaches and, after a heated debate with the organisers, they allowed us a lift home; not that they had any choice. There was no fucking chance we were getting off ! We settled down for the journey home, relieved after the stressful ninety minutes. I felt relaxed and comfortable on the coach until, after just a few miles down the M4, a car overtook us in the third lane, the occupants beeping the horn and giving us the finger. All the boys on the bus dived over the seats to the windows, giving it large back to them. The car sped to the front of the coach and one of its passengers climbed out of the window up to his waist. He produced a large house brick, pulled his arm back and with great force slammed it straight through the driver's side windscreen. The bus lurched from side to side as the driver struggled to control the bus after the shock impact at 60 miles an hour. It was only his quick thinking and driving skills that saved our lives. The nightmare of a trip had ended as it had started, in total fucking chaos ! We had to wait for four gruelling hours in the Services for a replacement coach to come all the way from Swansea. My love affair with the FA cup was strained to say the least.

I just wished the boys had made the journey. It would have been a hell of a row if they had. It was a lesson learned - just like Bognor a couple of seasons before - you never knew who you would meet when playing non-league teams.

It had been a successful season on the pitch, with our new manager Terry Yorath getting us into the play-offs. After a 1 - 0 victory at a packed Vetch Field in the semi-final first leg, we set off to South Yorkshire to face Rotherham at Millmoor. Two minibuses left on a glorious balmy evening, one full of our mob and the other full of the Mini Angels. After a long journey and a major drinking session, we arrived in Rotherham not long before kick-off. The beer was in and the brains were out as we decided to go on the home end. As we queued, a couple of lads came round while we stood silently in line, waiting by the turnstiles. They walked past one of the lads, Frankie and started giving him the evil eye, unaware that the whole queue consisted of Jacks. Frankie snapped and lashed out at one of them, catching him with a vicious left hook. Frankie dragged him down and started giving him a good stamping. Within seconds, it kicked right off as more and more lads appeared. Some of the boys were already in and the home crowd had turned on them as they came through the turnstiles. The corrugated doors thrashed back and forth as their boys inside tried to get out. There was confusion and pandemonium outside as Tracy smacked one of the new faces, Divy, as he came to help. We were coming a little unstuck by now as the odds against us grew and grew. There was frantic activity just inside one of the turnstiles as the operator decided enough was enough and he abandoned his post. I could see Ginger Stevens struggling to get back over the turnstile as arms grabbed and fists rained down on him. I ran over and grabbed hold of him and, with a big heave with my foot against the wall, I managed to drag him out to safety, leaving a Rotherham boy clutching the torn pocket of his C 17 jeans. Right behind him was John Longdon in an even worse position. It took a few of us a good two minutes to pull him through - it was like a game of tug of war with a human rope! Poor John was a couple of inches taller but minus one of his trainers. There was some consolation though as the turnstile operator had left all the notes and change when he fled. It wasn't there when he came back, that was for sure.

A big crowd of Rotherham supporters had circled us by now as the police had finally arrived on the scene. With the police was an old boy in a military tie and blazer dressed just like the Major from 'Fawlty Towers'. He chatted to the police at length until he pointed out Frankie and the police duly frogmarched him off to the cells. Poor old Frankie got twelve months for it, just because of some fucking do-gooder. Their boys had come looking for it in the first place and we all felt he was hard done by. We were taken to the away end by the Old Bill where a healthy away support awaited us. Our little adventure had cranked up the atmosphere to fever pitch and the Rotherham fans danced and sang while they taunted John by holding his trainer aloft in the packed home end. It was a cracking game that saw us draw one each, taking us through to a final against Torquay. We celebrated jubilantly at the end of the game - a step closer back to Division Three. We had the last laugh - or so we thought. The police held us back for a quarter of an hour after the game and then seemed confident enough to let us go off into the dark night alone. We made our way back to the van past the home end. Everything seemed deathly quiet; a little too quiet in fact. As we crossed the road, we made our way along some grass banking towards the Homebase store near where we had parked the minibus. There was very little street lighting and the lack of traffic and noise just added to the strange, eerie atmosphere. Somehow I knew it was coming but it still fucking shocked me when it did. The roar of the mob pierced the silence as their voices echoed off the empty streets. We turned round to face them and were greeted by an impressive sight. We couldn't make out any details but we could see that they were spread out right across the road and grass banking, coming towards us through the black Yorkshire night. We were right out of our comfort zone. We had a fair head start on them so decided to make a dash to the van where at least there was light and some weapons in the form of the wheel brace and jack. As we approached the van, a disheartening sight awaited us. Every single tyre had been let down and the windows smashed. As if that wasn't bad enough, when we got within spitting distance, another mob came charging out from behind the nearby houses. It was the perfect ambush ! There was only 17 of us and the shock pincer movement had us on our toes for the second time in the matter of just a few seconds. The Rotherham boys were perfectly organised, a very impressive outfit with plenty of discipline to boot. They chased us through what seemed to be some playing fields until we reached a row of houses. By this point, Tracy had regained a little composure in the ranks.

"Stop !" he screamed. "Stop fucking running !" He picked up a stick and dragged it across the ground. "Nobody goes past this point, OK ?"

Once again he steadied the panic amongst the ranks. The Rotherham boys had given up the chase and were a good 50 yards back down the hill. I was gutted. It was the first time we had been comprehensively run without any resistance whatsoever. All the results we have had in the past would be overshadowed by this one tragic performance. The trust we normally had in each other would be strongly tested after such a pathetic effort but, as the saying goes, if you fall off your horse you get straight back in the saddle.

Promotion was won after a tense 3 - 3 draw down in Torquay after we had beaten them 2 - 1 at the Vetch. The Devon police took no chances this time. After the violence the previous season, they made the game all ticket. They allocated us 1800 spaces but many more made it into the ground as the tickets were of poor quality and simple to replicate. The forgeries were everywhere and the police got wind of it, threatening to arrest anyone trying to gain entry with a forged ticket. As I queued to get in, there was a man on the gate checking for forgeries. I was studying my forged ticket, trying to decide whether or not to risk it, when I heard a familiar voice.

"Well, if it's not Mr Wallis !" It was Martyn Morris, with a sly grin on his face. "What we got here then ?" he said as he snatched the ticket out of my hand. "Got to be a forgery - what do you think, Phil ?" he gestured to his sidekick.

"Aye, it's a forgery." With that he ripped the ticket up into little bits.

"You fucking cunt - that was the real thing !" I protested.

"Don't you fucking swear at me," he said as he grabbed me. A local police sergeant came over to see what all the fuss was about.

"What's going on ?" the Sergeant asked.

"I'm arresting this man for abusive language," Morris said.

"He ripped my ticket up," I protested.

"Is this true ?" the Sergeant asked Morris.

"Yes, sir. It was a forgery."

"No it fucking wasn't," I said.

"Did you check the serial number against the list, Officer ?" the Sergeant asked.

"No, sir," Morris replied sheepishly. With that, the Sergeant ushered me into the ground, apologising for Morris' behaviour.

I turned round and gave him a victorious grin as I entered the ground. Not only had I got one over the smug bastard, I had also had a stress-free entry into the ground with my forgery blowing away in the wind.

'88 - '89

A step up the league ladder had us revisiting Bristol City but first there was a Littlewoods' Cup game against our nearest and dearest. After a failed attempt at getting past the now near impenetrable ring of police placed on every motorway exit, bus terminal and train station, the first leg at Ninian Park passed off unusually peacefully. So it was back to the Vetch to see if we could have a little fun in the second leg. As usual, when we played Cardiff in a night game most of us would take the day off work. We would then spend the day drinking in the anticipation that they might do the same and come down early for a surprise hit. Rumours were abundant as they always were when we played Cardiff. The afternoon was spent checking if the information was kosher by visiting many pubs in the city centre, all to no avail. The match went by without any major incidents; just a few attempted pitch invasions from both sides. So, when Alan Roberts, Cooney and I decided to go back to Cooney's flat in the Sandfields for a spliff after the match, rucking was the last thing on our minds. The game had been over for nearly 40 minutes as we walked through the now quiet streets around the Vetch. As we got near the flat, Cooney said "Come on, let's have a quick gander on the Mumbles Road for some stragglers. You never know !" So we walked down onto the Mumbles Road and up towards the Seabeach pub. To our complete surprise, there was a large gang outside the pub.

"They must be Jacks," I said, as we walked towards them. It was dark and you couldn't make out any faces.
"I don't think they're ours," Alan said, as we got closer.

Suddenly one of them noticed us coming towards them and the hurried voices had them all turning to face us one by one as the word was spread. The chant pierced the night. "CAAARRRDIFF !" Alan's doubts were confirmed in an instant as bricks started to fly in our direction. Facing flying bricks in the day is one thing but in the night it's a whole different ball game. The missiles went through windscreens and bounced off street signs with loud metallic bangs. I jumped as they skimmed across the pavement at great speed. We were outnumbered ten to one so we made a sharp exit into the maze of streets in the Sandfields. Once back at Cooney's flat, we jumped in his car and drove straight to the Queen's to get the lads. I ran in, out of breath and screamed ...

"Come on ! Cardiff are on the Mumbles Road !" Tracy looked at me and said "Seriously ?"
"Yes, fucking seriously !" I retorted.

Without hesitation, the pub emptied and we ran down to the Seabeach; about 70 of us in total. When we arrived, they were nowhere to be seen. We searched up and down the Mumbles Road and in every pub but they had vanished. It was now a full hour after the game so we felt that our chance had passed and that they must have gone home. We decided to go back to the Queens just in case we had missed them on the way down. Just as we were about to go back, one of the lads could be seen waving his arms, frantically trying to get our attention from the promenade. He came running down from the high prom wall and said "They're on the fucking beach !" Tracy went up to have a look, beckoning us all to stay quiet and sure enough there they were - on the beach, just fucking about. He came back down and said "Right, split into two mobs. One go through the tunnel down on the left, the other through the car park on the right and we'll hit 'em with no escape." His plan was faultless. If we had just gone charging in, they would have escaped, no problem. But as the beach was five miles long, this way the only escape would be to swim for it.

We filed through the two entrances silently until we could see there was no way out for them. The shout went up as we charged full pelt towards our foe with all escape routes blocked. Their shock was instant. I couldn't imagine how they must have felt as the roar came at them from both sides. To magnify their fear it was literally impossible to see your hand in front of your face as we moved further away from the street lighting. The dark could induce panic quickly as we had found out ourselves in Rotherham. The Cardiff mob were in total panic - so much so that they were now up to their waists in the sea. Reluctant to follow them in because we were all dressed in our finest gear, we started to stone them. You could just make out their heads as the moonlight glistened on the ocean's surface. The boys had found a stash of large pebbles in the sand and the stoning gathered pace. The gulping sound of the missiles landing around the bobbing heads had the boys cheering with delight as the humiliation continued. Newt and a few others decided to go in after them which forced them out further until we could now make them out, their arms thrashing in the water as they swam away. This was total humiliation; an event that would go down in football folklore. Every time we played each other in the future we would chant at them "Swim away !" How fucking embarrassing. I didn't even see the police come onto the beach as we were mesmerised by the spectacle of it all. The police rounded us up and forced us back onto the promenade where we watched them pull the Cardiff boys out of the sea like drowned rats.

"SWIM AWAY, SWIM AWAY, SWIM AWAY !"

We taunted them as they loaded them into the police wagons. What a sight ! They were cold and wet but unharmed which was lucky for them because if one of them had been hit on the head with a stone he would have drowned for sure. I couldn't believe that they had run into the sea. There was no chance I would ever have done the same. I would rather have a good hiding than be shamed like that. It was another result for Swansea against Cardiff. Surely they were sick of us now ?

Bristol City had never really come to the Vetch even though they had a good reputation in hooligan circles. During my time following the Swans, it was their neighbours, Rovers, who had always come down and kicked it off. We knew we would always get a row at Aston Gate and the memories of the ammonia trick of a few seasons ago was still fresh in our minds. But even though we only had a transit van with 25 of us jammed in the back, we still went looking for a row. Nonetheless, I just hoped we didn't bump into that huge mob that came out of the park last time.

Our first stop was in some dingy pub about two miles from the ground which sold real scrumpy. The 'Mad Apple' went down a treat as we chatted to some lads who happened to be Rovers fans. As we were playing City, they gave us a great welcome and a couple of hours downing the cider went by like a flash. We were in a right state going to the stadium and a fight broke out in the back of the cramped van when Newt called Tracy an 'old cunt'. They both got out of the van for a 'straighter', right in the middle of Bristol. The row ended up with Newt getting the right hump and fucking off on his own all because he called someone an 'old cunt'. But, then again, that was what happened when you drank cider. We lost Dustbin, Nobsy, Tim Richards and Johnny Fowler on the way into the ground but it soon became apparent where they had got to. Some sort of disturbance was happening in the terracing over to our right. We could see fists flying as the boys were being backed up to the perimeter fence, fighting off the Bristol boys. The police dragged them out and marched them round to our end where they received a heroes' welcome. We lost the game 2 - 0 but there was a good atmosphere in the ground with well over 1,000 travelling supporters. As we left the ground, there was still no sign of Newt. We got back to the van where we thought he might be waiting but he wasn't there either. "He must have gone home," Tracy said as we pulled off. Then one of the boys in the front seat shouted "There he is !" Sure enough, there he was, banging on the window of a pub and beckoning the occupants out. We stopped the van and called over to him. "C'mon, Newt, you fucking header !" shouted Alan Harris. He came bouncing over, mumbling in some drunken speech something about 'wurzel cunts'.

As he climbed into the back of the van, the doors of the pub flew open and a mob of Bristol came bounding out. The van sped off up the hill as the boys were shouting "Stop !" to the driver. "Turn round and run them over !" I shouted to Neil in the driver's seat. As Neil did a three point turn, a breeze block came smashing through the windscreen, hitting poor Alan Harris right in the lap who doubled up with pain. As we kicked the back doors open to get out at them, they instantly backed off down the road while we poured out of the transit armed with the breakdown tools. We lined up across the street and called them on but instead of coming back up the hill they started throwing bricks and bottles from a safe distance. The boys started ripping the plywood off the van lining and launching it frisbee style. It whipped through the air at great speed and would surely do a lot of damage if you caught it in the face. We continued to call them on but even though they outnumbered us two to one they wouldn't budge. There was only one way we were going to have it off - we would have to go to them. Terry Davies led the charge, jack handle in hand and fag in mouth as he ran down the hill towards the Bristol mob. Jacken, one of the Mini Angels, came hurtling past me using a 'Men At Work' sign as a shield to deflect the oncoming stones. As we clashed, Little Dai launched a huge road cone into the middle of them splitting the mob in two. Terry lashed out, swinging the jack handle like a fucking madman while Jacken just ran straight into them with his makeshift shield. Both mobs were dancing around each other, throwing kicks and punches, when a young mother, pushing a pram up the hill, shouted at us all in a comical West Country accent. "Grow up, you fucking animals !" She had a good point but it was falling on deaf ears ! The wurzels were backed off further down the road when a couple of cars pulled up. Phelpsy dived out of one, only to be set upon by Tebay who didn't recognise him and gassed him with a tin of deodorant he had nicked from the Services. Four strangers jumped out of the other car. Alan Harris smashed one in the face, splitting his nose a beauty. "We're Swansea!" he protested. The poor lad had seen it going off and stopped to give us a hand, only to get a fucked-up nose for his troubles. Alan said "Shit ! I thought I'd got revenge there for a minute," because he was still hurting from the breeze block in the groin earlier.

The police arrived on the scene sending the Bristol mob fleeing in fear of arrest. They pounced on Ginger as he gave chase and arrested him. The van was wrecked, the wing mirrors hanging off, the windscreen shattered and all the ply lining in shreds in the back. The street was full of debris as more and more police wagons navigated the mess left by our little spat. The Old Bill were trying to get us out as quickly as possible, afraid that a bigger mob was coming our way. But there was no way we were going without Ginger so we told them that, if they let him go, we'd fuck off otherwise we'd stay and they'd have to arrest us all. The look on Ginger's face as they let him go was priceless. He was smiling from ear to ear. One minute, he was facing a night in the cells and suffering a scrumpy hangover and the next he was free to enjoy a good night out.

We drove back to Swansea happy in the thought that we had done well against greater numbers. The ghost of Rotherham had been well and truly laid to rest and we were back on form.

It was a season of consolidation on the pitch as we battled to hold on to our Third Division status. The pacesetters in the league were Bristol Rovers who always seemed to turn up for a ruck and this season was no different. I had great deal of respect for Rovers. They had brought down an almighty mob in the Milk Cup when we were in Division One and kicked it off big style. We got wind of a mob of Rovers holed up in the Seabeach pub on the Mumbles Road. We approached the pub from the front with Jacken hiding by the side of the exit. As they saw us, they charged out of the door. Jacken roundhouse kicked the first lad and dropped him with his surprise attack. The rest came out tooled up with chairs, bottles and glasses. The traffic stopped as the Rovers boys hurled their ammunition, forcing us back to back off down the road. Bottles smashed around us as I skipped over one flying bottle only to be hit on the ankle by another. I winced in pain as it cut into my leg, sending blood all over my brand new blue suede Gazelles. As they ran out of ammo, we steamed into them. I caught one with a good punch, sending him into the garden of the Guest House we were fighting outside. Through the windows, you could see the guests' faces pressed against the glass, mesmerised as they watched the ruck unfurl. One new lad on the scene, Hoskins, was struggling with a couple of Rovers' boys on him so Laddie and I set on them to help him out. I grabbed one off of him as Laddie tackled the other. I punched him hard to the temple, hurting my thumb in the process and he crumbled and fell to my feet. As he did, he grabbed onto my legs, gripping on for dear life. I struggled to get him off me by trying to shake my legs free but his dead weight was impossible to move. I bent over and punched him repeatedly in the face but still he clung on. By now the sirens were getting closer and closer and I started to panic. I didn't want to get nicked again so I screamed at Laddie "John ! Get this cunt off me !" He grabbed him and pulled but his vice like grip held. I could now see the coppers jumping out of the vans. "For fuck's sake, John !" I yelled. With that, Laddie swung his leg and smashed the lad with a punishing kick, square on the jaw. He collapsed in a heap and we made off just in the nick of time. I turned round to see a few bodies on the floor after what had been a brutal encounter.

Even though they had run at us first, I think we just edged it due to the nasty beatings dished out. The adrenalin was pumping big style as we chatted about the off on the way to the ground. We gave Hoskins, the new lad, some stick as we had to save his arse but all he could do was moan about his torn Chippie jumper! Even though we gave him some shit, we were well impressed that he had got straight in - not that we would tell him, though. My joy at our success was short-lived. While watching the game, I saw the police shifting through the crowd, obviously looking for someone. Not for one second did I think it was me until they stopped right in front me.

"Come on, Wallis, you're nicked."
"What for ? I've done fuck all !"
"You were seen fighting outside, pal."

Off I went, once again, with my old mate, Martyn Morris. The season ended with us wining the Welsh Cup in a cracking 5 - 0 hammering of Kidderminster Harriers. This gained us entry into Europe so plans were made as we eagerly awaited the draw.

I was living and working in London at the time but used to get home as often as I could because I missed the weekends in the Queen's. I used to live for the all-dayers which were usually topped off with a ruck with gangs of Valley boys in town for the night life. This brought us into conflict with the doormen at various clubs in the city. My mate, Craig, lived in London and we had decided to go back for a celebration piss-up after one of the lad's baby's birth. On the way past Putney tube station, I told him to stop the car as I had decided to stay behind and work at the weekend. It turned out to be one hell of a decision because the boys got into a ruck with some bouncers which saw three doormen suffering serious slash wounds. One nearly lost his sight after being slashed through both eyeballs. Many of the boys were arrested and charged with some very serious charges. This one incident nearly destroyed the firm as a war broke out between us and the doormen. Punishment beatings were dished out as the bouncers picked off the boys one by one. The father of one of the boys was leading the punishment gang so we lost Duffy.

Cooney's wife's uncle was one of the victims and, as he and Toozey worked the doors, they were in a difficult situation. This led to a split because many boys were scared off from hanging around with us. The beatings went on for a few months until one night, after we had come back from Chepstow Races, an almighty row erupted in the Queen's which ended with us getting the better of a large group of bouncers. This put an end to the beatings but many of the boys still faced serious Crown Court appearances. The firm was never the same after this, especially after losing Terry Dustbin - one of our main leaders - after he was falsely charged with the slashings.

'89 - '90

The previous season's Welsh Cup success saw us thrown into the hat for the European Cup winner's cup draw. Apart from a tie against PSG in Paris back in 1982, our games in Europe had been lack lustre draws to say the least. So you can imagine the excitement when we were paired with Panathinaikos based in Athens, Greece. One of the Winch Wen boys, Hoppy, arranged a flight with his father's travel agency and 88 of us booked for a full week in Athens, accommodating the match in between. I couldn't wait for it. We had all seen the England fans performing when abroad and now we had the chance to put our mark on Europe. We flew out from London after a mega piss-up in the Queens, leaving for the airport after stop tap. The hangovers were abundant on the flight over which made for an unusually quiet journey. This was the calm before the storm. I was sure it was going to kick-off over there and I told everyone who would listen beforehand "You watch - we'll make 'News At Ten'," I said, a little tongue in cheek. Little did I know how right I would be.

The week started well with a routine of drinking by the pool by day and out in the bars of Glyfada by night. However, the boundaries were being pushed further and further day by day. The hotel management were getting sick and tired of our behaviour by the pool and it didn't surprise me when one of the lads, Brummie Steve, pissed over Tracy's shoulder into his breakfast as he tucked into his bacon and eggs. A full-on food fight erupted with sausages and fried eggs ending up floating in the swimming pool; the ketchup being used as a squeezy gun and, eventually, the crockery and poolside furniture being used in a mock mini riot. The proprietor, a stern-faced, middle-aged German woman, stormed out yelling at us to stop the fighting. "Look at this ! No wonder the other guests won't use the pool with you fucking animals here !" As we all stood silently, heads bowed like scolded school kids, Tracy sneaked up behind her. I thought 'Oh fuck, no, Tracy' as he pushed her mid-sentence into the pool. The place erupted in laughter as her slip over dress floated off her as she plunged to the bottom of the pool in her '50's style underwear. I was on my knees crying with laughter as were most of the boys. She dragged herself out like a drowned rat and fled in embarrassment. That was the last time we used the pool as we were banished to the beach. The nights were spent travelling through the nightlife that Glyfada had to offer. Often small scuffles would break out with the locals; motorbikes were kicked over and our general misbehaviour had the Greeks resenting our presence more and more as each day passed.

The day of the game was soon upon us and we were set to go to the Olympic stadium by coach at five. We'd spent all day drinking in the hot Greek sun and the boys were in a fair state on the journey to the ground. The coach was escorted to the Olympic Stadium by a heavy police presence and we ran all the red lights as they sped us through the heavy home time traffic. I had seen public awareness adverts on the Greek television channels warning about the perils of hooliganism and heard stories from the local barmen about the Panathinaikos mob, 'The Gate 13'. Apparently they had burnt down their old stadium after a bad season, hence the reason they now played at the Olympic Stadium. They had a reputation of being the worst football hooligans in Greece which was the reason we were being escorted so hastily, accompanied by a water cannon truck and several armoured police wagons. The escort slowed to a snail's pace as we hit the stadium traffic. The locals in cars around us looked on bemused as the boys traded insults through the skylights and small sliding fanlight windows. Brummie Steve, an old Villa boy who had joined us when he moved to Swansea, started ripping the curtain poles down and lobbed them through the skylights at the Greeks in the stationary cars. This caused the lads to start chucking all sorts of objects through the windows - lighters, coins, armrests and, finally, a beer bottle which smashed through the windscreen of a nearby car. The police boarded the bus, yelling at us in Greek, ordering everyone off the bus. We stood around until darkness crept over us at the side of the motorway while the police argued over what to do with us. They eventually decided we would have to fork out a couple of quid each to compensate the owner of the car. Once that was sorted, we were back on our way with only a few minutes to kick-off.

We pulled up at the car park of the stadium which was deserted as everyone was already inside. The huge stadium was shadowed in the dark Greek night, topped off with a white glow emanating from the open air ground. Figures danced around the top tier, arms held aloft as they chanted in unison. It was a truly awesome sight which made the 80 or so of us feel rather insignificant compared to their massed legions of fans. We entered the stadium flanked by riot police. The noise levels instantly rose as they chanted in our direction. We had no idea what they were saying but I was sure they weren't being friendly ! We chanted back and made a hell of a noise - especially as there was only 500 or so of us. They responded by unfurling a huge flag with the gruesome motor head motif in green ...

'GATE 13 - WELCOME TO HELL'

The chanting now became relentless as flares were lit in every part of the immense stadium. It was an intimidating sight which we countered with a loud chorus of "Who the fucking hell are you ?" The chanting back and forth continued throughout the whole match which we narrowly lost 3 - 2 with John Salako starring in a pulsating end to end game. The result sat us up for a real chance in the second leg with two precious away goals. This fact was not lost on the Greek fans as their anger prompted them to stage a charge towards our small contingent that was sandwiched between two deep lines of riot police. The cracking sound of seats being stamped on filled the air as the boys armed themselves ready for the inbound mob. When they got within 50 foot of us, one of the riot police blew a whistle and they charged towards the incoming mob of Greeks. This repelled their attack as the lads taunted them from behind the riot police. After a well planned security operation, we were dropped back at the hotel without further incident.

The next night Craig, Brummie Steve and I went out looking for somewhere to eat. As we walked past the main square, there was a huge team of Olympiakos fans, all decked out in red and white with flags flying, waiting to go to a Euro Cup tie with Rad of Yugoslavia. They eyed us up as we went past, hissing and saying "Swansea" in long drawn out, high-pitched voices. Craig shouted "Fuck off, you cunts ! You'd be speaking fucking German if it wasn't for us." They sneered at us as we walked on. We turned the corner, heading for the 'California Burger Bar' and an old restored American Cabriolet came slowly past with more Olympiakos boys in it. Two were in the front and another two were sitting up on the backs of the seats, practically on the boot. In between them was an odd-looking Staff mongrel. "Swansea, you die !" one of the Greeks said, mockingly. Brummie Steve threw his can of lager at them and in his broad Brummie accent shouted "C'mon then, you tossers !" They opened the back door and set the dog on us. Craig swung his leg back and gave the dog an almighty boot right in the nose. It yelped and fucked off down the road a bit sharpish. We charged at the car as the front seat passenger fumbled in his coat for what looked like a gun. The driver slammed his foot on the accelerator and sped off. Unbeknown to the driver, this action threw two Greeks on the back seat out over the boot and onto the road. We gave them a severe kicking as their mates drove off with no intention of stopping. We made our way back to the hotel to get the rest of the lads but the Olympiakos fans had already set off on their journey.

We still had two days of the trip to go and the locals were tiring of us already. The lads had been involved in smash and grab; general criminal damage to bikes and cars; pubs had been wrecked as beer fights turned a bit rough and Phelps and I had been in a ruck with a restaurant owner after we danced on top of his Mercedes. We had to fend them off with a length of chain with diamond shaped studs and narrowly escaped a possible stabbing. It was fair to say that one more incident could see the whole resort of Glyfada turning against us. I'll never forget the night that it happened. It's etched on my mind so clearly, as if it happened yesterday rather than almost two decades ago. We were walking up to the Ship Inn, a pub we were frequenting in the main square, when I noticed two familiar Greek faces walking towards us.

"Look ,Mike, it's those two cunts I was on about the other night," I said to Phelpsy, referring to the driver of the Cabriolet and his gun-toting passenger. As we passed, I pushed him with both hands in the chest and screamed in his face "Where's your fucking gun now then, cunt ?" He waved his hands, gesturing to me to leave him alone but I was having none of it. The rage had built up inside me and exploded as I hit him with all my might with a swinging right. He was out before he hit the floor, his head smashing with a sickening, dull thud on the pavement. His mate just cowered away in sheer terror as Snowy pulled me away and said "Leave him - he's had enough." We carried on to the pub, leaving the two Greeks behind on the street, one trying to revive the other. The Ship Inn was quite a large establishment which faced the square. It had an open terrace at the front, leading into the main bar area. In the far right hand corner was an emergency exit which led to an alley with a glass fronted canopy. We had been drinking for about 20 minutes when about ten Greeks walked in. At the front was a long haired man in a sleeveless T-shirt and shorts. He went on to some of the lads to protest about the lad I had levelled outside earlier. At first he was a bit animated as all Continentals tend to be but he soon clamed down. I couldn't be bothered to talk to them but for some reason some of the boys were trying to appease the Greeks. As I watched from the bar, everything seemed to be resolved and the long haired Greek was shaking hands saying something about us all being fans of the beautiful game. Then Lako shook his head, pulled the Greek forward with a sharp tug and butted him right on the bridge of the nose, totally unexpectedly. As this happened, Dolly smashed him over the head with a beer bottle, sending him to the floor with blood pouring from his scalp. We sprang off our stools and laid into the other Greeks as they fled into the streets, knocking over tables and chairs as they scrambled away amid flying glass and fists. They ran off up the road but we knew they would be back with reinforcements.

At the time of the first bout of trouble, there was only about 20 of us there. The sun was still shining as dusk approached which meant more and more of the boys would turn up in drips and drabs - a welcome sight, as we knew that trouble could be only moments away. By the time the second wave of Greeks came, we were 40 strong. Beer bottles had been kept for ammo as we had not allowed the bar staff to take away the empties. They came across the square, about 100 in total, armed with sticks and flash knives as they whooped and cheered at us. We were bouncing with the lads all jeering each other up, getting the aggression flowing till the pressure popped and we came bursting out armed with bottles, glasses, chairs and anything we could get our hands on. The Greeks were hesitant as we launched our weapons into the now darkened Athens sky. The sound of smashing glass was non stop as the Greeks danced around trying to avoid the spinning missiles. One aimed a stick at me as I smashed him in the face with a glass. I grabbed at another but got hit on the elbow as his mate lashed out with a lump of wood. I hopped in pain as I clutched my elbow, expecting a further barrage of weapons. As I retreated, I saw one of the boys, Sid, take my place as he decked one of the oncoming Greeks. The square was full of lads, toe to toe, as we fought for our lives. We were in a precarious position with our backs against the pub and nowhere to go except into the square filled with Greeks. So forward we went, backing them off, again and again, until they broke ranks and ran. We chased them out of the square, jubilant in our victory. We had fought against the odds and the British fighting spirit had won the day or so we thought.

This was when we made our biggest mistake. Instead of moving on, we went back into the Ship Inn and carried on drinking. Looking back now, with hindsight, we should have found a more strategic position than a pub facing a huge town square with no way out but through it. We should have known that they wouldn't leave it at that and would come back stronger. The chanting and singing rang out from the pub as we celebrated running the Greek mob,. We failed to notice the crowd gathering on the far side of the square as the Greeks came back, one by one. The singing soon stopped when we noticed the crowd had grown considerably. More and more kept flooding in as an air of angst came over the square. We sent some lads out to get all the Swansea boys who weren't already in the pub. There was no way out now but through the masses of Greeks and a terrible onslaught was unavoidable. We resigned ourselves to the fact that we would have to face this immense mob so we started dismantling the pub bit by bit until there was nothing left to get hold of. Big cheers went up every time a Jack walked in, until we were at full strength - about 80 in total.

When the charge came, the fight or flight concept never came into the equation. There was nowhere to go so everybody had to fight and there was no place for any shrinking violets. We only just made it out past the terrace as the debris rained down on us incessantly - bricks, blocks, glasses, bottles, planks of wood, chairs, tables, coins and even scaffolding tubes, came hurtling towards us. We were battered back into the bar where we were quickly running out of ammunition. Boys were down in the cellar passing up crates of bottles in a chain gang to feed the front line where we were desperately trying to keep them at bay. As far as the eye could see, there was a mass of heads that filled the square. We were trapped. The only thing that kept them out was our continuous barrage of bottles but the cellar was emptying fast. At the front of the Greek mob was a man on a moped, his headlight glaring into the pitch black pub. He pulled on the accelerator several times as if revving up to drive towards us. I grabbed a long bench along with a Dutch lad we called John the Clog. We ripped off the 2" thick timbers and waited either side of the pub entrance. Sure enough, the moped shot forward - the driver on some sort of suicide mission. As the moped came bursting through the doorway both John and I smashed the driver from either side. The bike careered into the bar and he flew off and landed motionless on the pub floor. He hadn't been wearing a helmet, his head was smashed in and to me he looked dead. We didn't have time to find out, though, as we had run out of missiles - even the till had been chucked. I looked over at Jeff Warren behind the bar who held up a tiny bottle of Tabasco sauce and shrugged his shoulders. "That's it !" he said as he threw the Tabasco at the charging Greeks.

We had no option but to jump over the bar. Everyone vaulted it in a single leap but the cellar door was open in the floor and an unlucky few tumbled down the long drop. Poor Brummie Steve hit his elbows on the hatchway on the way down. He landed on the concrete floor in front of the terrified bar staff who had locked themselves in a steel cage to escape the madness. Back upstairs one of the boys had discovered the fire exit door and we all spilled out into the lane, fleeing the mob coming through the bar. Once in the lane, our fate could not have been worse. The door had been jammed tight to the bar and we were trapped in a very small lane, around 20 foot long, covered by a semi-circular canopy. We fought to get out and made it just to the end of the lane, trading punches and kicks as the mass of Greeks struggled to get control of us as we tried to escape. We were literally fighting for our lives and it showed as the Greeks were getting knocked out as they came forward. We seemed to be getting the better of them as we inched ever forward. As I got my foot onto the street, I was suddenly smashed sideways. A Greek had welted me right in the ear with a brick. I stumbled around, stunned by the attack and I lost my hearing to a high pitched ring. One of the lads pulled me back into the lane and sat me down next to one of the Morriston boys who had been stabbed in the backside.

The boys were eventually forced back by the weight of the baying mob while around 40 of us were squeezed into a small space at the rear of the lane. The bombardment began as the Greeks demolished a wall outside the lane and showered us with rocks. The back of the lane was full of old tables and crates which we utilised as shields to deflect the projectiles. We all crouched down under our paltry shielding, glass showering down on us as the glass canopy was shattered. We were in a terrifying situation - our fate was now in their hands. I was just waiting for the petrol bomb to come in and torch us all. Our spirit had been broken after a long night of violence and I was physically and mentally exhausted. Some of the younger Mini Angels were panicking, almost in tears at our ill fated position. Recognising that spirit was low, Tracy burst into a chorus of 'Men Of Harlech' in a scene reminiscent of the film 'Zulu'. Even though we faced extreme danger, laughter filled the air as we joked with each other. The missiles mysteriously stopped as an eerie calm settled everyone's nerves. A flashlight shone into the pitch black lane as the figure of a policeman brought a welcome sigh of relief from everybody. The police had used tear gas to disperse the Greeks and brought a coach to the end of the lane. The police then formed a line each side of the road along our path to the entrance of the bus.

As the boys emerged from under the debris of rocks and glass it became apparent that hardly anyone had escaped injury. It was a bloody sight of stab wounds, cracked open heads and blood stained clothes and, as if we hadn't suffered enough, when we ran the gauntlet to the bus, the police beat us with truncheons. While the Greeks lashed out from the back of the lane, Craig and I helped Newt get out. He had been hit on the shins with a scaffold tube which had left a nasty wound and he was unable to walk. We carried him to the coach but the police showed no sympathy, beating him as we carried him shoulder high onto the bus. We sat at the back of the coach and I looked at the square through the rear window. The scene of devastation was a shock. Cars had been turned over, all the shop fronts were smashed in, walls had been demolished and rubble littered the whole square - it looked like a war zone. The coach sped off on the short journey to the police station with officers armed with machine guns overseeing our transportation. Craig whispered to me "Clean off the blood." We licked our hands and rubbed the blood off on the seats. I wiped my face on the inside of my T-shirt and cleaned the spots of blood off the white stripes on my Gazelles.

They put us in a holding room in the station and lined us up against the walls to search us. An officer walked in, twirling his nightstick, cockily walking up and down the line peering at us through mirrored sunglasses. The cunt looked like he just walked off the set of a George Michael video ! He walked past me and kicked my trainers. "Adidas. You're a hooligan." He walked the line a few times then said "You know, in Greece we fuck boys and girls. I would like to fuck you all but I haven't got the time." Seeing the way he was dressed, I wouldn't have put it past the cunt.

The mind games continued as they interviewed us one by one all throughout the night. I had swapped shirts with Snowy because I was sure I would be picked out as the one who had started it all. But, when the witnesses came in, pointing people out, I wasn't fingered . Maybe Craig's plan had worked because many of the boys covered in blood were pointed out. By the next morning, the police had whittled us down to 20 - letting others go throughout the night. I was so sure we were going to be flung in jail that I said to Terry Davies "We ain't getting out of here, mate." I was only 50 per cent correct, as at around nine o'clock, Craig, Brummie Steve, Tenko, Snowy and I were released. Before they let us go, a man claiming to be the British Consul told us to go back to the hotel, collect £2,000 and the police would release the others. We got back to the hotel to find all the flags missing from the balconies and bullet holes sprayed across the outside. We knocked everyone up and collected as much money as possible. The money was given to the police and we awaited the boys return. The hotel was surrounded by armed guards at all the entrances. There was no chance of leaving. We were packing our stuff when the police came bursting through the door. A copper walked up to me and said "Stephen Rowden ?" I shook my head and pointed to Snowy. With that, the copper grabbed him while another brought in Midge, one of the arrested lads. Poor Snowy had briefly tasted freedom, only to be snatched back at the last minute.

The bus arrived to take us to the airport but there was no sign of the boys. We thought they might be at the airport but, once we got there, it became all too clear that they weren't coming home and the Old Bill had pocketed all our money. We travelled back to London on a sombre flight.

Chapter 7 - LEE'S STORY

Our trip had incorporated the Swansea match at Fulham on the afternoon of return so I accompanied Craig to his office in Victoria before setting off to the game. As we waited for the pub to open, a few Chelsea lads turned up, laughing at the story on the front page of The Sun newspaper. I looked over their shoulders at the picture and there, in black and white on the front page, was Terry Davies, his T-shirt over his head with the headline 'Soccer Yobs Are Gassed'. I was thrilled that we had made the front pages of the national tabloids but, at the same time, concerned about the fate of the boys - especially as it was my actions that had kicked it all off. I felt responsible and terribly guilty. The Fulham game passed with our team losing 2 - 0; not that I really bothered watching it. All the talk on the terraces was about Greece and rumours were rife that the boys had been jailed. The bus left Fulham as we listened to the final scores. I just about managed a smile at Stuart Hall's mad ranting. Then silence enveloped the coach as the newsreader said "Sixteen Swansea City fans have been jailed for their part in a riot in Greece." My heart sank. I couldn't believe it. Less than two days after the row, they had been tried, found guilty and jailed. The speed of the conviction alone showed how corrupt their system was, not forgetting the £2,000 they stole from us. And we complain about our police ! In Greek law, you can pay off your sentence so, after a week, most of the boys were out of jail. Only two were left unable to afford the payment until, in a kind hearted gesture, Swansea's Chairman, Doug Sharpe, paid to get them released. The story had caused a media storm. The lads appeared on 'News At Ten' and, as I had predicted, footage was shown of them arriving back at Heathrow where Dolly attacked the cameraman. Old habits die hard !

The return leg saw us narrowly missing out on the next round by away goals. The mob we had out that day was the biggest I had ever seen. With the world's media watching and expecting a bloodbath, the police ran a well-oiled operation, taking the Greeks into the Upper East Stand from their buses. The only trouble happened when the Chief of South Wales Police came in the Queen's to address us about the game and he was bottled out of the pub. And later, when a small group of Cardiff came on the West Bank thinking it was holding the away fans, they were chased out of the ground.

It was time for another game against one of the Bristol sides. We had taken a 52-seater to City in October only for the police to stop us and turn us back round to Swansea. So, for the Rovers' game, we decided to go by train as there was no chance of turning round 125 ! Rovers had sold their ground and were now sharing Twerton Park with City. A trip to Bath included a change at Cardiff Central. Cardiff were playing at home so the prospect of a meet was very possible. We had an hour to kill at Cardiff so we left the station of the capital looking for some scum. To our disappointment, there was nobody about; only a few 'scarfers' here and there so we made our way off to Bath. Our frustration continued there as there didn't seem to be any firm about in the city centre so we made our way to the ground 100 strong. We passed a pub on the way up the hill to the ground. It was full of boys who banged on the windows singing "Sheep, sheep, sheep shaggers !" We called them out as we converged into the pub. They didn't make any effort to come out - all mouth and no trousers - as they bounced up and down behind the glass. Police vans arrived between us and the pub, forcing us back. The police now escorted us to the ground.

The away support in the ground was in the thousands with plenty of boys present so it was no surprise that, when the second Rovers' goal went in, we charged the fence and broke through the emergency gate onto the pitch. The Rovers' fans at the far side of us followed suit and it took mounted police to restore order. The boys fought with the police on the bank as they laid in a bit heavy handed after the invasion. Punches were exchanged and Little Dai was nicked. The highly charged atmosphere had us wound right up and we couldn't wait to change trains in Cardiff. The short journey had us at Cardiff central by 6:30pm. We disembarked, fully expecting a heavy police presence but we looked the length of the platform and there were none to be seen. We held our breath as we marched through the tunnel under the platform, in hope of a free passage. As we came through the concourse, it was plain to see that the police had made an almighty fuck up and lost track of us between Bath and Cardiff. We were free and on the streets of the capital. The blood was pumping through our veins at every step with the anticipation of an ambush at any moment. There was only one destination on our minds - The Philharmonic pub. This is where we thought the Soul Crew would be drinking.

As we turned onto St Mary's Street, a mob of Cardiff came bouncing up the road. We heavily outnumbered them but they still came forward. At the front was Bully Fulman and Sims from Neath. Sims was a familiar face. I had started work with him in a joinery shop in Neath and he was also good mates with Little Dai. Sims had been at the front of many of our recent conflicts. He was there at the Guildhall row. He was the one that had gassed us at Ninian Park. He was one of the game lads outside the Queen's and he had been in the car load that jumped me down in Mumbles. He still hadn't seen me when Ivy made a beeline for him. Sims backed off and put his hand in his Burberry jacket gesturing that he had a knife. This bought him a few seconds as the boys closed in around him.

"Run, Simon for fuck's sake !" He turned to me smiled and said "All right, Wall."

Ivy shouted "Is that the cunt from Neath ?" This made Ivy even more angry as he steamed towards him. Simon and his mob pegged it down the road with a few in tow. He wasn't very popular with the lads as you can imagine. The fact that he had influenced lads to follow Cardiff in a Swansea stronghold made him public enemy number one.

We arrived at the Philharmonic but the Cardiff mob weren't there. We were sure they would be along soon after our chance meeting with Sims and Co so we settled in for a few lagers. Time was getting on but there was no sign of any Cardiff which had us perplexed because they had played at home and were sure to be around. Ivy collared one of the bouncers, ordering him to get the Soul Crew on the scene as he professed to know them. We waited and waited but they never came. We had come to town and let them know we were there. We camped out in one of their pubs and waited for hours but still no show. So much for the 'famous' Soul Crew.

That season's FA Cup saw us drawn at home with Peterborough United after we had beaten Kidderminster in the first round. The trip to Kiddie had turned out to be an eventful one with us rowing with some Villa boys in the pub before the game. It was a rude awakening for a couple of new recruits who had made the trip with us for the first time. As the Villa boys came in chucking tables and chairs, they had reacted well by returning fire with glasses and bottles and seeing them back out of the door. One of the new lads, Waggy a shaven headed boy from Baglan was extremely eager to impress - so much so that when we were in the ground, Little Dai and I set him the task of running across the pitch to get into their end. We creased ourselves laughing as Waggy ran the length of the pitch and climbed over the perimeter hoarding into the Kiddie fans, calling them on. Little Dai said "Look at that fucking bozo !" which had us doubled up, crying with laughter. From that day on Waggy was known as Bozo !

There was a good turnout on the morning of the Peterborough game and, with the sun shining on a bright December afternoon, we made our way down the Sandfields for a nose. We had no idea that the Posh would bring a firm so you can imagine the shock we had when we entered the Badminton to see it chock a block full of Peterborough lads. We went to the bar and ordered some drinks as everyone eyed each other up, just waiting for it to kick-off. There must have been about 30 to 40 of them, matching our numbers to a man. Cooney turned around, pint in hand and looked at one of their lads and said "All right ?" lifting his eyebrows in acknowledgement. This lulled the Peterborough fan into a false sense of security as he didn't even see Cooney's flying head butt. The pub erupted in an explosion of voices, shouting and glasses smashing. We forced them out of the pub door, attacking them with pool cues and glasses. Once outside, the fight continued as they regrouped and came back at us. I singled out a tall blonde lad and traded punches with him. I was in trouble. For every punch I threw, he threw three back in quick succession. By the time I threw another, my lip was cut, my nose was bleeding and my ear was ringing. Seeing that I was struggling with my quick-fisted, sparring partner, Aggis came to my rescue, jabbing him right in the Adam's apple with the thin end of a pool cue. He went down instantly like a sack of shit. I booted him as hard as I could only to be sent reeling with pain as I was wearing flimsy suede Wallaby shoes. The Peterborough firm fled up the road with our mob in hot pursuit and escaped into the ranks of the South Wales police force. Our boys had smashed them outside the pub with a few nasty kickings dished out but I was disappointed with my own performance. If it hadn't been for Aggis, I would have had a right hiding.

I didn't fare any better in the next round. We drew Liverpool at home in what was the biggest game we had played since our brief spell in Division One. A massive firm turned out because everybody wanted to see this one. We had been searching the Sandfields all morning for some opposition but all we could find were 'scarfers' so the boys settled into a drinking session in the Queens and, once they got comfortable, it would take a sledgehammer to move them. Chrissy Neale came in shouting "They're up by the Quadrant !" I said to the lads "Come on !" but they wouldn't listen as we had been chasing rumours all morning. I was up for it so I set off towards the bus station with the youth firm in tow. As we came through the car park, they could be seen coming through the rows of buses. I charged at them across the car park and into the bus terminal. The next thing I saw was Chrissy Neale standing over me trying to lift me out of the puddle of rain water I had been lying in. Apparently a Scouser had hit me from the side as I passed the end of a bus. I never saw it coming and he knocked me clean out. I walked back into the Queens with a cracking black eye. I was furious with the boys for not coming with us and let them know in no uncertain terms; only to be met by a barrage of laughter and piss taking. I had to see the funny side, though, as I must have looked a sight; soaking wet, muddy, with a beauty of a shiner as I shouted at them - the bastards ! I had my revenge after the game when I knocked out one of their lads as we searched the dark Sandfields streets for some victims. We nearly came unstuck though as Little Dai, big Terry Davies and I had blades pulled on us as we challenged a small mob down Oxford Street. Once again the Scousers lived up to their reputation of dirty, blade wielding cunts.

The Boxing Day fixture was Cardiff at home yet again. The Queens had opened early as usual and we were 200 strong very early on in the morning. This fixture was so notorious now that 400 police would be on duty to combat the threat of violence. This would have its advantages for us because they had to draft officers in from all parts of Wales. Officers who wouldn't know us from Adam and couldn't differentiate between a Cardiff and Swansea accent. The boys had a tendency to get too settled in when beer was around so Cooney and I rallied the troops for a scan down the Mumbles Road. Sometimes, if nobody said anything, they would stay rooted to the spot. We left the Queen's in an awesome mob which stretched 150 yards, like troops on the move. As we approached the 'Swansea Jack', half a dozen police vans pulled up and emptied out alongside us.

"Where are you lot from ?" the Sergeant said in an English accent.
Quick off the mark Cooney said "Cardiff, mate."

With that, the police started escorting us towards the away end without a clue about out true identity. We marched along the Mumbles Road through the police lines at the street leading us to the away end. We would have made it all the way if it hadn't been for one of the local officers who protested "What the fuck are this lot doing here ?" We all laughed at the English copper's expense but were disappointed at not getting amongst the Bluebirds. All was not lost though because we had managed to get down around the away fans' area in one big mob. We noticed some dressers across the road by the County Hall car park. They darted back over the grass banking as we made our way across the Mumbles Road. One of the boys had sprinted over and was already on top of the bank, waving frantically and calling us over. We steamed over the grass banking and were confronted by a mob of Cardiff coming down the banking opposite us. The ruck was on as we clashed in front of the County Hall. The Mini Angels were the first in as Jacken traded punches with a lad in a Burberry bucket hat. We rounded the mob as a few were dragged down and battered. We were right on top of them now and the pressure was too much for them as they retreated up the bank.

The first clash had us wanting more and it wasn't long before we bumped into another mob. As we walked along the car park, we saw a gang led by a big black lad who came bounding over to us, confidently announcing "Santos here, live and direct !" With that, Cooney just smashed him down without a word. Without their main man, the mob melted. Once again we had won the competition off the pitch. It was just a pity the team couldn't do the same as we lost 1- 0 in front of a crowd of 12,500.

It was getting more and more difficult to get into Cardiff for our annual visit so, with the Easter Bank holiday fixture fast approaching, we held a meeting to decide how we would get into the Welsh capital undetected. We thought of going to Merthyr by bus and catching the train down. We also pondered the idea of catching the service bus straight into the main bus station but finally we all agreed on hiring a coach to Barry and catching the train into Cardiff. The plan worked a treat and we left Grangetown train station into the heart of enemy territory without a copper in sight. We hadn't been totally undetected however, because a station worker took it upon himself to get in his car and attempt to run us all down. Still dressed in his fluorescent orange British Rail jacket, he drove at speed towards us as we marched towards Canton, sending us all diving out of the path of the crazy driver. He weaved the little black Fiat towards his intended victims in a manner that showed this intentions were real. Unbelievably, he handbrake turned at the top of the road, revved his engine and came hurtling back towards us. Ivey spied a bike against the railings, picked it up and went into the middle of the road to face the oncoming maniac. He stood in the middle of the road with the bike raised above his head and, just as the car reached him, he slammed the bike right through the windscreen and dived out of the way. The driver swerved from side to side and continued off into the distance. We all agreed he must have been a right mad cunt to pull a stunt like that.

We approached the corner of the Grange pub as a few Cardiff boys came round the corner with gas at the ready. They obviously didn't realise how many of us were there because they suddenly came to a dead stop, bumping into each other as they struggled to turn around and run. The gas had been dropped without being used and was commandeered by Chrissy Neale. The police arrived on the scene and arrested Cooney and Pinto following a struggle to control us. We were now buzzing at the prospect of having to be led right through the maze of residential streets of Grangetown. The possibility of a row was at every corner and junction we passed and, when it did come, the police were in no position to stop us. They came at us out of a side street but were chased back instantly. A few of them carried on further than the rest and we caught up with them as they scrambled about in a skip trying to pull out some old door frames to use as weapons. I grabbed one by the shirt which ripped in my hands as he tried to pull away. He spun around, freeing himself, only to be tripped up by one of our boys. He went down as Laddie pounced on him, pinning him to the floor. He was knocked unconscious and dealt a full hiding. The Cardiff boys regrouped a few yards up the road, geeing up each other to come back to help their stricken comrade. The Cardiff mob now outnumbered us because the police had gained control of the rest of the boys. However, we had the controlling factor because we had the skip. They came back towards us as we emptied the rubble in their direction. Their fight back was short lived when we charged at them, armed with nail-studded door jambs. They didn't hang around and I didn't blame them.

At the ground we taunted them with a chorus of 'Swim Away !' with our crowd acting out the swimming action. This wound them right up and turned the volume up a notch or two but their crowd was silenced when we added insult to injury with a 2 - 0 win. At the end of the game the police had a dilemma. Normally they would send us out on coaches straight onto the M4 through Leckworth but, because of our successful plan, they would have to march us through the centre of Cardiff to the train station to send us back to our coach waiting in Barry. The police surrounded us on all sides and marched the 80 of us through Cardiff . It was a 'stop, start' affair as they cleared the roads ahead of potential ambushers. Once at the station, they put us on the Barry bound platform where we mingled with Cardiff fans, kicking them and dishing out sly digs when out of the policemen's glare. We boarded the train for the short trip to Barry, all packing into one carriage. Among us was one poor Cardiff fan. He was verbally abused the whole journey down but was safe because the police were with us on the train. When we pulled up in Barry, the police got off and lined the platform. As we disembarked, the poor Cardiff fan was covered in spit and slapped as the boys filed past him. I thought it was out of order but the hatred ran so deep that sometimes shit like that happened. I'm sure some Jacks have been in the same position.

Back in Barry, we had just boarded the coach ready to go back to Swansea when some of our boys, who had travelled by car, came running up the road. They had bumped into a tidy firm of Cardiff. Our bus emptied and we sprinted down the road towards the mob of scum. We met on the corner of the road, scuffling, as the police intervened to separate us. This was the gamest firm we had seen all day and it was a shame that the police were already on the scene because it could have been a cracking row. The Old Bill sent us packing. Although I thought we could have done better in Barry, we were well pleased with the day's work. As Tracy later commented: "I love it when a plan comes together."

We had played Bolton a few times over the last few years and they had always turned up. There was something about the first and last games of the season that always seemed to bring out the numbers and, as we had Bolton at home on the final day, there was sure to be a big turnout from both sides. It was a typical sunny end of season day, the T-shirts and shorts were out along with an array of designer sunglasses. It was the perfect day for a bit of bother. We sunned ourselves outside the Seabeach pub on the Mumbles Road, enjoying a few pints of cider as we awaited news from our spotters. All was quiet before the game so, at about two o'clock, we set off up the Mumbles Road in search of some Bolton lads. We walked through plenty of 'scarfers' who, as usual, all seemed to be decked out in England shirts. There seems to be a psychological trait that all Englishmen have which can be seen in any holiday resort throughout the world. Whenever they leave England, they feel it's compulsory to wear an England shirt as if they are some sort of invading army. They strut round with their chests puffed out as if to say "Don't fuck with me, I'm English." The thing is, though, that the 'scarfers' feel this way too. As if by putting on an English shirt it makes them a superhero to be feared. So, when we were walking down the Mumbles Road as shit-loads of 'scarfers' came by with puffed-out chests and smug grins, it was no surprise when Ivey lost it shouting "Look at all these cunts ! Who the fuck do they think they are ?" A Bolton boy stopped and looked at him as if he was offended. His fat, ugly bird pushed him towards Ivey and said in a broad Lancashire accent "Go on, Joe, fuck him !" Ivey exploded in a rage, smacking 'Joe' in the jaw. He turned to run but Simon gripped him by the collar, the shirt ripped in two and he fled in panic, leaving his charming wife behind. Ivey held up the shirt, laughing, as the boys chased the rest of them down the road. We had broken the so called 'Hooligan Code' by attacking shirts but sometimes it had to be done. You don't take shit off nobody, shirt or hooligan.

After an uneventful 0 - 0 draw, we got wind of a mob of lads on their way along the Mumbles Road, heading out to the East Side. We cut across the Quadrant Shopping Centre, down through the Megabowl in Park Tawe and headed them off by the New Cut Bridge. We charged across the open grassland between the two bridges. The sun blazed down as the two mobs clashed. Ivey was first in but was put down when the initial punches were thrown. They showed their mettle as they drove us back. Not enough of the boys were getting stuck in, leaving us thin on the ground in front. Eventually they ran us back as we conceded victory to them. Dejected, we headed back to the Queens. We had been beaten by the better mob but we were outnumbered and by no means at full strength so, when we arrived back at the pub to see that many more of the top lads had turned up, we decided to go back. We piled into the back of Lako's van and he made a few trips back and forth, dropping us off at the top of Morris Lane. The Bolton mob were in the Ship Inn at the bottom of the lane. The Ship was situated on an island between the main road and the Tawe river on one side and St Thomas on the other. The pub was the only building on the island and there was access around it, 360 degrees. There was a building skip in the lane so the boys tooled up ready for the ambush. We had passed the Bolton fans drinking in the sun outside the pub, basking in the glory of winning the earlier bout. Little did they know that a storm was on its way in the shape of a vengeful Jack Army. The plan was set. Half of us would come around one side of the pub and the rest around the other. We hurried down the lane, all armed with something from the skip. Not a word was spoken and we all knew our orders. We hit them in a perfectly executed pincer movement, coming around both sides of the pub simultaneously. A lot of them were sunbathing, lying on the grass and had no time to get up as blocks and bricks were dropped on them. They scrambled to get inside, fighting each other to get away from us as we bombarded them. The windows of the pub shattered as we gave them a lesson they would never forget. A few still lay on the floor as the police arrived to rescue them. They were a shadow of their former selves. They didn't even try to fight back. It just goes to show that a little discipline and good organisation will always win the day.

'90 - '91

The season started with a massive turnout at an away game at Leyton Orient.

Toozey, Bristol City away

Toozey on holiday in Bognor Regis. In the background is Martin King carrying his bag of vitamins !

Swansea, Cardiff & Newport fans in Milan, 2003

Wallis & Toozey in Milan

Swansea, Cardiff & Newport fans ...

... just released from prison, Milan 2003

Fans leaving Mansfield, 2004

Tebay, Peter, Grant & Ricky at Mansfield, 2004
before heading for The Royal Exchange, Cardiff

Scum head for the Queen's Pub ...

... Welsh Cup Final played at the Vetch: Scum v Wrexham

Trundle's minder is a soccer thug

AND HE HAS BNP LINKS

ON WATCH: Andrew Tooze (right) with Swansea City striker Lee Trundle

THE bodyguard and close friend of shamed Swansea City soccer star Lee Trundle is a convicted soccer hooligan who has attended a major right-wing BNP party rally.

Top striker Trundle was arrested for displaying an obscene T-shirt and waving an offensive flag at rivals Cardiff City after his side lifted the Football League Trophy last weekend.

On Thursday, he and Swans defender Alan Tate were given a police caution for public order offences and still face a Football Association of Wales probe.

Battle

Now the News of the World has discovered his minder and friend Andrew Tooze, 39, was given a prison sentence after a pitched battle between fans before a Wales international in 2003.

More than 50 fans from Swansea, Cardiff and Newport clashed after booing in bars near the Milan ground.

Twenty-stone skinhead Tooze was found guilty of violent disorder and sentenced to 12 months' jail, suspended for a year. He was kicked out of Italy and didn't even see the match.

But Tooze, a security guard and weightlifter who also runs a coffee shop in Swansea, went on to become a close pal of Liverpool-born Trundle and claims to be his "unofficial minder".

Defended

He defended Trundle, saying he had merely picked up the flag and T-shirt thrown by supporters and held them up for a few seconds.

Father-of-four Tooze has also admitted attending a British National Party meeting in a Swansea church hall where its leader Nick Griffin was the main speaker.

But the former nightclub bouncer denied any other links to the BNP.

He said: "I wanted to hear what the BNP had to say but I decided they were talking a load of rubbish."

Swansea's Finest

Forest away, 2005

Wallis, Trevor, Toozey, Mojo & Jez in the back of a police van.
Newport away

Millwall away, 2007

... and this is Daz's first trip !

Skinheads, alive & well in Swansea, 2007

John the Bank with Buller

*Michael Buller
in the
Seventies*

Two of Swansea's finest, Thomo & Wayne

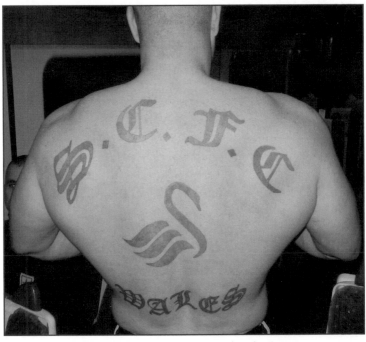

Dai Lloyd gets his wings out for the Boys

The Youth outside the Garibaldi

Don't fuck with the Baldies !

Gaz, Nobsy, Phelps, Coombsy, Boxer & Haggis.
Soaking up the sun outside the Gari.

The Boys, 2007

The Lads under escort at Paddington

The Youth at Millwall

Say Cheese !

*The Shipwright Arms at London Bridge.
First one at the bar gets the drinks !*

We had a firm of 250 boys among the travelling support. It just showed our potential to compete with big boys. We found no opposition at Orient or in the centre of London on the night. We were disappointed not to get the chance to flex out muscles with such a good firm at our disposal.

Just before Christmas the inevitable happened and we lost some top faces when they were jailed for their part in the row with the bouncers. Most notably we lost Tracy who was the veteran of the firm. He was the glue that held us all together. We also lost Terry Dustbin who was probably the gamest lad we had and always willing to go the extra mile. We also lost Johnny Longden. Jack, as we called him, was the joker in the pack and there was never a dull moment with him around. Along with five others, they all received twelve months. All, that is, except for Terry. The cunts stitched him right up and he faced eight years for a crime he did not commit.

That season off the pitch turned into a disaster as we failed to really organise any trips. The whole winter passed incident free until the visit of Stoke City. I stumbled upon them by accident. We had been drinking more frequently down the Sandfields on the Mumbles Road in the Seabeach and the Swansea Jack. You can imagine the shock when I went in the 'Jack' looking for the boys to find it was jam packed full of Stoke's firm. I walked to the bar, acting as if nothing was out of the ordinary and noticed Big Rog seated at the other end.

I went over to him and said "Fuck me, Rog, do the boys know about this lot?"

"Tebay's gone up to the Gari to get them," he replied.

I hurried down my pint, ready to leave by the side door, when one of the Stoke guys shouted "Come on they're outside !" I looked through the front window and there was Jacken swinging a steel bin over the heads of the Stoke boys. For some reason, only a handful went out to join in the ruck and the few who did came back in screaming at their lads. One of them, whose head was cut open, was furious at their lack of bottle. "Come on, drink up. We're going up there now !" he commanded. I slipped out of the side entrance and sprinted up to the Garibaldi to warn the boys of the incoming mob. When I reached the Gari, it was plain to see that we lacked the numbers but nonetheless we ventured out to meet them at the end of the lane. Fair play to them, they meant business as, within seconds, they forced us back into the lane at the side of the Gari. Our boys were really on the back foot as many retreated through the side entrance of the pub and shut the door, locking a handful of us out. Phelpsy hammered at the door, screaming for them to get back out as I found myself trapped against the wall along with Laddie and Little Dai. Luckily for us, the police arrived just in the nick of time !

We were gutted. This was the first time we had been run so comprehensively at home and at our own pub. There were no excuses; we had bottled it in the face of a real game firm of lads. The recriminations flew in the pub afterwards with Phelpsy incandescent with rage because the door had been shut on us. A few home truths were found out that day and it showed that we struggled without some of the top boys around.

The season ended with us in the Welsh Cup Final at the National Stadium in Cardiff against Wrexham. We all thought that Cardiff were sure to turn out for a row, especially after all the embarrassments we had dealt them in the recent games. We trailed through the pubs in the city centre and around the stadium looking for them without luck. Unbelievably, we didn't see anybody all day. They had spurned another chance to challenge us in their own backyard ! The main opinion among the lads was that Cardiff might turn up against the teams with lesser reputation but when it came to some real opposition they were left wanting.

'91 - '92

The new season was preceded by an unbelievable decision to stage a friendly at Ninian Park because Cardiff had been relegated to Division Four. It gave us the opportunity to carry on the derby festivities. About 100 of us boarded the train at Swansea Station without any police attention. It was the same at Cardiff Central - not a copper to be seen as we came out of the station. We walked down towards Canton unopposed. I was desperate for a slash so I stopped off and used a toilet in a pub on the way. When I came back out, the lads were way off down the long road through riverside but someone had shouted my name. I looked behind me. It was Simon, the Cardiff lad I'd worked with along with his mate, Sandham. I told them how many of us there were and told him to rustle up a mob.

It was still early so we stopped off in the Riverside Club for a few bevies. The boys were well tanked up now and they got more and more boisterous as the lager flowed. It was time to go before the police were called. We set off towards Canton where Simon had said most of their lads would be. We piled into the Canton Cross to find it deserted with half-drunk drinks abandoned and fags still burning in the ashtrays. It was like a scene from the Marie Celeste. They must have seen us coming and left to find some boys. We left the Cross and crossed over by the large pub, The Corporation. The doors were locked shut as we swarmed around the pub. Their mob was inside and they were pressed against the windows, all chanting at us with empty threats, locked inside their own pub ! We called them out time and time again but they stayed inside and made no attempt to come out. The boys pulled at the doors, hammering on them and shouting "Get out, you wankers !" The doors weren't unlocked until the police wagons arrived. Then, to our surprise, Stacko came out of the pub. He had got in ahead of us and witnessed them panicking as they locked the doors at the prospect of our mob coming down the road. What a fucking embarrassment. They had the chance, with no Old Bill, to settle the score once and for all and they just bottled it. Unless they had massive numbers, they just didn't want to know. We weren't the toughest mob around and certainly didn't claim to be. Not like this lot, the self-acclaimed number one firm in the country - my fucking arse !

The FA Cup draw came around again and, as soon as the draw was made, the phone started ringing. "It's Cardiff at home!" I must have had 20 phone calls as the excitement swept the city. Playing Cardiff was enough excitement on its own, let alone in the FA Cup. The rumour mill was at full pelt all morning. Stories were coming in thick and fast about mobs being spotted in various locations around the city. One such rumour had been confirmed by a reliable source so we headed off up the High Street to the King's Head where some early visitors had set up camp. We charged up the High Street, full of confidence, the

'Operation Vetch' scores

POLICE move in to control fans in the centre stand next to the Jewson family enclosure at the Vetch.
PICTURES: Steve Phillips

Police boss hits out over cup-tie rampage

'SUB-HUMAN ANIMALS!'

POLICE CHIEFS were today deciding whether tomorrow's Swansea v Cardiff Cup clash should be called off because of rioting by 'sub-human' fans when the two sides met in Swansea at the weekend.

350 police stopped the fan clashes

POLICE today hailed last night's massive security operation at the Swansea versus Cardiff Allbright Bitter Welsh Cup quarter final a success.

A total of 350 police officers were drafted in for the game at the Vetch following trouble at a previous clash between the two sides in November.

firm at full strength with all the top faces present. The Cardiff boys came out of the door as we steamed in. They didn't get very far as we hit them hard in the doorway. One had been dropped as Cooney held onto the door frame with both arms and stamped on the chest of the lad stuck in the doorway. They tried to fight back but were knocked back as Frenchy, Toozey and I traded punches and kicks in the cramped entrance. Cooney had knocked the lad with curly black hair senseless by the time the police arrived on the scene. We walked away doing the 'I haven't done anything, hands in our pockets' walk' while more and more Jacks were still arriving on the scene. It was first blood to us and once again we felt as if Cardiff had nothing to offer.

We were so used to coming out on top that we totally underestimated them - dismissing them totally out of hand. It wasn't until about half an hour before kick-off that we found out how wrong we had been. We were waiting on the corner by the Queens when the police came steaming into us for no apparent reason with their new telescopic truncheons drawn, beating us and screaming "Get back!" It was obvious that something was coming - something big. We ran down the lane by the Gari and out onto West Way, looking back up towards the Queens. I couldn't believe my eyes. The police were escorting the biggest mob I had ever seen in my life. There must have been 800 or more of them. They stretched across the four lanes of the road and the snaking army of hooligans went back as far as the eye could see. We could see the smug grins on their faces as the Old Bill marched them closer. They were obviously dictating the route to the police as they would never march them down past us in normal circumstances. The police, once again, laid into us as we battled to get at them. It was our turf so we weren't going to let them walk through it without a fight. Beaten back once more, it was obvious to us that the police found it easier to control us than them. So we made our way to the next junction with West Way, then the next and the next. Each time we got within a few feet of the gigantic mob, only to be beaten back by the truncheon-happy coppers. Not once did the Cardiff mob try to get at us or to break free from their escort. In my opinion they missed an opportunity to give us a good hiding. They outnumbered us many times over and, if they had broken free, the Old Bill would have been powerless to stop them. It would have been a bloodbath.

We finally broke through the police cordon onto the Mumbles Road, sending the police sprawling as they gave under the sheer weight of our numbers. We brawled on the wide expanse of the Mumbles Road until the police regrouped, sending in the dog handlers. Tracy was nicked as four coppers dragged him to the van, struggling in a rage. Fair play to him, he was only just out of jail on licence but was straight in regardless of the chance of losing his liberty once more. Still shocked at the sight of the Cardiff mob, we made our way up to the North Bank as kick-off was imminent.

As we queued in the long lines, another mob of Cardiff came up, calling the odds. This time there was no Old Bill to stop the clash. This mob was the PVM. I had respect for the PVM because they would always turn up and have a pop. But, at the same time, I held them in contempt as they had dished out a beating to me when I was training at the Skill Centre in Port Talbot. They had called at me from the street as I had waited for a train. "Oi, Wallis. Don't run !" Anton had shouted at me. There was no way I would ever run have from them. As about ten of them had came onto the station, I had plenty of time to make my escape but I would never have given them the satisfaction. I stretched out my arms and said "Come on, lads - there's fucking ten of you !" Tino had laid into me and they had smashed my nose with a boot. I felt it was a cowardly act and, when the boot had been on the other foot, both Tino and Anton had run against far less odds.

Cardiff Fans in the Vetch

This day was payback time as we flattened them. They were smashed all over the place with at least two laid unconscious as they were beaten and stamped on. The police laid into us and we turned on them. There was no stopping now. The line had been crossed right in front of the CCTV cameras and it was shit or bust.

The only time there was any calm was when the match was on. We were ecstatic with the 2 - 1 win with Cardiff's ex-striker Jimmy Gilligan scoring a cracking wining goal. The word had been spread to meet outside the Queen's after the game. There was a massive mob gathered - around 400 of us. We knew we had our work cut out but, with this mob, we would certainly have a good chance even though Cardiff still outnumbered us two to one. A shout went up that the police were escorting the mob back up the station by a fleet of double-decker buses. Stacko said we should stay here as their main lads were sure to give the police the slip. His plea fell on deaf ears as 300 or so went chasing after the buses, leaving less than 100 of us protecting the Queens. Stacko's prediction was spot on as a mob of about 300 came down the Kingsway. They came through us without any problem, sending us across the road as confusion reigned in the dark of the gloomy November night. For a few moments, I was swamped in the Cardiff mob as they filled the street. Our boys just vanished into the night as I searched for a friendly face. The police had driven a van into the middle of the street, the blue lights pierced the darkness and I saw Stacko in the flashing lights being dragged away by the police outside Martha's Vineyard. I felt totally alone and extremely vulnerable and needed to get out of there before I was recognised. I watched as the mob of Cardiff were marched back up the Kingsway, past the smashed windows and broken shop fronts. I was totally gutted with a sense of shame that they had smashed our city centre and we had failed to protect it. We had had our victories throughout the day but the result certainly belonged to them. I hadn't seen them in a mob like that since the late 70's and even then they weren't together. In a mob like that, all together as one, they were unstoppable.

40 VETCH FANS TO PAY £4,000

FINES TOTALLING MORE THAN £4,000 were today imposed by Swansea magistrates on 40 Swansea and Cardiff soccer fans following Saturday's derby between the two teams at Vetch Field.

The fines, ranging from £50 up to £170, were each backed up with binding-over orders.

In addition, juvenile court magistrates in Swansea were also dealing with 16 youngsters.

Other supporters are scheduled to appear in court at a later date following applications in them for an adjournment at today's hearings.

Anthony Graham Bevan, aged 21, of Solva Road, Morriston, Kevin Coure, aged 22, of Millers Arms, Ynystawe, Charles Leslie Davies, aged 19, of Tegid Road, Mayhill, each pleaded guilty to using threatening, abusive, insulting words or behaviour and were each fined £100.

Christopher Paul Davies, aged 18, of Llanllienwen Road, Morriston, was fined £170 for using ...

The media scrum after the day of violence saw the police calling for an end to the derbies. As we were due to play Cardiff again in three days time in the Auto Glass Trophy, the game was in doubt because the police were threatening to refuse to police it. It eventually went ahead, trouble free.

We had all anticipated getting arrested for the row with the PVM and the police because it had happened right outside the ground in front of the CCTV cameras. Luckily for us, because the police themselves had used so much violence, a source told us that the footage was too risky to use in any prosecutions. Stacko wasn't so lucky though and he was sentenced to twelve months for the clash on the Kingsway.

'92 - '93

With Cardiff still in the lowest tier, we faced another season with the possibility of not playing them. That was until we drew them away in the Auto Glass trophy once again. I took the day off work and headed down to the Garibaldi at twelve noon. Everyone had said they were coming but it became apparent that this was not the case. Only a handful of the main boys had turned up with the rest made up of a mixture of youth and up and coming boys. In my eyes, it wasn't a mob worthy of going to Cardiff so I got a few Strongbows down my neck to steady the nerves. The only trouble was that cider made me a little unpredictable and a tad more violent. We had our doubts about going and Little Dai said "We can't go with this lot, Wall."

I agreed with his concerns but was determined to go. A couple more of the boys turned up in the shape of Craig Chapple, Ginger and Harold so we decided to go but instead of taking the train we were going on the service bus. We prepared to leave - there were 45 of us - that is until Lako decided he needed his coat from the car and never came back ! As we queued for the X5 direct bus to Cardiff, one of the boys who wasn't a regular, nicknamed Eric the Viking, was spouting off about how "we didn't have enough" and we were "going to get killed". I told him to shut up several times but he wouldn't be quiet. With all the youth with us, all we needed was some muppet unsettling their nerves so I smacked him in the mouth and told him to fuck off home. This seemed to pull everyone together as we set off on our short journey up the M4.

As we approached Cardiff on the bus, I decided to make a speech. I'd heard Ivey do it at Millwall and Bristol in the past and it always had its desired effect. I stood up and addressed the lads on the deck of the coach, telling them in no uncertain terms that we were to stick together at all costs. I told them that we could not afford to run because the lack of numbers meant that, if we dispersed, it would be disastrous and would be sure to lead to a kicking. I also told them to keep a low profile; no singing and fucking about until we had a base in a pub where we could arm ourselves. We all got up, made our way downstairs and queued up by the door waiting to arrive at the station. I recognised the driver of the bus. He laughed and said ...

"Going to the football, Wall ?"
"Yes," I replied. And he asked if we wanted to get off before the station in case in the Old Bill were there.

We jumped off at the lights and I spotted a black Cardiff lad. The cider was controlling me and I ran over and booted fuck into him. So much for my speech about keeping a low profile !

We settled into the pub on the corner of Mary Street opposite the castle. We had arrived at about 4.30pm and there was plenty of drinking time until kick-off so we got some much-needed Dutch courage down our necks. We had been in there an hour with the boys getting a bit rowdy. Someone had ripped the plumbing out in the toilet and flooded the place so it was time to leave. One of the up and coming boys, George, said that some of the Cardiff mob drank in the 'Owain Glyndwr' so we made our way down to that pub. We arrived outside but the lads were a bit hesitant - all waiting for someone else to go first. It was time to step up to the plate so I opened the door, only to be confronted by a bearded bouncer with grey hair. He put his hand on my chest and asked where we were from. I grabbed him, gave him a punch which sent him reeling backwards and ran into the pub shouting "Jack Army !" with my arms outstretched. The reaction was instant as all the boys came flooding in behind me. The Cardiff lads in there scattered, heading for the fire exits and windows to escape. Suddenly I was rugby-tackled from behind as the bouncer tried to wreak his revenge. As I lay on the floor, wrestling with the ageing doorman, the boys were ripping the pub apart. I struggled with the bouncer and feared the police would be in at any minute. Frenchy realised I was having trouble breaking free of the bouncer's iron grip and duly kicked him off, setting me free.

It was a scene of devastation. The boys had demolished the pub. When we got outside Craig came at me, screaming in my face. Apparently he had told me to walk into the pub and suss it out first but when I'd kicked it off, he had been forced out against the fire exit by the fleeing Cardiff fans. The exit wouldn't open and Wayne had walked up, opened a Jiff squeezy lemon and sprayed them all, including Craig, with ammonia. Police had to separate us as the argument got heated but fortunately they just moved us on.

We made our way through the narrow Victorian walkways where someone smashed a shop window. The manager came out shouting and received a broken nose for his troubles. We exited the Arcade and bumped into one of the Soul Crew boys, Dai Jones, who had a group of Wigan lads with him. They tried to say they were Jacks but Little Dai knew better and they were chased off down the road.

The police were back on the scene as we went in the pub around the back of the train station. The Old Bill camped outside and, within ten minutes, they walked in, accompanied by the bouncer from the 'Owain Glyndwr'. My heart sank as I turned to the bar to hide my face. I dropped my Aquascutum scarf and pulled off my hat and jacket. The police walked him round us all slowly. He gazed at everyone until his eyes fixed on mine. I could tell just by his look that he recognised me instantly. The policeman asked him a question out of earshot and he shook his head. They walked out without another word. He had seen me but not dropped me in the shit, God bless him.

Cardiff boys were walking past the windows with ever-increasing frequency and one, with blonde hair wearing a red puffer jacket, walked through just sussing out our numbers. A few moments later the window came crashing through. They jeered from outside as the police moved on them. The Old Bill decided it was time to move us on and we began the marathon march to Ninian Park. As it was only the Auto Glass trophy, the police were thin on the ground so it would be an eventful walk. The Cardiff first came into us outside the bus station but were fucked off straight away. The police came in and nicked a couple of boys. Our numbers were now down to 35 with the ones we had lost outside the 'Owain' and the Arcade. The walk seemed to last forever as we were shadowed by lads the whole way. The familiar sight of the Ninian Park pub came into view, along with hundreds of lads. Our police escort was pathetic and it was sure to be a bloodbath. There was no way out now. We had no choice but to weather the storm.

I shouted "Fuck it, come on !"
George started bouncing, jeering the boys up. "Let's do it !"

With that we began the charge. If we were going down then we were going down in style. As we got closer and closer to the army of Cardiff lads, something told me 'they're going to run'. They could see we weren't going to stop. We were like cornered rats and we were on the attack. Before we reached them, they were on their toes. I couldn't believe it. 35 of us had hundreds of them running in fear, right through the railway bridge as the voices of anger echoed off the walls. The chase continued right around the corner to Sloper Road with boys fighting and brawling in the gardens of terraced houses. A voice shouted out "Egan, we know where you live !" For fuck's sake ! We were on their turf, heavily outnumbered and they still made empty threats as we ran them past their own end !

I got to the entrance of the Grange End where a Cardiff lad swung a punch at me. I grabbed him and swung him round, kicking him in the side. A copper grabbed me and threw me into the turnstile. Someone grabbed me from behind and said "Get in, son before you're nicked." I walked through the turnstile and out into an unfamiliar part of the ground. To my horror, I was walking up the concourse behind our end into the huge Bob Bank. If I was caught in here, I was a dead man and I could already see a few familiar faces in the bank ahead. I eventually managed to persuade a couple of coppers to let me back into the Swansea End after twenty questions. The boys were on top of the world at the result we had outside. After I had gone in the turnstile, the Cardiff lad in the puffer jacket, who we'd seen earlier, congratulated the boys at "coming through them like a dose of salts". What had seemed like a possible disaster turned into a famous victory. Never again would I dismiss the youth lads. They performed like veterans and the legend of the Naughty Forty was born.

The team was having a successful season and the crowds showed it. The firm was nearly back to full strength after the trouble with the bouncers. It was a Tuesday night and the visitors were Stoke City. Their result against us in the Gari lane was fresh in our minds and the boys were out for revenge. We searched the pubs around the ground looking for them in the vain hope that they would turn up on a Tuesday night. We made our way back to the Gari only to find a few casuals walking through the lane - big mistake ! Talk about wrong place, wrong time ! Luck was certainly not on their side as they received a hell of a kicking and were left for dead.

The game was lost 2 - 1 which only added to the tense atmosphere. As we left the ground there was only one thing on our minds - to dish out some retribution. The police had their barrier systems in operation as we converged at the corner of Western Street, facing down towards the away end. As luck would have it, there was a building skip full of rubble just in front of the barriers. Once the first brick was thrown, the barrage of missiles increased every second until the sky, lit up by the bright floodlight above our heads, was full of flying objects. The Stoke fans took cover in the turnstiles, the doorways of nearby houses and underneath the police vans. The bombardment continued as cast iron drainpipes were ripped off houses and hurled like javelins. It was a fearsome sight that sent flashbacks of that night in Greece twirling through my mind. The police finally hit back as reinforcements arrived; driving the boys back with brute force. It had appeased the painful memory of the episode in the Gari lane slightly but we were gutted not to have had a proper row.

The season was coming to an end and promotion was a real possibility so, when we played Reading on May 1st, we took a huge mob up on the train. There were 250 on the first train and another 200 on the second. Reading didn't know what had hit it as 400 plus boys marched through the town centre. The lawlessness of the day was incredible. Every pub we visited was wrecked, the fag machines were ripped off the walls and looted of their contents, pool tables the same and the boys pulled their own pints as bar staff were terrorised. The Reading mob was non-existent so the lads took their frustrations out on fixtures and fittings. The anarchy in the town was transferred to the ground. When I got there, the police had closed the Swans End as it was too full, so Craig and I decided to go in the Reading End by the side of the Swansea fans. The scene inside was incredible. The Swans fans had scaled the fences and were sitting on top of them. The high advertising hoardings behind the end were covered in climbing supporters and the floodlights had lads perched halfway up them. It was reminiscent of a scene from the 70's when chaos was the norm.

As the kick-off approached, Madness blasted out from the tannoys and Cooney did the Moon Stomp in the centre circle. The boys were on the pitch, in the goals and in every end of the ground. The police were escorting Porters and Terry Davies' brother around the pitch side. The Reading fans gave them some stick as they went past, causing them to jump in and start brawling with them. They were dragged out only to jump back in at the next load of abusers. Suddenly I saw Laddie and a few others coming across from the Swansea End to help them out. I ran down from the back of the Reading End as they were hit from all directions. The ground was now erupting in all corners as Swans fans were brawling with the police in the penalty area and scrapping and ripping the fences down in the away end. I managed to get into the Swansea End as the game started and stopped in between pitch invasions.

There was a false rumour going around the End that a Swansea boy had been killed after the police had beaten him unconscious. This was the catalyst that fuelled the riot. The perimeter fence was ripped down and rammed into the police. Lumps of concrete were ripped out of the terrace floor and rained down on the police and Reading fans. One Asian copper in a turban and wearing a badge became a favourite target. I bet he wished he'd forgotten about his religious rights and worn a proper helmet when the biggest cheer of the day came as he was hit on the head and carried away. The second biggest cheer came when Johnny Longden scaled the full height of the floodlights and conducted the crowd from his lofty vantage point.

The violence got worse when an outhouse containing lawn mowers, garden tools, bags of lime and tiles was broken into. The air was thick with missiles as the attention then turned to the Reading fans. The boys had invaded the no man's land between the two Ends and had scaled the corrugated fences, ripping off the chicken wire to throw the ammo through to their fans. Pliers and shears were now being thrown through the asbestos cladding on the Gable end of the bank as the Reading fans backed away from the melee. The riot was getting out of control but the police had one last trick up their sleeves. They had tried truncheon reinforcements and dogs and now it was time for the riot police. They came in the end of the bank stretched from top to bottom - not the ordinary Robocops but fully armoured riot police with six foot plexi-glass shields. They moved as one, shields ahead of them like a walking wall of clear plastic. Reports in the media later, said that it was the first time in British history that this type of officer had been deployed at a football match. The game was lost 2 - 0, putting an end to our automatic promotion hopes.

As we left the ground the police sent in snatch squads to nick offenders caught on camera. Cooney was carted away again - for what must have been some sort of record. I had been arrested many times at football before earning myself the nickname of 'Bailhead' but Cooney took the biscuit with a record as long as both arms. We made our way through town looking for a watering hole but most of them had shut down so that the police could get rid of us. The only place we found open was some sort of club but the occupants weren't keen on us coming in. A standoff took place outside as they brandished pool cues. Longden threw a glass at them, only to hit one of our boys, Maggsy and cutting his ear on the way. We edged towards them across the road and then I was suddenly smashed onto the bonnet of a police Volvo. The cunts had seen us in the road and just run me down, giving me one hell of a dead leg.

It had been a chaotic day for everybody involved. The old adage 'a mindless minority' certainly didn't apply to that day. Over half of the travelling support of 2,500 were involved at some stage or another. We had certainly come a long way from my early days in the firm where we would only just fill a transit van for our travels. The numbers had grown tenfold and we weren't the only firm any more. Jacken and the Mini Angels had grown up and were practically veterans now. Even though they had lost a few numbers to the drug industry, Tracy's older boys had merged with our original casual firm 'The Baby Squad'. George was coming through strong with the likes of Wayne, Albert, Egan, Owain, Hilton and Bozo, who had all shown their bottle in a superb performance against Cardiff with the Naughty Forty. And there was still an even younger firm on the horizon. The football factory was in full production in West Wales.

'93 - '94

The season had been eagerly awaited since Cardiff's promotion back to what was now called Division Two. The fixture list had us up there just three days before Christmas and back home at Easter.

Our first trip of the season came in early September with a visit to Brentford. Any game in London was worth a trip because you never knew who you would come up against. Two minibuses were ordered, George running one and Tracy the other. George was now regarded as one of the top boys. He was a great personality with a wicked sense of humour. A day out with George would have you in stitches one way or another ! Before the game, we drank in pubs around Kew and didn't really expect any trouble as Brentford didn't have any sort of reputation. The plan was to watch the game and spend the night in London's West End. On the way to Griffin Park, we passed a cricket pitch where the Middlesex Cricket Cup Final was being played. It looked like a formal affair with players and supporters clapping politely as the runs were clocked up. All of a sudden, a shocked silence swept across the pitch as George ran onto the pitch and vaulted the bails totally bollock naked. The boys all cheered with laughter as he picked up the forgotten ball and ran off back towards us, giggling like a twat.

We made our way to the game without any opposition. The game was a boring encounter and the lack of atmosphere didn't help so we decided to leave early. After a few beers, we made our way up to a pub we had passed earlier. I was trailing behind in the rear, talking to Little Dai, when a shout went up. Tracy was up front calling everyone forward. About 30 yards in front of him was a mob of lads bounding towards us, arms raised in the 'come on' position. We sprinted forward, to be faced with a strange collection of dressers. There were 70's throwbacks and a half-caste lad in a vest, camouflage trousers and Doctor Martens. "Come on, we're Chelsea !" said a black haired lad wearing a black turtle neck sweater. He brandished a pool cue in front of Tracy while the half-caste waved a broken Pils bottle. Tracy stepped towards them and the lad broke the pool cue right over his head with a sickening crack. The blood was streaming down Tracy's face as he wrestled the broken cue off the lad and started laying into them. Once again he showed us why he was still the top dog after all these years. We rounded them and forced them towards the door of a nearby pub. I grabbed hold of the arm of the lad with the black jumper as he tried to escape and swept him to the floor with my foot. The half-caste boy dropped his bottle and ran as another lad was punched to the floor outside the pub. A framed sign was picked up and smashed over him until it broke into pieces in an act of extreme violence. I watched in shock as a pool of blood flowed from his head like a pot of paint spilt on the pavement. It seemed like far too much blood for anyone to lose and still survive and we were all convinced he was dead.

I heard Tracy shout "Let's go !" It took me a few seconds to come back into the real world. I was still shocked at the bloody sight in front of me. "Wallis, let's fucking go !" he shouted again. The sirens could be heard in the distance as we fled the scene. Tracy decided that we should spilt up into pairs and make our own way home. I shot off down a side street with Little Dai and we walked the unfamiliar streets, panicked by the thought of being picked up by the police. We decided to make our way to Paddington for the train home. We hadn't been walking for more than ten minutes when an unmistakable roar of a rampaging mob echoed off the walls of the terraced houses. We looked up and down the road but couldn't see them although we realised they were close by for sure.

We decided to split up to give ourselves a 50/50 chance of avoiding them so Dai went one way and I went the other. I walked nervously to the end of the street only to find that I had been given the short straw. Coming towards me was a fully-armed mob of lads, about 50 in total. For a split second, I contemplated walking on past them as if I was just an innocent passer-by but my identity was known instantly when one shouted "It's that ginger cunt !" I turned and ran as the baying mob pursued me, screaming down the road. I had a good 50 yards head start on them so I sprinted as fast as I could, turning down as many roads as possible to try and lose them. To my horror I ended up on a long street with no exits and could see them closing in on me as my stamina started to fail me. Luckily I saw a break in the terrace and dived down it to be confronted by a large complex of flats. I was at the rear of the flats and the ground floor ones all had gardens with tall wooden fences and gates. I hit one of the gates with my foot, flew in and the gate shut behind me on the latch. I saw a back door and ran full pelt towards it and shoulder-barged it until the lock jamb split and the door flew open. I tumbled onto a kitchen floor and a large black woman came out screaming at me in a West Indian accent. I pleaded with her to be quiet because I was being chased by a gang of hooligans. She peered out of the kitchen window and saw the mob running around looking into the individual gardens, frantically searching for me.

"My God, boy, they got a chopper !" she exclaimed.

I looked out to see a man in a yellow polo shirt carrying a fucking huge machete. I breathed a big sigh of relief that I had narrowly escaped a revenge killing. I was sure I wouldn't have lived if I had been caught. The kind woman gave me a glass of water and phoned me a taxi. I apologised for damaging her door and gave her £20 to get it fixed. I waited for 20 minutes but the taxi never turned up. I was nervous about the prospect of going back out on the street. Not only about the possibility of meeting up with my pursuers but also about getting picked up by the Old Bill. The lady could see I wasn't relishing the prospect of going back out and brought me a T-shirt to change into. I put it on and must have looked a right state with 'Starlight Express' emblazoned across the tight-fitting shirt. But if it would help me get safe passage I didn't give a fuck.

I walked through the streets nervously, checking around every corner to make sure it was safe, until I reached the main road and a bus stop. The wait for the bus seemed to last a lifetime. I waited anxiously until the silence of the night was broken by a voice shouting "Oi !" My heart missed a beat for a second until I turned round to see George. "What the fuck is that ?" he said, pissing himself with laughter. "I don't know, we've been up here having it off and you've been swanning off down the theatre !" "Fuck off, twat !" I replied.

All the way home, the piss was ripped out of me. We found out later that the lad with the head injury was OK which was a relief to us all because he looked like he was in a bad way when we left the scene. We all loved the buzz of the fighting but nobody really wanted to see anyone seriously injured, let alone killed.

The Cardiff fixture was upon us once more and some of the lads had left early on the train. I had been committed to stay at work because I had a new job. I went down to the station as soon as I finished. The boys who had gone up earlier had been on the phone to tell us that, as soon as they had got off the train, a big Cardiff mob had steamed into them. There were only 25 of the boys and Cardiff had a big result after scattering them. The police had flooded the station in Swansea,

stopping us going
on any of the service
trains. It was the first
time in a decade that

FLARE THUGS HIT SHOPPER

A 63-YEAR-OLD man suffered burns after being hit by a phosphorus distress flare following the weekend soccer clash between rivals Swansea and Cardiff.

THE SEASON OF HATRED

Fans clash again in big match

NINE people were arrested as violence erupted last night at the soccer derby between Swansea and Cardiff City.

Hooligan

Crush could have led to disaster

they had decided to
put on a 'Football
Special' for the ever-
increasing numbers
outside the station.
By the time the
old shed of a train
pulled into the
station, there must
have been 1,000
waiting to make the
journey east. I met
up with Ivey and Toozey in the Pullman pub opposite the station and we chatted
excitedly about how many had turned up. There were boys who hadn't been
down to the football for years turning up in their droves. This was sure to be an
eventful night.

The journey was a nightmare as the piss-stinking train was far too full with
lads jammed in like sardines. As usual with the special trains, they stopped the
train at Ninian Park Halt and we all spilt out, charging down the concrete stairs to
the streets full of police and Bluebirds. The Old Bill failed to hold us back and
the weight of the crowd sent the small line of coppers at the bottom of the steps

Soccer fans kept in line

Cardiff fans are escorted to the Vetch Field, Swansea.

Derby operation
hailed a success

THIRTEEN soccer fans were arrested last night at the Swansea versus Cardiff cup derby at the Vetch Field.

But high profile policing again stopped any serious disturbances.

Eight Swansea supporters and five Cardiff fans were arrested for offences including assault on police, obstruction, drunkenness, disorderly behaviour and breach of the peace.

The policing operation was hailed a success by Assistant Chief Constable Bob Evans who had around 500 officers on duty in Swansea, Cardiff and at rail stations in between.

He said: "Although it was evident that a hard core of Cardiff hooligans without tickets got into Swansea, because of the manpower deployed they were quickly identified and escorted from the city centre.

"It was obvious there were individuals from both sets of supporters who were bent on trouble but our policing operation enabled us to contain it."

A force spokeswoman said: "Around 110 Cardiff fans came by rail and the rest by road.

"Between 40 and 50 Cardiff supporters without tickets for the match were turned away from trains by police at Cardiff Central railway station.

"Around 20 known Cardiff hooligans were rounded up in Oystermouth Road, Swansea, and their cars escorted out of the city and on towards Cardiff.

"Another 20-25 supporters, most of them without tickets, came to Swansea in a rented van. They ran through the city centre but were rounded up and escorted beyond the city limits.

"Two of those were arrested outside the city centre for public order offences."

out into the street under the intense pressure. We were out on the street and looking for anyone who was up for a ruck. I was up the front of the huge mob along with Ivey and Toozey. There were a few Cardiff lads in front of us, back-pedalling and a few trying to mix in as we walked past the main Grandstand. One of them called us on and Ivey laid into him. They were swamped by lads up against the Grandstand wall. Ivey nearly pulled one lad's nose off after ripping at his nostrils with his fingers in the ruck. I saw Toozey punched in the nose from behind by a little man, almost a dwarf, with odd, long hair but balding on to. I chased the little cunt around a police van but he got away, dodging my kicks like a fucking crazy Oompa Loompa ! The police regained some sort of order but sporadic outbreaks of fighting continued because it was hard to determine who was who in the packed dark streets.

Inside the ground, they had made a bad decision to hold us in the main Grandstand right next to the Cardiff fans. They also underestimated our travelling support and had to lock out over 300 more before the game had kicked off. The boys had got wind of the decision to lock the gates so we moved down to the entrance in the depths of the decaying old Grandstand. There were a couple of stewards manning the big blue gates. Tebay told the steward to open the gates but he refused. "Open the gates, you fucking Cardiff cunt !" he said with more intensity.

Behind the scenes with the soccer peacekeepers

Police plans halt thugs

BACK in February a small group of senior officers met in room 27 in Central Police Station to lay initial plans to deal with the hooligans expected to try to hijack the derby match.

Superintendent Steve Gird this outlined the history of violence between the two sets of supporters, and allocated senior officers to special tasks on April 2.

Two weeks later worried leaders and the major retailers were ushered into Room 27. Mr Griffiths frankly admitted that police had "lost it" a few years previously when there were violent clashes.

He was able to tell the business community in confidence there would be up to 500 police on duty across South Wales. On the day he eventually used 500, excluding Special Constables.

Last week the police operation was planned in fine detail.

It was finalised by Assistant Chief Constable Bob Evans, Chief Superintendent John Knight in Swansea, and Chief Superintendent Alan Greswey in Cardiff.

On Tuesday, local councillors and Swansea supporters organisations were told of the policing arrangements around the Vetch, and left satisfied.

On Wednesday, senior officers from all over South Wales were summoned to headquarters in Bridgend for a final major briefing.

But the police were wrong-footed by Cardiff chairman Rick Wright's decision to sell his club's allocation of 3,500, and the police were worried. They no longer knew how many of Cardiff's hardcore thugs would try to get to the game.

Elaborate plans were needed to outwit them with the help of railway police.

By 8am on Saturday police were already manning the barrier system, and in the control room messages were flashing back and forth on five different wavelengths.

Cardiff police reported they had turned away around 80 fans at the station, but some had gone to Newport in an attempt to get on another train. They would never reach Swansea, even though some unexpected to get match tickets.

Five Cardiff supporters were turned back at a road block on Jersey Marine Ferrymoustier later they were arrested in breach of the peace for a second attempt to get through.

As the Vetch a gang of ticketless Swansea fans — nearly all known to police on the barrier — hung round near the North End.

They were filmed by the National Criminal Intelligence Service Football Unit who have come from London to monitor the match. Two were later arrested for public order offences.

Some Cardiff fans had already been intercepted coming off the motorway.

"Tell them it is in their best interests to re-join it foot-bound," said Mr Knight.

Chief Constable Robert Lawrence arrived to brief his troops before the game, and then went to watch the policing unfold.

After the game, the anxious police commanders had just one more major scare. A group of around 50, suspected of being Cardiff supporters, had been in a Neath pub but have disappeared. "We'll find the buggers," warned Knight.

By 2.45pm they were on a train back to Bridgend haven't where they came, but others turned out to be ready on lovers on their way to the Heath-Llanelli match.

After the game the police

operation was wound down quickly, with a contingent staying in Swansea city centre just in case.

There were a total of 11 arrests.

A relieved Bob Evans commanded around 500 Cardiff fans who had been sorted away.

No believers a warnings to plan the previous Thursday evening Pam warning parents to know exactly what their children were up to had been a big help.

"I still find it sad we have to deploy this number of

officers for what is supposed to be entertainment"

"At the end of the day it too worked and I am pleased about that," says the stretcher Chief Constable.

The success of the operation had spared him considerable police from coming to plan.

But at 5.30pm a tragic nearly scoured the whole operation when a 65-year-old man was injured with a flare.

It could have been as much as worse.

On the bedrow — police and fans during Saturday's big anti-hooligan operation.

Police search fans on the way to the match.

They didn't budge as we laid into them, dragging them away from the doors. The big wooden gates were pushed open and the locked-out Jacks came flooding in, free of charge. The old Grandstand creaked and groaned under the weight of the extra fans. The two sets of fans exchanged insults over the line of police separating them and the atmosphere was unbelievable. And for the first time in a while, we were under a roof instead of the open-air Grange End.

After a delay, the game kicked off amidst threats and taunts from every corner of the ground. The chants flew back and forth all game until a Cardiff goal silenced our end. The silence gradually broke into individual shouts of "smash it up !" followed by the sound of splitting wood. The first two inch thick, heavy wooden seat went flying over our heads, beyond the police lines and into the taunting Cardiff fans to our left. The cracking sounds increased in frequency until the air was full of spinning wooden missiles. The Cardiff fans ran the barrage until they, too, were ripping out the seats and throwing them back in retaliation. The destruction continued and whole rows were being ripped out with the seats still attached to their metal rails. As far as you could see there were men with their backs to the pitch, stamping out the seats for more ammunition as the missiles rained back and forth. The Cardiff fans in the Bob Bank were so incensed by the destruction of their ground that they came steaming over the fence and across the pitch towards us in the Grandstand. The players were taken off the pitch because it was now full of supporters. The police held them back on the pitch as we made our way down into the empty terrace in front of the Grandstand. The police forced us back into the Grandstand and finally cleared the pitch of Cardiff fans. After what seemed like an age, the game was finally concluded. As we left the ground the scale of the damage became apparent with rows and rows of missing seats. Afterwards the Cardiff lads would criticize us for bombarding the so-called Family Stand but it certainly didn't look like women and children throwing them back.

This latest violent outbreak at the South Wales derby was the straw that broke the camel's back. After the scenes were shown on GMTV and other national news programmes, there were calls for us both to be kicked out of the English League, consequently the FAW and the police had to act. All away fans were banned from future matches for the foreseeable future. What a joke ! They could police The Glasgow Derby, Man U vs Liverpool, Chelsea vs Spurs and Newcastle vs Sunderland in 40,000 plus crowds but they couldn't control 10,000 Welshmen.

'94 - '95

With the ban in place, we had very little to look forward to. Our first game of the season saw us at home to Brighton where the pitch was invaded in the first few minutes of the game. A few lads jumped into the away end and laid into the visitors. They didn't try to fight back which was unusual for them as we would normally have a crack with Brighton. The season before, we'd had a tidy little ruck with them in the Paxton pub near the Vetch. We had gone in and kicked it off and, as they came out of the door, Terry launched into one just as Laddie raised his arms above his head and smashed down with an aluminium beer barrel. But instead of hitting the Brighton fan, he pole-axed poor Terry. In true warrior fashion, Terry was back out a couple of hours later, bandaged up like he was wearing a turban ! It's safe to say that the sympathy was fleeting and he had the piss ripped out of him all night.

Our next visitors to the Vetch were Birmingham City. We had a few rucks with them outside that scrap yard up there in Division One but they hadn't really impressed when we played them at home. Unusually, we had trouble with West Brom and Wolves but the Midlands team with the biggest reputation never seemed to turn up. That was until that day. We had been out down the Sandfields, drinking in the Seabeach on a fine, sunny day when someone came in to tell us that Birmingham were in the Queens. We knew straight away that this was a deliberate pop at us because the Queens had been our base for many years. We now tended to split between the Seabeach and the Garibaldi but, as it was such a glorious day, we had decided a pint by the sea was in order. There was a big firm out that day, more than likely due to the Zulus' reputation and the boys were itching for it big style. A few of us set off ahead to suss out the opposition. I walked in the Queens along with Ivey and Tracy. Inside were about 40 to 50 Brummies but not all of them were firm. Maybe 30 boys, tops. As we waited for a pint, I heard one of them shout in a strong Brum accent ...

"Fucking hell, look at this lot !"

We all looked out of the window at once to see an awesome sight coming up the lane from the Garibaldi. The boys stretched back over 200 yards, all dressers in their best summer gear. Their speed gathered pace as they neared the Queens. I was mesmerised by the sight and thought to myself, 'this is what we look like when we're steaming towards the enemy'. It was so impressive that I was still watching as if hypnotised when the windows came crashing through. The Birmingham fans were now under the tables and up against the far wall. I looked at Ivey and Tracy and we all laughed as every window in the pub came in. We went back outside to rejoin the lads as the Brummies inside were little opposition.

We were soundly beaten 2 - 0 by Birmingham. They had a healthy support, including many lads in the front of their end giving it the big one. A meet was arranged on the Mumbles Road after the game and, when we arrived, our numbers were phenomenal. As the Brummies came out of William Street onto the Mumbles Road, they were charged. We had too many for the police to handle as we swept through. Some of the Brummies fled up behind the centre stand as others were caught against the prison wall and beaten. A police horse came over the central reservation to intervene, only to trip and fall, sparks shooting from its shoes as it threw its rider. The Birmingham boys were routed and they knew it. We has been far too strong and would have seen off any firm with the mob we had that day.

I had been nicked at the home game against Bradford after a set to with the police and was banned for the rest of the season. This hit me hard as I missed the Swans beating Cardiff 4 - 1 at home and a cracking FA Cup run, beating Middlesbrough away after drawing at home, then Newcastle away. Even though I was banned, I couldn't resist coming out for Boro at home. The last time we played they had brought down a game firm despite the distance. It was no surprise when they came outside the Queens, early doors. Once again they proved a formidable foe as we battled with them outside Harper's Nightclub. We had run down from Quid's Inn to face the Boro mob all dressed in black leather jackets. It's fair to say that they backed us off at first until Harold laid back into them. Boro always seemed to be a nasty looking bunch and just the first glimpse of them close up was enough to score most off. They had faces only a mother could love and must have been the ugliest bunch of hooligans on the planet !

Even though we hadn't been done, we were all disappointed with our performance and felt we could have done better. With this in mind, we set off down the Sandfields, following their escort, to see if we could have Round 2. This time we had 200 or so lads marching down, as the boys had come from all over the place after the initial clash. We came down the street parallel to them, only to be forced back by the Old Bill who laid into us. Mounted officers rode their horses into our ranks. Simpson, one of the lads, was stepped on by one of the horses and later on nearly lost his leg. The police were nicking people left, right and centre and I decided it was best if I fucked off because I was on a ban. Once again, Boro had made an impression on me. They had come a long way in good numbers which was more than some of the nearer so-called top firms had done.

'95 - '96

Our first game of the season was home to Shrewsbury Town. We knew they had a tidy little firm called the English Border Firm but they hadn't been down to our parts for years and we had played them many times in the Welsh Cup without any bother. So it came as a surprise when one of the lads came down to the Swansea Jack, where we were enjoying a pint outside, to say that a mob of Shrewsbury had been in Martha's Vineyard dishing out calling cards. We left 100 strong. On the short walk up to Martha's and with a perfect piece of timing, we got to the corner of the North Bank just as they did. They were in a bad situation. They had been confidently dishing out abuse to all they saw, knowing that they were safe in their firm but now they were face to face with a bigger firm who they had just disrespected by dishing out calling cards on their turf. We steamed into them mercilessly. They were hit all over the back of the North Bank with bodies littering the floor. A few were kicked senseless as their mates jumped the turnstiles into our main end. Once inside they had to run the gauntlet once again until they escaped across the pitch. They were taught a harsh lesson that day. We had to admire their front but, if you haven't got the muscle to back it up, you could end up on a hiding to nothing and that's exactly what happened.

'96 - '97

Following the ban on the South Wales derbies, things had calmed down considerably. CCTV was everywhere and banning orders were being dished out for trivial offences. The mad scenes we had witnessed at Reading and Cardiff seemed to be a thing of the past. Our European adventures had also been stopped forever with the invention of the Welsh Premier League and our expulsion from entry to the Welsh Cup. Things would never be the same again. It looked like the authorities had put an end to our fun. The only problem was that football was our heroin and we needed a hit every now and then to liven up our mundane existences. It hadn't helped the situation that we had been relegated to the lowest tier. The only game to look forward to was Cardiff but, with the ban in place, even these fixtures became non-events. Games which used to attract 10,000 plus crowds, now fetched less than 4,000. We had a ray of hope when we drew Bristol City at home in the first round of the FA Cup.

We found out that a mob of Bristol were on their way down Oxford Street accompanied by the Old Bill. We decided to go up the Kingsway, parallel to Oxford Street and hit them from the Arcade which connected the two streets. The plan worked perfectly and we caught the police off guard as we charged out of the lane. But the Bristol fans were ready for us. They showered us with bottles as we exited the Arcade. I turned my back as a bottle was unavoidably coming my way. It hit me on the back leaving a perfect circle of a welt mark. The police waded in as usual, hitting the fuck out of us and pushing the mob back up the arcade. George had only just bought a new stone Island jumper that morning and had it ripped as the police tackled him. Bristol would see this as a result but in our eyes the police had won the day.

Wales were playing Holland at the Arms Park and the boys had decided to go in an unusual show of Welsh patriotism. A lot of the boys couldn't be bothered one iota about Wales, seeing it as a Cardiff thing. The FAW didn't help by changing the traditional away kit from 'yellow and green' to the 'blue and yellow' of Cardiff. The whole international set up had a Cardiff bias which alienates our fans so it wasn't surprising that we weren't too fussed on the international scene. We left for Cardiff by train with a good 150-strong mob. The police liaison officer for Swansea, Lyn Phillips, was at Cardiff Central and his face was a picture when he saw us roll off the train. We walked up towards Mary Street singing "Jack Army"; announcing our arrival in no uncertain terms. We walked past various pubs in the city centre with Cardiff lads threatening us through the windows but unwilling to come out and play. We made our way down the main street as a crew of Cardiff came shouting down the road behind us. We all turned round and charged up the road towards them. They didn't even wait until we got to them and were on their toes before we got any closer. We carried on, as the police escort arrived, to a pub called the Golden Cross and settled in for a few pints. It wasn't long before we were scuffling again outside with Bazzy glassing one of them in revenge for a nasty facial scar he received on the Naughty Forty episode. We made our way to the ground as kick-off approached. By this time, there were Cardiff everywhere but we stood strong, forcing them back into a pub after they had steamed out. Apart from a few scuffles in the game, we hardly faced any test whatsoever and had showed Cardiff that we were still an active firm who would face them any time.

'97 - '98

This was the quietest season on record. Apart from the authorities allowing away fans to travel to the derby games again there was little to get the blood pumping. The derby games passed off quietly. This was because it was the first time that the 'Bubble' trips were operated with fans only allowed to use official coaches and no tickets issued. You just got off the bus and walked in !

'98 - '99

This season's excitement was dominated by the FA Cup. When we drew the likes of Millwall, Stoke and West Ham you would have thought we would have had a right old punch up - but how wrong were we !

Our numbers for the first round against Millwall were outstanding but, despite no mean effort from both sets of fans, we never actually met. The closest we came was on the Mumbles Road when a rocket flare was shot towards them. A bus from Millwall had been stopped on the motorway, absolutely chock a block full of weapons and a stash of petrol bombs was found near the Mumbles Road but neither of us got to use them.

At the Stoke game we had a huge mob out waiting. After speaking to them on the phone, they informed us that they didn't feel as if they had enough boys with them and wouldn't come into the city centre.

As for West Ham - they were a joke ! The boys walked right through the East End, mob-handed, without opposition. It had gone from the dodgiest place to visit in the early 80's to an easy walk in the park. We had more trouble at Exeter than West Ham.

In the League, the only trip of any note was to Southend United. Toozey had organised a couple of minibuses for the trip to Essex. Toozey had been around a long time but, because he had worked on Saturdays for many years, he wasn't a regular on the scene. He had come to the fore in the last few seasons and was fast becoming known as a top boy. He was a formidable sight at around 20 stone of muscle with a shaved head. He had worked the doors with Cooney for many years and was not shy of a row. Just the sight of him would have most lads on the back foot so he was a very handy person to have around. We arrived in Southend just after lunch and found a Yates Wine Lodge that was run by a lad who originated from Swansea. We had only been in there for a couple of minutes when in walked Lyn Phillips, the Football Liaison Officer. How the fuck he did it, none of us knew but, wherever we went, he was never far behind. He would just appear as if by magic. Either he was very lucky or he was fucking good at his job. The drink flowed as we enjoyed the landlord's hospitality probably a little too much. When it was time to leave, we were a little the worse for wear.

Southend wasn't known to have an active firm so we didn't really expect any action at the game. On arrival at Roots Hall, Toozey, Alan and I decided to go on the Southend Bank behind the goal, just to liven things up a bit. As we walked through the home stand, a few lads started giving us the eye. They were wearing Stone Island so they were fair game. We walked over and offered it to them but they were having none of it. I clipped one round the ear and called them mugs. I hated those fucking impostors who wear Stone Island just to look tough and this stand was full of them. We walked the length of the stand, just the three of us, and must have passed 50 boys in Stone Island jackets but not one of the fuckers stepped up to the plate.

The game was halfway through when 'Fred the Fish' came walking down the side of the pitch. Fred was an odd little fellow that trouble seemed to follow wherever he went. As he went past the Southend fans, situated to our right, they started abusing him. No shrinking violet, Fred just started giving it back to them. A fan leant over the stand wall and took a swing at him and that was all it took. We charged across the empty terracing between us and into the stand. Scuffles broke out along the short wall between us all. Suddenly I was pulled down from behind as a couple of stewards jumped on me. I thought I was nicked but Lyn Phillips came charging down and said "It's OK, I've got him." With that he took me to the back of the stand and said "What the fuck are you doing ? Lee, you're going to get yourself nicked." And with that he let me go. All the years that I had been involved in the scene, I had never met anyone as confusing as Lyn. He would treat you like a mate but, if he had a chance, he would put you down without a second thought. He had just had a chance to get me on a ban but let me go. He was so unpredictable.

The only other trouble we had this year was when Hull City visited the Vetch on a very wet final game of the season. The rain had been non-stop all day and the kick-off had been delayed until 5 o'clock so they could work the pitch. If it hadn't been the last game of the season, it would have been postponed. But the season had to end that day. By the time 5 o'clock came around, the whole crowd was pissed up. The Hull fans were in fine fettle with a huge King Billy flag erected in the corner closest to the North Bank. Their lads were giving it large in the corner, winding the boys up so much that, just as the game kicked off, a mob of the newly formed youth firm called the SRS ran over to them and started attacking them through the fence. The violence escalated when they started smashing up the advertising hoardings and using the timber as missiles. The Hull fans just took it and made no effort to get over the fence to join in the melee. The new arrivals on the scene showed that they were well game and had little regard for the CCTV cameras. The future looked bright as another chapter of the Jack Army began.

'99 - '00

The season started all quiet on the hooligan front but, on the pitch, we were having the most successful season in years. It wasn't until we went to Plymouth at the later end of the season that we had any sort of action. We took 200 down by train and set up camp in the city centre. After we had been drinking in a pub in town for a spell, Toozey and I decided to go for a little scout about. We had walked around the town for a few minutes when a couple of lads jumped out from a shop and started giving it large. We went for them as they chucked a bin at

THIS was the scene of shame when hundreds of football fans had to be escorted along Royal Parade in the lead up to Saturday's fixture at Home Park.

Seven people were arrested and hundreds of pounds worth of damaged caused in incidents involving Plymouth Argyle and Swansea City football supporters.

Police kept opposing fans away from each other after trouble broke out in the Noah's Ark pub on Courtenay Street where around 130 Swansea fans congregated at lunch time.

More than 30 officers from the Tactical Aid Group were called in to contain them.

A hard core of supporters tried to break through the police lines but were forced back into the pub after minor scuffles.

Yob rule?

ANTHROPOLOGISTS should get on the case of the new generation of football hooligans responsible for the huge rise in arrests at grounds around Britain.

UNACCEPTABLE The unwanted face of British football.

us. We told them that we were in the Lord Nelson pub and for them to get a firm together. As usual, as if by magic, Lyn Phillips turned up once again, laughing at us chasing these two idiots round a set of table and chairs. Back in the pub we waited for another hour but there was no sign of them. Out of sheer boredom, the boys just started smashing the pub to pieces.

The police arrived and we were evicted from the wrecked pub. They marched us off towards the stadium on a marathon walk. We went past a club of some sort where a few Plymouth came out but were soon chased away. On the way to the ground, a photo journalist took a picture of us marching by with me in the front doing what looked like a Nazi salute. But it wasn't until the next Saturday that I realised the full impact of it all.

I had a phone call at six in the morning from my mate, Davis, who worked at Swansea train station. They had just received the newspapers and he had seen the front page of the Daily Mirror. On it, in full colour was a photo of me leading the boys through Plymouth with the headline 'Name This Thug'. I couldn't believe

consternation of shoppers on Saturday afternoon

Football violence is still a threat

ANYONE who thought the threat of violence had disappeared from British football should have been in Plymouth on Saturday.

Sadly, they would have discovered that there are still troublemakers who are hell-bent on causing destruction and mayhem, given the chance.

Fortunately, police were geared up to dealing with a large contingent of visiting fans from Swansea, and did well to nip trouble in the bud.

However that did not prevent groups of so-called fans from smashing up the Noah's Ark pub in the city centre and the beer garden of the Britannia Inn at Milehouse.

The sight and sound of chanting Swansea fans being escorted through Plymouth city centre to Home Park brought shoppers to a halt.

Many were frightened by the demeanour of the supporters, some of whom were clearly spoiling for trouble.

It was a sad sight. But it was a timely reminder that although the behaviour of fans has improved immeasurably over the last ten years, there is still potential for violence.

Well done to Plymouth police for containing the minority of thugs who came with the intention of causing mayhem.

If nothing else, Saturday's experience graphically underlines the need for continued vigilance, and shows we cannot – and must not – become complacent.

it. The accompanying article was even worse and went on about the new wave of Neo-Nazis sweeping through Welsh football. What a fucking joke ! My phone was red hot with threatening phone calls from anti-Nazis, Cardiff fans and anybody who fancied abusing me. Simon told me that my picture from the paper and my telephone number had been put up all over Cardiff and every Tom, Dick and Harry was ringing. I went to the game against Torquay in the afternoon and found out that I was on the front page of the Evening Post and the Western Mail. This was getting out of control. The following day the papers revealed my identity as people had phoned in to name me. The Evening Post had talked to the Swansea Football Club Chairman who said I would be banned for life. Sure enough, a letter was delivered to me before the penultimate game of the season banning me for life.

The final game of the season was a title decider at Rotherham which I wasn't going to miss for all the tea in China so I went up and kept a low profile. There was trouble in the lane behind the ground where Swans and Rotherham fans exchanged missiles. A mounted policeman took it upon himself to charge down the lane full pelt on his horse, killing a Swans fan called

Terry Coles. He was the third Swansea fan to die due to football violence and it made me think long and hard about what we did. My time was coming to an end. My desire and willingness to do anything for the cause was fading fast and in this game there's no place for hangers on. I kept going for a few more years until around 2003 but the stories are better coming from the lads who keep on carrying the flame. I had been at the forefront of football violence in Swansea for 20 years. I had stood toe to toe with many firms and shoulder to shoulder with many of our main boys. We had run some top mobs and had results against all odds. I had been run, beaten, stoned and battered and loved every minute of it. All my friends were hooligans and I would have died for any one of them.

The friendship and camaraderie was second to none and I don't regret a second of it.

CHAPTER EIGHT
JOHN THE CLOG

When Swansea were in the old Second Division, I went with my father to watch them play Fulham in London. Earlier that day we'd been to see Chelsea v Spurs in a midday kick-off. I was still at school and wrote to Swansea Football Club to see if they could put me in touch with a pen-pal so that I could improve my English as I am Dutch. Two people wrote back to me and one of them is still a good mate to this day. I then came over for a home game at the Vetch and that was it - I was hooked and became one of the boys.

There are now a couple of Swans Supporters' Clubs in Holland and the Swans are very popular in Den Haag. I am also a Director of Swansea City Football Club now. About five years ago, I put some money into the club, along with some friends, to help save it. I've got to know a lot of the boys over the years and they're a great bunch.

A few years back, we qualified for Europe by winning the Welsh Cup. We were drawn against the Greek side Panathinaikos and a few of us booked a week's holiday out in Greece. The day after the game, a few of us went for a meal and a few beers when someone in our party noticed a huge crowd of locals had gathered outside. Next thing, a bloke rides into the bar on a motorbike and all hell breaks loose. We came under attack for a good 30 minutes while the police stood outside watching. We had some British girls with us who worked out there and it was frightening. I feared for our safety - I was sure someone was going to die. It was later estimated that a 2,000-strong mob of Greeks were outside and there were only about 50 of us inside that bar. When we came under attack, one of our lot jumped the bar to get away and fell straight down into the cellar where the doors had been left open. It was wave after wave of vicious attacks, then all the boys were arrested. Me and another bloke and three girls locked ourselves in the toilet and managed to keep out of the way.

My Dad was sitting at home in Holland watching the late evening news when it came on that 52 British football fans and one Dutchman had been arrested in Greece. In the end, the ones not arrested, like myself, offered to pay for all the damage done to the bar, even though we were the innocent victims. We had to pay in order to get the boys released from jail. We paid up in full even though not one Greek person was arrested. They took the money and then the next day they denied that we'd paid up. "Money ? What money ?" they said to me.

In the end,
we managed to get everyone home
but it was one scary trip.

CHAPTER NINE
ALAN

I'm 41 now and I've been going to games since I was about ten years old. My first game was against Hartlepool United and we beat them 8 - 0. I went with my uncle to that game, then I progressed to selling the match day programmes and that's how I got to know a lot of the boys.

When I was about 15, I started tagging along with a few of the boys and started becoming a bit of a runaway train. I had been brought up by my grandparents and had lots of problems in my childhood. I became violent in school, had attacked teachers and was expelled. I was so angry. I was just full of pent-up anger. Football was one way of venting that anger. I had so much anger and went through so much trauma. Nowadays there's counselling and the like. When I was a kid, you were just left to cope with it. I never knew my Dad and didn't see my Mum so I rebelled. I became a skinhead and, at one time, I weighed 22 stone. I was a fucking huge, angry young man. I looked like Buster Bloodvessel. I went from a fresh-faced, young kid at the football to a nasty bit of work. I had many scrapes with the law even before I went with the mob at football.

In Swansea, we didn't have many ethnics like Africans or Asians to fight with so we used to do battle with the local Gypsies or Pikeys as we called them. One night we had a big row with the Pikeys in our local pub. One of them got hit on the head with a breeze block and got well fucked up. He was in a bad way and was in a coma and very nearly died. It was around the same time as the Toxteth riots in Liverpool. The Pikeys lived on a caravan site not far from the pub and turned up one disco night and it just kicked off. It was a really nasty night. Ten of us were arrested and all of us were jailed. I got 12 months for affray but that sentence made me worse. I had numerous fights inside and was fighting with black guys because, at that time, I was very racist. I have mellowed with time.

I was banged up when the system changed in 1981 from Borstal to Young Offenders and the rules and regime changed - and what a shock it was. One good thing that came out of it was that I lost a load of weight and came out fighting fit. When I came out of the jail, a lot of the boys had changed from skinheads to the casual look. Times and fashions change very quickly in nine months. My mates at football were, basically, my adopted family, so when I came out I went straight back into the flow with them. I felt at home and comfortable with my mates from football. When I first came out, I went straight up to London and bought a couple of Taccini tracksuits from a shop in Shepherds Bush and I thought I looked the dog's bollocks. It's the sort of thing Cliff Richard would have worn when he was playing tennis with Sue Barker. But anyway, I was the nuts in my newly acquired outfits. I was now into football violence in a big way. I sorted out some calling cards and was one of the main faces in the younger lot I knocked about with.

> CONGRATULATIONS
> *You have just been serviced by "THE SQUAD"*
> Please Call Again

Over the years, I've been involved in some right scrapes - the obvious ones like Millwall and Cardiff and others like Hull City, Stoke, Shrewsbury, Reading, Plymouth, Northampton and even places like Torquay away in '86.

SWANSEA: Hooligans cause thousands of pounds of damage

Rival fans clash before match

RUNNING battles between rival football supporters marred Swansea City's Second Division clash with Bristol City last night.

Fighting broke out in pubs near to the Vetch Field before yesterday's game with thousands of pounds worth of damage caused to windows and furniture.

Hundreds of Bristol City supporters hurled missiles at passing cars and police officers on Swansea's Oystermouth Road.

Gangs of supporters, who had travelled to the match wearing casual clothes rather than their team's colours, fought in the Garibaldi, Eli Jenkins and Potters Wheel and Glamorgan pubs.

And, despite a heavy police presence, after the game's delayed kick-off at around 8pm, sporadic violence was still being reported in the Sandfields area of Swansea.

A member of staff at the Potters Wheel in Swansea said the trouble had flared suddenly and for no apparent reason.

"It was a big gang of men, none of them were wearing football colours and all of a sudden all hell broke loose," he said.

"Tables and chairs were flying around, windows were broken, but it was over almost as soon as it started and by the time the police had arrived they had moved on."

Despite a tense atmosphere there was no trouble within the Vetch Field itself and after the match, which ended 2-2, riot police escorted around 1,000 Bristol supporters from the ground.

One that sticks in my mind was a night game against Bristol City. We'd heard nothing from their boys about turning up and coming down so we all took it that they wouldn't be making a show. They go to Cardiff for games but, for some reason, they'd never turned up in Swansea. The main bulk of us had arranged to meet in the pub once we'd finished work. As far as we were concerned the day was already written off as a non-event. I'd got in from work and was just getting changed at home when I got a call from one of the lads to say that Bristol City had turned up 100 handed and smashed up The Potter's Wheel pub. I got picked up and we drove down to The Garibaldi where a few of the lads were drinking. It emptied out and we went looking for the Bristol lads. We were told by the coppers waiting outside that there was no way we'd get anywhere near the Bristol mob. As we came up the road, we saw a mob about 80 strong coming out of the Eli Jenkins pub. We ran at them and they came at us but, as we got closer, we realised both mobs were Swansea. Now we had a good 200 strong mob out on the streets and the Old Bill weren't very happy.

Then the news went up that the Bristol firm were in a nearby pub. We raced up Oxford Street only to be met with lines of coppers and metal crash barriers. The first amongst us grabbed the barriers and launched them at the police. The

Old Bill came back at us with gas and batons but you could tell they were shitting themselves. One copper stood there with a video camera filming the whole lot. Next thing, another group of coppers was leading the Bristol fans out of the pub, some still carrying their pints of beer. They were taken under escort up the side of the ground and we tried to come at them from side streets and alleyways. A few of the boys had armed themselves with lumps of wood and bits of fencing and were trying their best to launch attacks but were being beaten back by the Old Bill.

CITY'S THUGS CAUSE CHAOS

A night out with my mum ends in terror

We were split up by the coppers into smaller groups. The bulk of us managed to go quickly anti-clockwise around the ground and, on our travels, we discovered a builder's lorry delivering bricks. Next thing we heard was that the Bristol boys had been put in another pub as the ground wasn't yet open for business. The pub they were in came under attack with these house bricks and a few of the boys got up a side alley next to the pub and were having toe to toe with the Bristol fans. There were cars caught up in all the chaos and

Police plea to catch thugs

A CAMPAIGN is launched today to track down the football thugs who sparked a riot when Swansea City met Bristol City.

Detectives have drawn up a picture album catalogue of people they want to eliminate from their enquiries.

Five police were injured and a tracker dog blinded in one eye in disgraceful scenes when the clubs met in a night match at Vetch Field.

Detectives have studied around 16 hours of video footage from closed circuit television in the city centre and from security cameras at the Vetch Field.

The films were sent to a specialised studio in Cambridge to be enhanced by a firm which carries out work for the National Crime Squad and Government agencies.

And on both sides of the Bristol Channel a major enquiry backed by dozens of the photographs of men has been set up.

Today the South Wales Evening Post publishes pictures of people the investigating team want to talk to.

Our colleagues at the Bristol Evening Post plan to do the same in an attempt to track down a large number of hooligans from the West Country, some of whom launched an attack on the Potter's Wheel pub causing serious damage.

Detectives from Swansea were travelling to Bristol today to meet football liaison experts from Somerset and Avon Police to co-ordinate the operation.

The release of the photographs marks a crucial phase in an investigation which has been going on ever since the match three weeks ago.

All the pictures the Post is publishing today come from cameras in and around the ground.

Detective Inspector Julian Williams, who is in charge of the inquiry, said today: "The scenes witnessed before and after this match are totally unacceptable."

"We are determined to track down as many people as possible. If your picture is published in the course of this investigation and you have done nothing wrong you have nothing to fear."

"But we would still like you to come forward because you may have vital information."

Nobody was arrested on the night of the match but anybody convicted of offences as a result of the photographic evidence will be banned for life by Swansea City.

The club, which has been hauled before the Football Association of Wales and fined over the behaviour of its fans in recent seasons, has pledged to publish pictures to track any more troublemakers belong to supporters.

SMASHED UP A Bristol City supporter's car is abandoned at County Hall after being vandalised after the football match at Vetch Field on Tuesday night.

they got smashed to bits.

That was it before the game but afterwards we had a 500 to 600 mob out on the streets. The police were drafted in from everywhere and the Bristol had lines and lines of Old Bill around them. There were dogs, vans, the lot wrapped around them. I'll give it to the Bristol mob, they were all geezers with no shirts or youngsters with them. In the end, our crowd got so pissed off that they attacked the coppers and it went on 30 - 45 minutes. It was just mental. A police dog was injured that night and it was in all the papers the next day how this police dog, Major, had lost an eye. There were loads of arrests, many having been caught on CCTV. A few of the Bristol boys were also arrested but later had their charges dropped. One of our boys even turned up in court on the day of their appearance and offered to take the biggest one among them outside for a chat. He declined his offer but shook his hand and told him he had real balls for coming on his own. Our boy asked them why they hadn't told us that they were coming and why they smashed up a pub with none of our boys in it. He couldn't answer but did say they didn't want to blow their chance of getting into Swansea with no police intelligence. We've had our run-ins with Bristol City over the years but never on a scale like that.

Football fans admit violence

FOUR Swansea City football supporters have admitted violent disorder on the day of a match between the Swans and Bristol City at Vetch Field last autumn.

But five other fans pleaded not guilty to violent disorder when all nine appeared before Judge John Diehl QC at Swansea Crown Court yesterday.

The four who pleaded guilty were Mark John Davies, aged 24, of Gwynfor Road, Townhill, Christopher Spencer, aged 36, of Maes y Capel, Pembrey, Robert Daniel White, aged 22, of Westland Close, Loughor, and Lee Glyn Howells, aged 21, of Dyfed Avenue, Townhill.

Howells also admitted possessing a tube designed to look like an imitation firearm in Swansea on March 18 this year.

He intended to use it to make others fear unlawful violence would be used against them, the court heard.

The four have been bailed and will be sentenced after the others are tried.

The five who pleaded not guilty are Douglas George Shannon, aged 44, of Llys Gerginam, Swansea Marina, Andrew Paul Davies, aged 35, of Aberdyberthi Street, Hafod, Paul Sullivan, aged 28, of Oakford Place, Port-

mead, Richard Edwards, aged 27, of Wimmerfield Avenue, Killay, and Andrew Lee Bate, aged 18, of Ystrad Einon, Gorseinon.

They were released on bail until a pre-trial review and trial on dates to be fixed.

Police in riot gear were deployed in the city centre on the evening of the match when trouble broke out and a police dog, Major, was blinded in one eye and later retired from duty.

We had a good row with Bristol City in '84 at Bedminster. We took 200 over there early and took over the Red Lion. Then, give Bristol their due, they turned up but spoilt a perfectly good row by pulling out these Jiffy bottles filled with ammonia. A lot of our boys suffered burns and injuries to their eyes but, as soon as City ran out of ammo and the coppers appeared, they were off. In five minutes, it was all over. Nowadays the Old Bill have got a grip on the fixture so nothing really happens.

Jury clears fans in violence case

FOUR Swans fans have been cleared of violent disorder on the night of the Bristol City match at the Vetch Field last season.

The Nationwide League Division Two clash on October 31 last year led to the four appearing at Carmarthen Crown Court.

Douglas George Shannon, aged 44, of Llys Jernegan, Swansea Marina, Paul Sullivan, aged 28, of Oakford Place, Portmead, Richard Edwards, aged 28, of Wimmerfield Avenue, Killay, and 36-year-old Andrew Paul Davies, of Aberdyberthi Street, Hafod, all denied violent dis-

order. Mr Shannon, Mr Davies and Mr Sullivan were accused of running down Clarence Street, near the Vetch, and charging police lines to get at Bristol fans.

Mr Edwards was said to have been part of a group threatening opposition fans, having been seen in the city's Quadrant bus station gesticulating at visiting supporters.

But the trial was stopped on the third day after the prosecution decided to offer no further evidence.

Judge Gerald Price, QC, directed the jury to return not guilty verdicts against all four and they were discharged from the dock.

Over the years I've also been interested in British politics. At one stage I looked at the BNP and what they had to offer and even went up to a big rally in North Wales. But, at the end of the night when all the cameras had been switched off and all the press had fucked off, they went into their big marquee and sang pro-German songs and anti-Jewish songs and songs about Auschwitz that weren't for me. My Grandad fought against the Germans so I realised what a bunch of nutcases the BNP were. A few of our lads also follow the politics in Northern Ireland very closely and go out on some of the Marches but again that's not for me.

I've lived, breathed and loved football - watching it and fighting at it. I don't fight around town, I don't mug old women but I love to scrap at football. Pure and simple, I'm a football hooligan - I can't explain it. I've been nicked, fined, jailed and banned but it's in my blood. I'm 41 and just can't get it out of my system. I can stay away for a couple of months but, sure enough, I get drawn back like a moth to a light.

I just can't resist it.

CHAPTER 10
MAD DOCTOR

We walked into the Railway Inn at about 4 in the morning. Looking around I could see there were a good 30 or 40 reliable lads already there drinking and talking about the days plan of action. Madness was already blasting from the jukebox and there was boozy, party atmosphere more reminiscent of a nightclub rather than a back street boozer. We had already been in touch with a hooligan contact in Hull who said their firm would be 200 to 300 mob handed. We were expecting a few more lads than we had but it looked like the night life and female clubbers had seen off many of them. But there was no question we weren't going even if the numbers were going to be 4 to 1. The buses were booked, everybody was bouncing and we were ready. A couple of the lads looked a bit worse for wear as they'd stopped out all night. George had been to a wedding and was still dancing round in his Granddad's suit covered in pizza. I then spotted a younger lad whose eyeballs were in the back of his head and was virtually licking the walls after taking 8 pills during the night. I was then reliably informed that he was one of the fucking drivers !

I decided to take my mate Kiddy Dan with us, English as fuck which is not his fault but was welcomed and respected by the lads. We left Swansea in 3 minibuses plus cars and met up with another minibus from Neath/Valleys, always easy to spot as you could see the lads pissing against the bus at the side of the motorway. After all the usual drinking, singing and other nonsense during the journey we were informed that the Old Bill were waiting for us on the motorway at the Hull turn off, so we made a detour towards Goole approximately 20 miles outside Hull. We mobbed up in The North Eastern Hotel opposite the train station and contacted the Hull lads of our situation. We were told that there were no Old Bill at Hull station so we left the pub and went to board the train for Hull station. Just as we were about to make our move, a plain clothed copper walked into the boozer. For some strange reason he didn't believe that 60 lads from South Wales were on a sight seeing day out in Goole. He tried to persuade us to stay but we just left and boarded the train.

I sat with Ivey on the train and we both agreed that we were too old for this running around and then we both laughed as we knew this was a great buzz and then just concentrated on what was going to happen next. By the time we arrived in Hull there must have been over 150 Old Bill who stopped and searched us before slowly marching us through the back streets of Hull. This was a nightmare now, as the chances of it kicking off were drastically reduced.

Still in touch with the Hull lads, we managed to get in sight of each other on the Great Thornton Street Estate and, as soon as they saw us, about 200 of them came charging down the street but the Old Bill drew their batons on both mobs, smashing whoever was in front of them, trying desperately to keep the two mobs apart. There was a stand off for a couple of minutes before the Hull lads launched their ammunition of bricks and bottles instead. Everything that rained down on us was given back to them by us until the Old Bill had had enough and charged the Hull lads back down the road. We were then circled and held by the Old Bill for over a fucking hour as they'd called for buses to drive us to the ground because they couldn't trust us or the Hull mob on a walk to the stadium. It was here that we were introduced to Hull's rubbish re-cycling system as the friendly local residents in the high rise flats chucked dirty nappies, used condoms, their mothers best china and their dead pets at us.

We got to the ground and were escorted straight under the stand and then left to our own devices. We were talking about what we should do next when a load of Hull lads came charging down from behind us. A ruck broke out and it lasted for 2-3 minutes before the Old Bill piled in to break it up. Kiddy Dan and myself were being fronted by a couple of Hull lads until one big Northern lump smacked him from behind and called his fellow countrymen a "Welsh Prick". Being called a Welsh prick hurt him more than the smack in the face. More Swansea lads joined the ruck and Hull were well beaten especially when Toozey came steaming in and double punched two Hull lads which sent them reeling. Somebody then stole one on Wallis and his nose exploded but he just carried on until the police stopped the chaos. Once again the Old Bill drew their batons and it was game over.

After the game, we all tried to leave the ground but there was no way the Old Bill were having us back on their lovely streets of Hull again. So we were put back onto buses and escorted back to Goole while a mob of about 300 to 400 Hull lads were waiting for us down the road. We had a couple of pints in Goole and got in touch with the our Hull contact but there was no way the Old Bill were going to let them on a train to meet us. He said we had their respect for showing up with a mob smaller than we would have liked and agreed to meet us again. We then started the drive home and decided to stop off in Nottingham for our evening's entertainment. When we got to Nottingham, we parked up and piled into the city centre. We visited several bars and made our presence felt but the locals weren't taking the bait. We then went to one bar and, within a couple of minutes, we were soon spotted by a couple of Forest lads who, once they knew who we were, said they would try and get a mob together for a meet later. We stayed put in this bar waiting for Forest to arrive and stockpiled our ammunition of bottles, glasses, ashtrays and fire extinguishers whilst giving the locals a bit of stick but, unfortunately, an hour or so later the two Forest lads returned and said they couldn't raise a mob and congratulated us on our stand in their city. The trip was complete with a few more beers and leaving George in Nottingham as we had lost him. Full of booze, I sang to Toozey and Ivey who were driving for the whole trip home which really got on their tits and we arrived back in Swansea at 4am. We all wandered home in different directions while George headed for the nearest taxi rank in Nottingham for a taxi to Wales ...

and yes, still in his Granddad's suit !

CHAPTER 11
SRS & YOUTH

The early to mid 90's saw the emergence of a new and younger set of lads come onto the hooligan scene in Swansea. Before that it was a lot of the same faces getting involved that had been doing it through the 70's and 80's with the exception of the bigger games and derby's which attracted a lot of lads that normally wouldn't take part in fighting and disorder at games (which I think is common for all mobs) but for the added spice and passion. Added with the beer was a recipe for aggro, especially if you had another group from elsewhere looking for a ruck. However that changed at the start of the 90's. This was also the peak of the drug and rave scene and, at most clubs, numbers in mobs/firms started to fall and so did the number of incidents of disorder at games. This also was also the case at Swansea but it wasn't all love and ecstasy at that time. Far from it.

By the mid 90's, the number of younger lads (by that I mean under 30s) getting involved was rising and, together with the re-involvement of some of the older lads, football related incidents in Swansea were increasing again. By the turn of the millennium, we had a good set of lads under the age of 30 and, though at first there would be some friction between the older and younger set of lads in our mob, it was generally never a problem. Soon, a few of us started making names for ourselves and with it came a lot of attention from the local Old Bill. CCTV and banning orders were also making things hard for the 'new breed' but for some, myself included, we couldn't give a fuck about all that. If you don't want to risk fines, bans and a prison sentence then this 'way of life' isn't for you. And that's exactly the way it was and still is for many of us, a way of life, we live and breath it, the music, fashion and above all the violence at football. But only at football, don't ask me why but that's the way it is. Most would never go looking for bother at any other time. What's the point ? But at football, well that's different init !

It was around this time that the name SRS - SWANSEA RIOT SQUAD came into being. We would often talk about why we never had a name though years back there were calling cards done with the name 'The Squad' but it never took off. The fans in general were called the 'Jack Army'. Nothing to do with a mob or firm, just a name that the travelling support had been called. So the SRS was thought up as a joke more than a serious thought and it stuck. However, the new youth of today sometimes call themselves by another name but that changes from time to time and SRS is still used today.

Apart from the emerging youth element in the 90's, there was another factor that was emerging within the mob. This was the support for the BNP and even links to Loyalism, though not all agreed with either especially as some of the lads were catholic. Now I don't want to get side tracked by this subject as this is a book on Swansea's hooligan following not politics but some of the lads have their own beliefs and as this is (well supposed to be) a democratic society. They can vote for who they want. The BNP is a legal party just like Labour, Conservatives, Lib Dems, etc and people should not be judged on who they vote for, as surely that too is a form of racism also. I will leave it at that.

The following accounts are from various games and incidents involving Swansea's younger followers though most are now a lot older and can no longer be considered 'Youth' and are well established faces themselves. Some may argue that some of the incidents were not with the top firms, fair enough but you can only fight what's in front of you. I'd love to have been at it with the best but sadly, due to our teams position, this was not possible. That's not intended to disrespect the mobs that did want it with us, after all a fight is a fight.

LUTON AWAY

The game against Luton was looked forward to as it would be a day trip to the big city which is always a good piss-up and a laugh but we also knew Luton had a firm at home and would be up for a row. There were two mobs that day, one of older lads and another of younger lads with ages ranging from 19-28 and it was arranged for both sets of boys to meet up when in London.

We were the first set to arrive on train at Paddington numbering around 40 boys and, as usual nowadays, we had a few Old Bill with us keeping an eye on what we did and where we went. As soon as we left the train, there was a sizeable presence of Old Bill, larger than I had expected for a game at Luton. Two officers came up to me and it turned out that Middlesbrough were playing Spurs that day and they wanted to know if we had much history and how many we had coming. Strange as they normally don't have to ask with their 'intelligence' these days. Needless to say I said we had no history with them (we did a little) and this was all we had that day. It was then that our liaison officer, Lyn Phillips, came up and asked me what our intentions were and asked where the 'others' were - as if I was going to tell him, twat. I grumbled 'dunno' and we all kept walking out of Paddington and, to our surprise, no Old Bill followed which was a shock as normally they stick to us like glue.

We made our way to a pub called 'The Flying Scotsman', quite a well known bar that has some dodgy looking strippers/pole dancers. We had a few beers there and made contact with the older lot who said they'll meet us later. After about

20 minutes, one of the Neath boys who had popped out to get some grub came rushing back in to say it was going off outside with some of our lot. We all poured out onto the street to see riot Old Bill by a pub further up the street and, as we made our way up, a line of Old Bill formed in front of us, extended their coshes and we were told to back off and that none of ours were involved but it was the Yids and Borough at it. They seemed to have had the incident sorted and, as none of us wanted a pointless nicking, we went back to the pub. As it was still early, we decided to stay for another beer and enjoy the strippers, one or two of whom I'm sure were actually men. I remember one having a go at one of my mates as, before a strip, they'd collect tips from customers and, while everyone else was giving a fair bit, my mate gave 1p which didn't go down too well. A bit of an argument started but soon got calmed down though I think the manly faced stripper was game for a ruck too. The same mate then decided to do a strip himself and got chucked off stage by some dodgy Greek-looking guy if I remember right. It then almost went off and the Old Bill came in - it was time to move on.

We got to Luton and met a few others who had gone up by van. It was now about 1 o'clock and we asked if they had seen anything. They hadn't so we had a beer and went to a different bar. Me and one of the lads decided to go for a scout as no MIGS had been seen though there were a few Old Bill with us. As we left the bar, a guy in a silver Stone Island jacket across the road called us over. "You two Swansea" he asked. "Yeah, where's your fucking firm then". We were expecting a few to arrive but the guy told us to stay where we were and they'd be there shortly. It was left at that as the Old Bill were just across the road and was not worth any hassle. The others were informed and we waited for the MIGS to show. Then the Old Bill could then be seen running up the road. We left the pub thinking it was Luton's firm only to see one of our lads who I shall call 'Mr skin' being nicked as he had slammed one of their lads who must have been seeing what we had as no other Luton were around. More Old Bill had now arrived and a few MIGS were now seen walking past the window making wanker signs but nothing more.

Time was getting on, the older lot had gone elsewhere and the Old Bill made sure nothing was going to happen before KO. As I was on a banning order at the time, about eight of the lads missed the game and stayed with me. We went to the back of the pub while the rest of the lads were rounded up and taken to the game. The Old Bill stayed outside for 10 minutes and then went. Great we thought. We gave it another 10 minutes before leaving to look for any Luton that also gave the game a miss. As we left, there were two coppers at the corner of the street. Just by the pub was a shopping centre and, as we walked past, the Old Bill followed. We made our way into the shopping centre and managed to lose the Old Bill. As we got out the other side, who do I spot by the cashpoint on his own but the guy in the silver Stone Island top who I had spoken to earlier. I tapped him on the shoulder. "Oi twat ! Remember me ?" I said. The look on his face when he turned around and saw 8 of us there was priceless, he totally shit it. But unlike some who were bullies, we didn't do anything; what was the point. He was on his own and it was broad daylight. "Where's your fucking boys then mate" said one of ours. To be fair, he kept his nerve and said he would take us to a pub where their lads go though none were there at that point. One of the lads who I shall call 'G' said that it was dodgy and why don't we make the twat give over all his cash in his account. As I said, that's not us and I said no and, maybe a bit foolishly, followed this guy who we don't know to Luton's so called main pub.

Once there, it was pretty empty apart from one or two people drinking. This guy then started ringing about on his mobile. "Fuck this" said 'G', "He'll have all their lads here now and there's only 8 of us". 'G' then went up to him and tried to grab his phone. "Who the fuck you phoning twat". "Lets fucking do him" someone else said. The guy, who was now beginning to look a bit too relaxed, said he wouldn't set us up and he was sorting a row for after the game. 'Fuck this', I thought expecting all of Luton's mob to walk in. "Right we'll go and get our other lads and be back here before end of game", I said. He agreed and we went back to the pub we were first in by the shopping centre where some calls to the boys were made. Within 15 mins, we had around 25 lads who had left the ground, also closely followed by about 5 Old Bill. Most of us left the pub and made our way to the pub where we had been with Luton's lad. I say most as for some reason a few decided to have a drink first. This happens with a few people quite regularly and it pisses me off. As soon as there's a hint of actual aggro, some lose their bottle and want to hold back a bit or are 'in the toilet' and missed it or some other shit excuse. Truth is, and I think that all mobs have them, that some people just like to wear the gear, look and act hard when Old Bill are around but, when it boils down to the nitty gritty, the truth shows and they shit it. Why fucking bother, I don't know, as they look absolute pricks and it's fucking embarrassing !

The walk to the pub is about 10 minutes and, as we got near, there were approx 10 of us in front. Also shadowing us were the Old Bill but they kept their distance. As we got to the bottom of the road where the pub was, we could see a guy by the doorway who pretty obviously was waiting to see if we would show. We did. Then as we got outside that's when it went off as one of the port Talbot boys 'T' ran up and smashed the guy by the door in the face. Out they came and I remember they had a black lad who, I'm told, is a bit of a knife merchant and a known face in the MIGS, though not that day as he too had a few good smacks. They didn't have that many, well not that actually came and had it with us anyway; probably about 15 max - about even numbers. But it was them that came unstuck. One fat cunt took a good few boots when he went down, this went on for a good

2/3 minutes which, for a ruck, is pretty long. Both sets went at it with boots and fists and, though they did have a go, they ran back into the pub as they saw more of ours come around the corner. This was when the Old Bill dived in with their coshes and dogs. For some reason they had Doberman Pinschers instead of the usual police dogs and one of them decided to sink his teeth into the leg of my mate while another took a fancy to me and chased me down the road. One thing that sticks in my mind is that, while the ruck was going on, I caught a glimpse of the Old Bill and they were just stood there with arms folded, letting us go to it. I ain't complaining but it seemed strange why they did that and, thinking back, no one ever got nicked for that day bar Mr Skin. I can't remember anyone else there bar the both sets of lads so maybe the Old Bill thought 'Fuck it, let 'em smash each other up'. Personally I think the Old Bill overreact and will make a big deal out of fuck all and the media don't help either. Apart from the most serious of cases, all that is needed is an 'On the spot fine'. That's what happens on a Friday and Saturday night so why should a ruck at football be any different ?

Once the Old Bill took control that was all the fun to be had but, for this day and age, a ruck and no arrests is a bit of a good day though I came close to being nicked. A copper grabbed me and pushed me up against the van and told me I was nicked. Then, from nowhere, 'G' jumped against the van and said if I'm nicked then so is he. The copper looked at him dull, then at me and said "Both of you, fuck off before I change my mind". I couldn't believe it but I wasn't gonna argue and fair play to 'G' though I would have pissed myself had he got nicked too.

Later we went back to the 'Flying Scotsman' pub and met up with the older lads who had done their own thing and told them what had gone on. They were impressed and already had heard at what had gone on and now the 'younger' part of the firm were showing they could do it without the help of the older lads, we too were now slowly building a reputation of our own.

BRISTOL CITY HOME (2001)

In recent seasons there hasn't been many mobs apart from a few that have come to us with a firm and actually had a pop. To be fair, City have a game set of lads and, when given the opportunity, they will always turn out down here. One of those games was on a cold October evening in 2001, the game was on a Tuesday and it was arranged by a few of us to meet up early straight after work. I had sorted it with my foreman so that I could leave work early about 4 but, if the boss saw me, that he knew nothing about it. At the time I was working in a builder's yard so I had a quick freshen up in the bogs then sneakily got changed in a warehouse that was full of broken bricks, timber and rats. Fuck the rats, I didn't want miss any of the fun. Bristol City to us is the second derby behind playing the Scum and there was always trouble when our clubs met.

I left work and made my way to the city centre and had a quick scout around to see if I could see any worrzels. As it happened there was fuck all about so I went to the Potters wheel pub. The pub was fairly busy when I got there, mainly people having an after work drink mixed with a few winos after the cheap beer they sold there. There was already about 5 of the lads at the front by the door having a drink. I got mine and joined them. I asked if anyone knew if City were showing that night. One of the boys said that they had already been in touch and that they would be in Swansea shortly. This was exactly what I wanted to hear and the adrenaline started and that funny feeling you get in your stomach when you know its gonna kick-off; a mixture of anticipation and excitement. I was due to meet more of the lads at the Gari (a well known pub that was always used by the boys for as long as I can remember and had seen many an incident, though at that time it was no longer our main pub). I finished my pint and made my way over.

When I walked in, it was dead apart from my mate Driscoll who was also waiting for the other lads, though bearing in mind it was only just after 5 on a Tuesday night. I told him what I had heard and asked where the rest of the boys were. He said he had spoken to some and that they would be down shortly as they had only just finished work. As it was still early and I had seen no sign of any Bristol, we decided to have a game of pool and wait for a few more of the boys. We played a game and there was still no sign of anyone so we decided to give it 10 more minutes to see if anyone showed. It was at this point a fella walked in shaking his head as if he was unhappy about something.

"Alright ?" said the barman.

"Bloody mad out there, a gang of Bristol boys are looking for trouble." Me and Driscoll both stopped talking and looked at each and then at the guy who had just walked in. I wasn't sure if I hear him right.

"Who's out there ? What's happening ?" I said, praying I had heard him right the first time.

"Load of Bristol City fans are on their way to the Potters Wheel. It's gonna kick-off now," he replied. That's all I needed to hear.

"Come on, it's going off. The boys are in there," I said to Driscoll.

We both ran out of the Gari and up the lane beside it towards the Potters Wheel. As we came around the corner, all I could see was around 100 City lads by the Potters all shouting and beckoning some of our lads inside. At this point I didn't know what to do; after all, there was only two of us and roughly 100 of them - 50 onto 1, not good odds in my eyes.

"What the fuck do we do," I said to Driscoll.
"Fuck knows, where's the boys ?" he replied.

I could see a few things being thrown from inside the pub back at the City lads but no actual fighting, though they never actually entered the pub. Another guy appeared by us who we both didn't know. By the way he was dressed, he must have been a doorman or security guard.

"Come on, lets do the fuckers," he shouted.

Was he mad ? Just three of us ! We didn't have a chance. There was too many of them for us. They then suddenly turned their attention to us and what started as a brisk walk towards us soon turned into a mob surge. We had no option but to run. I'm no coward and neither is Driscoll but what choice did we have. As we got back outside by the Gari, I turned around and didn't see any Bristol.

"What we going to do ? Where the fuck are all the boys ?" Driscoll shouted.

He was right. Where the fuck was everyone ? We decided to go back to the Potters Wheel but via another route. When we got onto the Kingsway (the road that the pub is on), we could see no sign of Bristol and, in fact not even any Old Bill. Some of the windows were smashed and you could see chairs and tables overturned inside. I then saw some of the Townhill boys, a tough council estate not far from the city centre. They came over and it turns out they were in the pub when it had kicked off. They said there was only a few of the boys in the pub but they still managed to hold their own against the City lads. In the distance the sound of sirens could now be heard. It seems it wasn't only our lads who were out late that day. There were now small groups of Swansea lads appearing by the Potters Wheel, attracted by the wail of sirens that now filled the air. Word soon spread what had happened but no one seemed to know where the Bristol firm were so we decided to go to the Eli Jenkins pub. We were now numbering around 20 but it wasn't long before we had around 150 lads. Everyone was pissed off at what had happened but credit to Bristol, even though we only had a few lads in the Potters, they weren't to know that. They came with a firm and had a pop which is a lot more than most clubs do these days. I was on my phone in Eli when someone said there was a large group coming up the road. Everyone poured out of the pub. In the darkness, a group of around 40-60 lads were making their way to us but, before anything had happened, someone shouted that they were Swansea. This now swelled our numbers to 200+. We were now fully charged with adrenalin. "Fuck this, lets find the English cunts" someone shouted. As the pub emptied so too did half the contents of it. Bottles, cutlery, ashtrays; even stools were taken, everyone was up for it and wanted revenge. We made our way past the Grand Theatre down the street and, even though it was a dark October's night, we stood out like a sore thumb but there was no sign of the Old Bill. It was then someone shouted that City were in the Singleton pub. This was just around from where we were. That was it. Everyone just charged. As we got near the pub, 4-5 Old Bill were outside and they totally shit it. All you could see was objects flying through the air at the pub. Fuck knows where everything came from. Inside, you could see Bristol in the pub but made no attempt to get out. A hand full more Old Bill showed, spread out and battened us back. We went down a side street and up another road to get at City's firm another way. They were now out of the Singleton and being escorted past the club shop. Again, everyone charged. We now numbered around 300 and getting bigger and again Bristol's lads made no attempt to get at us. People were ripping fences down, ripping off wing mirrors, picking up bricks; not just kids but men in their late 40s. Everyone was going mental and didn't give a fuck. Fair play to the Old Bill, there weren't many of them but they stood their ground. If it wasn't for them, Bristol would have been slaughtered that night. In the distance sirens could be heard and finally the Old Bill got their act together and more arrived. City's lads were escorted straight into the ground and most of our mob made their way into the ground also.

In the game there was a strong presence of riot police that went right along the perimeter of the ground. Throughout the game, Bristol's players were bombarded with objects including fireworks but, apart from that and the odd person running on the pitch, nothing of note really happened.

After the game, it was different. Everyone left early and made their way to the away end. The Old Bill now had it sorted and had a heavy presence in the streets this time with dogs and horses but again, no one gave a fuck and charged towards the away end. We were forced back and then it was the riot Old Bill who made a charge. There were people running everywhere. Again, boys and men alike were ripping things down and using them as missiles. We started to regroup and made our way to the Mumbles road - a main road by the vetch that has seen its fair share of battles over the years. Along the way, there were several skips that were full to the brim of bricks, wood, concrete, etc but not for long. As we turned the corner by the Mumbles road, we could see a line of Old Bill at the end of the road where the away coaches left. We all steamed at them and let everything go but the thing that shocked me was that the Old Bill just picked up what was thrown at them and threw it back at us. It was our turn to turn and run as bricks and wood came crashing around us. Cars and house windows nearby were totally smashed. Thinking back, it still makes me laugh at the sight of the Old Bill picking up wood, bottles and bricks and throwing them at **US**.

Bristol were escorted away by a heavily protected police presence. With them gone, it was now the Old Bill to bear the brunt of our anger. For the next hour and half it carried on with us attacking the Old Bill and then them attacking us. In the end, the Old Bill finally gained control and regained order.

In the papers the next day it turned out that the Old Bill made a fuck up and classed the game as category A - a game with no expected trouble ! How they made this fuck up I don't know as there is always trouble when we play either Bristol clubs, especially City. There was a public outcry as the residents of the Sandfields had, not for the first time, their cars and property smashed. Several police officers were injured including a police dog called Major who last an eye as a result and had to retire. This ensured a mass investigation, followed by dozens of photos of lads involved put in the paper which is common nowadays. One of the cases collapsed due to a lack of evidence; not the first time this has happened with Swansea Old Bill but several lads received prison sentences, one of which was a good mate of mine, Willkie. Since this game, Bristol City fans now have to travel by official coach only when our sides meet and vice versa. It's had the desired effect and trouble has declined dramatically since, largely due to the fact no lads from either side bother with the official coaches, though maybe one day we will ?

CARDIFF

At every club, there is a game more than any other that guarantees trouble - the local derby. For us, that game is against the Scum (Cardiff), our hated rivals just up the M4 who we hate with a passion. Much has been said about them over the years and, in recent times, largely due to the Hooligan documentary and their book, 'Soul Crew' (complete crap in my eyes). They seem to have this big opinion about themselves, that they're this top firm in football and that we live in their shadow - we completely disagree ! Though I will say this, they can pull the numbers when they want and, on their day, be a match for 'most' firms. But they don't always get it their own way and we don't give a fuck for their so called reputation and that's what pisses them off. In fact, we've taken it to them more times in the last 16 or so years than they have to us. The history between our two sets of fans is well documented. However, it's not just at football where it kicks off between our two cities. Music gigs, darts tournaments, clubbing/rave scene, boxing and cricket have all seen disorder between our followers. But it goes deeper than football. Even non football supporters hate them and their city. Jealousy they say and, to a degree, they're right. You only have to see how they get all the grants, lottery funds and whatever the fuck they want while we're left to rot (finally though that's slowly starting to change with a mass building regeneration in the city). A good example was when their shit city had a vote on whether to have the Welsh national assembly situated there and the result was a resounding **NO**. So Swansea was to have it and the city's Guildhall was to have a multi million pound revamp. However, as soon as this was announced, Cardiff suddenly had a change of heart and decided they wanted it even though their city voted against it. This was hotly debated for some time but, in the end, the outcome was the usual one - Cardiff had their own way and got the Welsh Assembly situated there while Swansea was pushed aside once again. What follows is an example of when disorder between the two sets of fans happens and how it's not only on match days when the two clubs meet that trouble occurs.

NEATH (2003)

It was the Sunday of a bank holiday weekend in May and, as a lot of people do on bank holidays, a group of us decided to meet up at the city's Wind street for a drink. Also, on this particular day, our hated rivals Cardiff were playing in the league 1 play-off final at the Millennium stadium against QPR. I met up early with my mate Muto, a good lad who's as game as they come. He was one of the Clydach lads (a wild bunch), a small village just outside of Swansea. It was still early (about 11 o'clock) so we decided to grab some food first to line our stomachs as being a bank holiday it was certain to be a big drinking day. Once we had eaten, we made our way to the Wind Street to meet a few lads at the Walkabout pub. On our way there, we met up with one of the Baglan boys (a town not far from Swansea), Barry, who said he too was meeting a few more lads in town. When we arrived at the bar, there was around 5-6 of our lads already there. We ordered some drinks and went to chat with the others. Talk quickly turned to the Cardiff game and if anyone had spoke to them about a meet after the game but no one had and, to be honest, we were just out for a piss-up and watch the Scum hopefully lose.

All of a sudden, I heard someone say "Who the fuck are they with the flag ?" I turned around and outside I saw four lads with a blue flag talking to each other. We looked at each other and all thought the same. Were they Cardiff who were living in our city - we couldn't be having that ! Out we went ready to kick the fuckers out of our city but, as soon as we got outside, I recognised 2 of the lads as Swansea boys.

"What the fuck's that flag then mate ?" someone said.

I explained they were Swansea and it turned out the flag was for support of QPR and almost immediately the situation calmed. The night before, a large banner was placed on a bridge on Fabian Way, the main road into Swansea off the M4 which had "**Good luck, QPR, WE HATE CARDIFF**" sprayed on it and also had a feature in the local paper on it - the cities just hate each other.

We all went back in the bar and carried on drinking and, as time went on, more lads were turning up. It was now approaching 2 o'clock and we were deciding where to go and watch the game. A few left and went to several pubs to see if they were showing the game. I had a call from them and it turns out that only one pub on Wind Street was willing to show the game. I think it was mainly due to worries of how drinking customers would react to having that shit team on their screens. We all drank up and made our way to the Toad pub. It was pretty full when we arrived. It was becoming apparent that a lot of our mob had the same idea as us and, by kick-off we had a firm of 80 or so boys; not bad for a non match day ! People were now fairly pissed and sniffed up, newspapers of pre-match write-ups were being set on fire and objects being thrown at the TV screen. It wasn't long before doormen turned up. One of the younger lads got thrown out but he was to be the only one. They did try and eject more but they were surrounded and sensibly walked away and left us to it. We weren't doing anything major but you could start to feel the atmosphere change and it would only a take something small for it to kick-off. And that it did. The Scum scored and some twat jumped up and cheered. He was smashed straight in the mouth by one of our youth and then a few more went for him. The bouncers piled over and there was a minor scuffle. The bloke was now outside and was covered in blood. From what I could make out, he was just a fan of Welsh football, cheering on a Welsh club but why the fuck he cheered for them cunts and, of all places, in a Swansea pub full of lads who anyone could see were up for aggro, is beyond me. Within minutes the Old Bill had arrived and were talking to the door staff and the prick who was hit. Someone came in and told me that they heard me being described to the police as one of the ones who was causing the trouble. I quickly done one and went to a nearby pub around the corner from the Wind Street. I waited there for 10 minutes before ringing and finding out where everyone was. I met up again at Yates where most of the lads were. Also there were around 15 of the Neath Jacks who had come down for a drink in Swansea for a change. The Neath lot were a mad bunch who just loved the aggro and there were some good lads, Chenko, Andy, Penny, Twinny, etc. It turned out to be Chenko's birthday and they asked if I wanted to go back to Neath later for a few beers. As I always drank in Swansea, I thought it would be a nice change for a few hours and Neath wasn't bad for a drink either. Once the game ended the rest of the lads met up with us. We now had around 100 boys but we were pissed off that Cardiff had won and gained promotion to the championship. We were now having a few calls and texts from the Scum who were taking the piss and rubbing our noses in it. I mentioned to the boys that a few of us were going to Neath for a drink and more decided to come along. The prospect of going to Neath also had the added bonus that a few Cardiff lads were from there and would at one stage be going back there. A message was sent to them telling where we would be going and if they wanted a row then that's where we would be. Despite the numbers we had, only two minibuses were booked as most didn't expect any Cardiff to show as they would probably be celebrating and not be back till late.

We arrived in Neath and went straight to the Big Cam pub, situated on the corner of the main stretch of road by the train station where we met up with the rest of the Neath crowd. We now numbered around 45 lads, mostly made up of the Neath Jacks but also of lads from Swansea, Baglan, Port Talbot and Llanelli with ages mostly under 25. By now, most of us were pretty much pissed up and we just had a drink and a laugh with the Neath lot. For about an hour, nothing of note happened. Cardiff had said their lads from Neath and Port Talbot would meet us but, other than that, we heard nothing. And to be honest, we didn't really expect anything but, despite this, you could tell something would happen. There was that feel in the air. A few of the boys were watching by the window as the train station was directly opposite and that's where the Scum were sure to arrive. Now the rest of what happens is to be honest a bit of a blur as I was pretty pissed by now and, with all the commotion, it is hard to remember exact details. I was at the back of the pub by the pool table when I could hear shouting at the front where the boys were watching by the window. I went to have a look and, as I got near, I could hear what sounded to me like "Blue army, Blue army". People were running outside and others were shouting that the "Fucking Scum were here". That was it. I ran outside and I remember someone chasing one guy up the read while there was this other guy laughing at me. I went up and asked where he was from. "Cardiff," came the reply. I smashed him in the mouth and he ran straight in the pub next to the Big Cam called The David Protheroe. I ran after him into the pub. Inside it was packed and the guy quickly disappeared. All of a sudden, a glass flew over my head and smashed by a pillar next to me. By my side was a table full of empty glasses. I picked one up and threw it in the direction of a group a blokes who were staring at me and where the glass that was thrown at me had come from. Unbeknown to me, all the other Swansea lot had followed me in and now it really kicked off. Bottles, tables, chairs, ashtrays, stools, etc were now flying around from all angles. The whole pub was kicking off. Everyone was fighting. It was like a scene from a old western movie. Due to all the glasses and other stuff coming at us, we went outside and offered whoever wanted it outside but no one did. They just stayed in the pub with their weapons and shouted "Blue army" - wankers ! Most of them in the pub were men in their 30s and 40s while we were mostly young lads but they wouldn't even have a pop outside.

We then went to go in a second time. A few got in and, as we opened the door, a glass smashed into my head. I backed off, blood poured from my head and I could feel glass in the corner of my eye. At first, I couldn't see out of my right eye properly and started to panic. Luckily I got the glass out of my eye and, after a few seconds, my eyesight came back. Inside, it was still going off and, as I went back to the doors, I saw Muto have a stool slammed over his head. He stumbled out. As he opened the door, you could see bodies on the floor and that the pub was wrecked. Muto collapsed outside and Gypo (one of the Swansea lads) and me went to his aid. At first Muto didn't answer but then opened his eyes and tried to get up only to fall down. This was largely due to the fact he was so pissed but I don't think the stool helped matters either. It was only now that the first sign of Old Bill turned up, mostly plain clothed, about 4 of them. The road was packed with people who were looking to see what was going on and more of the boys from the Big Cam pub next door who hadn't known it had kicked off. I was pulled aside by a copper as I stood out like a sore thumb with blood all over me. He asked me if I was ok and what was going on. As is best in situations like these, I said I was fine and nothing else. Finally more Old Bill turned up. They had to shut off the main road due to the large numbers of people congregated there and had finally got some order out of the mayhem. Two of the lads got nicked on the day but one was de-arrested later. The rest of us got questioned and names and addresses taken (the usual crap) and told to go back to Swansea. Most of the boys did but me and a few others stayed for one more pint before heading back.

I got myself cleaned up, ordered another pint and had a chat with the Neath lot about the day's events. When I looked outside, I saw an Old Bill van across the road by the station but thought they were there just to keep an eye on us. Due to the weather being nice, we went outside and finished up our drinks. This was when a copper came up asking me why I was still there. I told him I would be going when I finished my drink and asked what the rush was, to which he said

"Just finish your drink and get on the next train."

He went back to van and then one of the doormen at the bar said that they had told him a group of Cardiff were on their way to Neath now. I told the rest of the boys and we got a group of about 12-15 of us in wait for them. Sadly though, the Old Bill had had enough for one day and quickly came over and escorted the remaining 6 Swansea onto the platform. As we got onto the platform, the train was pulling in. It was then that I noticed there was a group on the train and this was the mob we were meant to meet - 2 hours later than hoped ! Being pissed up and still pumped full of adrenalin, we attempted to get at the Cardiff mob but the Old Bill were having none of it. Out came the truncheons and also the dogs were now on the platform too and we were forced into a waiting room on the platform. The scum got off the train, about 25 of them, and tried a half hearted attempt to get at us but the Old Bill had it sorted. We were put straight on the train and went back to Swansea where word had already spread about the events in Neath. Trouble continued in Neath town centre all night and more police had to be brought in from Cardiff to help out.

The local papers were full of it the next day and in the weeks that followed photos were published to try and identify people involved. The inevitable happened and a large number of boys got nicked including myself. Nine of us were bailed and charged with violent disorder whilst inquiries continued. The thing though that gets me is that it was only Swansea fans nicked, not one from the crowd in the pub who attacked us was nicked even though they were clearly seen on video ! Months went by and we attended various court hearings before finally being given a trial at Swansea Crown Court. Most of the boys went guilty apart from myself and 2 others but we were, as I expected, found guilty. I was remanded in prison until sentencing, the main reason was that I already had a long record for football related incidents and Wales were due to play England that weekend. On the day of the sentencing, we were all given prison terms ranging from 4 to 27 months. I had the longest but, strangely though, not one of us received a banning order.

SOUTHEND (away)

We met up early at a cafe in Swansea High Street and waited for the lads who were driving to turn up in the minibuses. Three were booked and were all full come the day of the game. As usual, everyone started drinking early and arranged that whatever bus got there first, they would find a pub and the rest would meet there. This we did and met up at a pub just inside Southend. We had a few beers and waited for the third minibus to show. About an hour later than the rest of us, they finally showed as they somehow got lost even though they were right behind the other two minibuses most of the way. There was no sign of much happening where we were so we went to the city centre and to a Yates bar. For a game from which we didn't really expect much opposition, we had a good turnout of around 80+ lads with about 25 'youth'. It wasn't long before the Old Bill spotters found us and gave out the usual warnings but left us to it and just shadowed us. Time was getting on and, if I remember right, a few of the younger lot started playing up and we were told to leave. So off we went and into a bar right by the ground which turned out to be the Southend supporters bar. Inside there was your typical shirt-wearing supporter. This was not what we were after so we left them to it and had a drink and a bit of a sing. Still nothing of note had happened so about 20 of us decided to make it a bit more interesting and go in the home end to see if we would have some fun there. At first I thought we'd be sussed straight away by the Old Bill but somehow there were none about and, with the dodgiest Essex accents you've ever heard, managed to get in. The stewards let us pass without question and we went straight in.

"Come on then you English cunts. We're fucking Swansea" shouted one of the boys.

More of us were coming into the stand but no one wanted to know. Again there were no stewards or Old Bill. You could see the Southend that were there were shitting it and didn't seem like they had any boys in that part of the ground so up we went onto the pitch and walked the perimeter of the pitch towards our away end. We offered the whole length of the terrace the chance of a pop but they didn't even shout back. Boos rang around the ground and only a few stewards came over and politely asked us to go in with the rest of the Swansea crowd who were loving it and cheering.

The game started and to our right there was finally a group of around 20 Southend who started to give it the big one. All that separated us was a handful of stewards and some empty seats. There was the usual banter but you could tell our lads were just up for it and wanted any excuse for a row. Within a few minutes we got the excuse we wanted as Southend scored. Two of the boys, Muto and Leigh P, were off over the seats. I was next with them closely followed by about 30 others. Some of the Southend shit it and done one but, fair play, a few stood and fought back and even two of the stewards had a pop which was quite funny. Everyone was having a fair scrap but we had too many for them as more Swansea piled in and Southend quickly backed off. Some Swansea were now on the pitch and trying to get at the Southend at front of the stand but again they just done one and legged it. Finally the Old Bill showed (fuck knows where they'd been) and sorted it out but didn't nick anyone which was a bonus.

As I got back in the away end, I noticed blood coming from my hand. I went to the toilets to wash it off but couldn't move my thumb - I later found out I had somehow broke it. The Old Bill were now keeping a close eye on us so we decided to make a move and go back to the Yates bar that we were in earlier. Just as we got out, we bumped into a few of the lads who didn't bother going to the game. They also had been at it with some locals as was evident as one had his Stone Island badge ripped off and was literally hanging by a thread. The doormen at Yates said they wouldn't let us in. This led to another confrontation and the Old Bill quickly showed. By now they had had enough and out came the batons and they started being heavy handed which was to be expected as most of us were now pissed up and causing problems from nothing. We then split up and found another bar in which were a few of the older lads. Again it kicked off but this time with each other as one had chucked a pint glass which narrowly missed one of the other lad's head which he didn't find funny. It was soon broken up and we made a move before the Old Bill showed. Outside there was the usual crowds as the game had now ended. Muto was off his face and was offering everyone and anyone outside. He then laid into a few lads who got a bit gobby and they quickly done a disappearing act. The Old Bill now turned up in numbers and were taking no shit. They rounded us all up and took us to where we had parked our minibuses. We were then told to leave and not come back which we did. One bus went and stayed in London for the night while the other two went home. One lad who I won't name decided to ring up talk sport on the radio and tell them about our day's events. Strangely though they didn't seem interested and cut him off.

WREXHAM (away)

Once again it was an early start and we travelled up in 4 minibuses, 3 from Swansea and 1 from Neath. On the way up, we stopped off to get more beer which was already flowing fast. As we got back on our minibuses, one of the Neath lads looked pissed off. It turned out that he had lost his wallet with not only his cash in but also a bit of 'powder' and a few 'pills'. We all chipped in and sorted him out. Lucky for him, he had his wallet back a few days later as someone had handed it in to the Old Bill and they sent it to Swansea Old Bill. Even luckier for him, somehow the Old Bill had missed the powder and pills which were still in his wallet !

It was nearly midday when we pulled into a large bar/hotel just outside Wrexham. As we got near we could see there was a wedding function going on with a few of the guests outside laughing and having a joke. We pulled into the car park near to where they were and it was funny seeing their smiles slowly drop as they saw about 60+ drunken lads get out, one of whom was spewing up his guts and who then quickly apologised saying he was travel sick; they didn't seem too happy ! We had a few pints and made a few calls to the Wrexham lads to let them know we would be arriving shortly.

We arrived at Wrexham just before 1 pm. We parked up and made our way through the city centre. There were no Old Bill about, just shoppers. So, to avoid standing out, we split up into small groups and tried to blend in. The first pub we came across was a Yates bar. We went in and rang the rest of the boys to meet there. In total, we had around 70 lads as a few had driven up in cars to meet up with us. Still there was no sign of the Old Bill. I rang one of Wrexham's lads and said where we were and that no Old Bill were around. They said they were in a pub not far from where we were and to go there. 'Fuck that,' I thought. We had done our bit by getting into their city with no Old Bill so the rest was up to them. Wrexham's lad agreed and said for us to wait there. The rest of our lot were told and everyone was ready. There were two doormen working and, by the worried looks of their faces, you could tell they knew what was going on. So they were politely told to keep their mouths shut and not ring the Old Bill or they would not have a pub by the time they turned up. Wisely they agreed and waited nervously for the expected KO. We waited and waited but no show. Then after about half hour, outside you could see a few of their lads walk past looking in.

"They're fucking here," someone shouted. We ran to the doors but the bouncers had already locked the doors.

"Open the fucking door, cunt," shouted one of our lot.

The doormen were totally shitting it now as people started to breakdown the doors. You could see them shaking with fear as they tried to unbolt the door. The Wrexham lads were calling us on outside but didn't make any attempt to come in. The bouncers took forever to open the door due to the fact their hands were shaking so much. Then one of our lads, 'Jez', found a fire escape around the corner and steamed through it with the rest of us right behind. It kicked off and both sets laid into each other. Wrexham's firm was soon on the back foot and down an ally on the opposite side of the road. In fairness, it was more a reaction than trying to run as they didn't know how many we had as we all ran out into them. There were a handful of Old Bill which were shadowing Wrexham's lads and quickly ran in to break up the fighting. Despite this, fighting still carried on for a few more seconds and I can remember a Wrexham lad having a few boots on the floor. Two of our lads were nicked and with the help of more Old Bill who were now on the scene we were forced back into the pub. We were now held in Yates by the Old Bill while Wrexham were moved on. For now, that was it so we ordered another drink before being escorted to the ground, an hour and half early !

Due to me being on a ban I couldn't enter any football grounds. I explained this and was asked why I was up there. I said it was for nothing more than a day out with the lads and, after the usual name and address bollocks, I was allowed to leave the escort and went to a pub right by the ground. I was now in the dodgy position of being on my own and risk being spotted by Wrexham's mob who would now be looking for any of our lads. Inside, the pub was packed with 'normal' supporters of both clubs. I got a drink and went down by the pool table near by the door. Just then a about 10 of the boys walked in who managed to slip the escort and said they saw what looked to be some of Wrexham's boys coming up the road. After 10 minutes though, there was no sign of them so I went back to the bar when I noticed two lads dressed in Paul and Shark. Now any lad knows this is a popular brand of clothing amongst football 'lads'. I then recognised one of them from the fight earlier by Yates.

"Where's your fucking boys then ?" I asked.

"I dunno what you mean mate,' he replied in that irritating scouse accent they have.

There was only two of them and not wanting to get nicked for something small I left it and told them we were in the corner by the door if they wanted it. As I walked back to where our lads were, I noticed a few other lads walking in, though these weren't 'normal' fans like the rest of the pub. These were their lads.

"Wrexham's boys are here," I said to my lot.

You could now see a few more of them outside making their way in. Me and a lad called George were the first outside and it kicked off again as we fought by the doors. Due to the pub being packed, the others got there a few second later. The Old Bill were already there with truncheons drawn and forced us back in. Some of the boys who couldn't get out started putting the windows through. Others who weren't with us also joined in with wrecking the pub. Glasses and pool balls were flying around and it wasn't long before the Old Bill shut down the pub on safety grounds. Outside, there was glass all over the floor with the odd pool ball rolling around. Riot police were now on the scene and were pushing people around. I was then spotted by our liaison officer who come up to me looking well pissed off.

"You lot, get in the fucking ground," he said to the other lads with me. He then turned to me.

"Go on then, hard man, fuck off on your own," he said. He then turned to the other officer with him.

"Come on, let's show the Wrexham boys who he is." With that, they both started pushing me towards the city centre and shouted.

"He's Swansea. If you want him, he's going to the city centre."

I couldn't believe what they were saying. Across the road, more Wrexham lads were turning up and were staring at me with the Old Bill still informing everyone who I was. 'Shit,' I thought, 'that's me done'. Then, just as I started to expect the coming hammering, I was grabbed from behind.

"Is this him ?" I heard someone say.

"Yeah, that's the one," said another voice.

As I turned around, I saw that a riot copper had hold of me and it turned out that I was pointed out by the landlord as one of the people involved in the trouble. To be honest, it was the only time I was glad to have been nicked; the only other option waiting for me was a hammering by Wrexham's lads who were now mobbing up across the road fully aware of who I was thanks to the Swansea twats in blue !

I was arrested under suspicion of criminal damage and violent disorder. I was kept in the cells until after the game ended. I asked if I could call someone so that they would wait for me to come out and get back to Swansea.

"We've already sorted it out and your mates are going to wait for you outside," a copper explained.

Great I thought. That was until I got outside only to find out the prick was lying and no one had waited as they had told the boys the opposite and that I wouldn't be out until the morning. I was then bailed for two week before having an 'ID' parade. Outside I was now stuck in Wrexham with no lift and not enough for a train home. Most of the boys were on their way to Blackpool for the night and were too far gone to come back but luck was with me though as the Neath lot were on their way home and were only 15 miles away after having to wait for the two that got nicked earlier. I rang Trevor who was driving and he said they'd come back for me which they did. Fuck knows how I'd have got home otherwise. A week later I had a letter telling me not to go to the 'ID' parade and that the charges had been dropped due to lack of evidence. My only guess was the landlord didn't want the hassle of a court case so cheers to him too.

There are many other accounts of Swansea younger hooligan element being involved in disorder at football in recent seasons. Below is a brief account of a few of those games.

OXFORD (away)

Several thousand pounds worth of damage was done to a pub before the game. While it was going on, the landlord strangely found it funny and was still serving drinks as everyone wrecked his pub. During the game, there was a minor pitch invasion and several attempts to get at the Oxford fans. Returning back on the train from the game, we had incidents at Swindon with their youth; Bristol where we had to change to a coach and a few mouthy twats got brave while we were on the back of the coach. About 9 of us jumped off and attacked the gobby twats; 2 got knocked out while the rest abandoned their mates and ran. Then, at Cardiff, a guy got on with his missus and thought he was the bollocks until he tried it on with us and it badly back fired on him. Though I will admit he was game as fuck (so too was his missus come to think of it), fuck knows what they were on that night.

WALES V POLAND (Cardiff)

Had a mob of around 40 boys, mostly under 30s and had no opposition for about 45 minutes before the Old Bill escorted us out of the city (and they say we never show !). We then went to Newport where there was a bit of bother with the locals and 2 arrests were made. Arrangements were made with Cardiff that we were now in Newport, about 25 minutes away, and would meet them there. They didn't show after saying they would ! We were then again escorted out of the city and then went to Port Talbot. As we left the train, a group of locals recognised one of our lot and started shouting Cardiff. We chased them backed into the pub and smashed them all over including one guy who, after having a traffic cone slammed over his head, then had it stuck on his head. Due to this, he couldn't see a thing and was running around like a headless chicken and bouncing off the walls while he was kicked to fuck; very funny. Again for a third time, we were escorted out of the town and back onto the train. The Neath lads got off at their stop only to run back to tell us that a group of Cardiff-based Neath lads had tried to bottle one of ours. The train was just about to go so someone pulled the emergency cord. We all piled off and up over a bridge to get to the where the Scum had run. At the top of the bridge, two Old Bill were assaulted as they tried to stop us getting past. We caught up with some of the twats that had a go at the Neath lads and gave them a few slaps. A few of the boys got nicked. While this was going on, the rest of us made our getaway only to be picked up on CCTV and all nicked moments later. Due to lack of evidence, all but two of the boys were released. These two were charged with violent disorder but luckily escaped prison.

NOTTINGHAM FORREST (away)

A mob of around 150 lads made the journey North to Nottingham which included about 40 'youth'. There was fighting with Forest fans before the game but the Old Bill soon sorted it out. A pub allocated for away fans had the light fittings smashed and ripped out, a pool table overturned and Swansea fans helped themselves to drinks from behind the bar. An English flag and posters advertising the Rugby six nations was set on fire and the police then shut the pub down. The landlord of the pub told the media that she was disgusted at the behaviour of the Swansea fans and they would never again be welcome at the pub. An eye witness said there was a young crowd of boys in their late teens and early 20s that caused most of the problems. Inside the Ground, there was more trouble with Swansea fans invading the pitch when we scored. The Old Bill then started to get heavy handed and fighting between us and the Old Bill happened throughout the remainder of the game with over 20 arrests made.

MILLWALL (home)

Around 50 youth met up as early as 9am in search of Millwall fans though there was no sign of Millwall before the game. During the game, a few Millwall pulled down meshing between the fans and made an attempt to get at Swansea. Then Swansea fans tried to attack the Millwall fans from both sides as police tried to regain control. Millwall fans then had to be escorted away early for their own safety as around 600-800 fans tried attacking them. Most were under 30 and it was the police that then bore the brunt of the attacks and were pelted with tyres, car wing mirrors, bricks, bottles and coins in what was described as the worst football disorder in Swansea in recent times. Local papers displayed photos of those suspected of being involved in the riot and dozens of arrests were made in the coming weeks including a child of nine. Most of the cases collapsed due to lost evidence and those that were found guilty only had fines and bans imposed.

ON RAMPAGE

TYRES, wing mirrors and broken bottles were hurled at police during a violent clash with around 300 Swans supporters yesterday.

Four arrests were made and three police officers and two fans were taken to hospital with minor head and leg injuries. Nearby businesses were forced to close and pull down their shutters as the trouble escalated in Siloh Road.

It came just minutes after the Swans' 2-0 win against Millwall. Swans fans said violence erupted on Siloh Road, near the Liberty Stadium, when police closed off the dual carriageway to home supporters after the game.

Witnesses said there was chaos in the streets as the police tried to control the crowd of Swansea supporters.

More than 200 police officers, some in riot gear, were drafted in.

One Swans fan who wanted to remain anonymous said: "It wasn't the Millwall fans, it was Swansea fans against the police. Bricks and bottles were being thrown, it really got quite frightening."

Violent history repeats itself

TROUBLE between Swansea and Millwall is nothing new.

Back in February 2001, police confiscated knives, knuckle dusters and even an axe from Millwall hooligans as they headed to the Vetch Field.

In September 2000, Swansea soccer thugs forced part of a London underground station to close when CS gas was hurled at riot police escorting them.

The incident happened as 150 hooligans were being taken on a special train after Swansea City's away game with Millwall.

Four police were treated for the effects of CS gas after a special train from Bermondsey, arranged to keep the yobs away from ordinary people, arrived at Victoria Station.

The supporters were being transferred to another train to take them to Paddington when the gas was thrown. One Swansea fan was arrested.

On the same day a massive police operation was mounted after the troublemakers tried to make their way to a battle with Millwall pre-arranged on the internet and by mobile phone.

The Swansea hooligans were contained by three lines of riot police at a pub close to London Bridge.

There were bottle throwing incidents before and after the match. Twenty fans were ejected from the match and a Swansea fan was arrested.

The South Londoners have one of the worst reputations for football violence over the years with clashes all over the country including Bristol and Cardiff.

One of the most notorious hooligan elements at the club is the Bushwackers, and they were once described by the Metropolitan Police as "the most dangerous firm in the country".

However, in recent years Millwall have gone to great lengths at improving their reputation.

At the 2004 FA Cup final at the Millennium Stadium, where they have had numerous running battles with Cardiff's Soul Crew, there were no arrests among the Millwall supporters.

ON PATROL Mounted riot police try to heard Swansea City fans along Stloh Road and away from the Liberty Stadium.

CROWD TROUBLE A tyre is thrown at the police line on Siloh Road after the Swansea City fans were herded away from the Liberty Stadium ground following their 2-0 win against Millwall.

Police to tackle troublemakers

POLICE in London will be coming down hard on any troublemakers at this weekend's Millwall versus Swansea game.

The fixture has seen a number of flashpoints in recent years, but police are confident that Saturday will be a trouble free game.

Some Swansea supporters clashed with police after Millwall played Swansea at the Liberty Stadium in October and officers are hoping to stop any repeat.

Despite no Millwall fans being involved in October's trouble, some Swansea fans feared revenge attacks in this fixture.

One club insider speaking after the violence said: "There were no Millwall fans involved in Sunday's trouble, but they would have

heard all about it. These so-called fans turned up and appeared to have an idea to get at Millwall fans and I'm afraid it could mean trouble for genuine fans who want to travel to the away match.

"A section of Millwall fans could be on the lookout for some revenge."

However, Met officers say they will be on the lookout for anyone wanting to stoke up trouble again.

"The Metropolitan Police Service, Millwall and Swansea City have all worked closely to organise this match," said a Met spokesman.

"Police are sending a clear mes-

sage to fans that they are aiming to police fairly, but firmly, in order to ensure the match passes without incident and allow true football fans to enjoy the day.

"We will be providing a high visibility presence to reassure the crowd and community, and using tactics to deter and identify any troublemakers."

The fixture has seen a number of high-profile incidents in the past few years and is always a potential flashpoint.

In August 2000, police had to be called in after punters were pinned and put up around Swansea before their away game urging fans not to back down from fights with Millwall fans.

Part of the Underground had to be closed after hooligans hurled CS gas canisters at police.

One Swansea fan was arrested. The previous season saw a mass brawl when Swansea fans attacked around 30 Millwall fans in a Sandfields pub after the match.

In 2001, a massive police operation was launched in Swansea and police seized more than 20 weapons from hooligans.

Swansea City director David Morgan has urged fans to behave and said only those with tickets will be allowed into the match on Saturday.

He said: "Only fans with tickets will be allowed in on Saturday, there will be none available on the day.

"Tickets will be going off sale tomorrow evening, so anyone who wants to go needs to buy one before the ticket office closes at 6pm."

Search for sixth football target

POLICE have tracked down five men they have been hunting in connection with violence after a Swansea football match.

But detectives are still trying to discover the identity of a sixth person.

Officers investigating the trouble within Bristol following the derby match are keen to identify a sixth man thanks to their recovery of CCTV images of the six men.

They had asked for help from the public identifying them but decided the big blurry against turned an honest one of the men have now wanted to come front person.

Detectives are currently waiting for the Crown Prosecution Service to decide whether any of the men have a case to answer.

More than 300 Swansea fans went on

could help close Swansea with their inquiries.

He praised the public for helping police identify fans following the riot.

"Since the incident we have received support from the football club, the watchers, Swansea football fans and the local community," he added.

"We would like to thank them all for this. Those men who we wish to speak to might be out continue the progressing this inquiry even further."

A spokesman for the police added: "Five of the eight have now been identified. They we are still working to identify the last one.

"Nobody has been arrested although four of the men have been contacted for detention.

"We are seeking to hear from the CPS before deciding how to proceed."

THE FUTURE

The future as I see it for Swansea's firm is in very good hands indeed. On our day and for the big games we can pull in easy 400-500 lads of which there would be upwards of 150 'youth'. Times have changed a lot since the football violence heydays of the 70's and 80's. Better policing (most of the time, well over the top), CCTV, harsh prison sentences, modern new grounds and banning orders have all taken their toll on trouble. But, despite this, there is still trouble and fighting amongst the fans. It's pretty much agreed that football violence will never go away completely. We are, after all, human and football has a way of changing the most timid of person into a raging mad man (or woman). We are now well into the new millennium but violence and trouble at games involving Swansea is still on going. There is a new batch of lads waiting to take over when and if the older lads decide to call it a day. Some already have banning orders and have served prison terms by the time they reach their mid twenties but still they come and look for trouble. I know of lads who have lost jobs, relationships and their freedom over their antics at football but that still hasn't stopped them. Some will say it has stopped them going for a bit but you never know when its going to blow and, before you know it, you're back in the thick of it. Deep down, they're lying to themselves as they know the buzz and excitement will never go. It's not something that you just give up and stop going. Trouble in Swansea has gone quiet over recent times but that's largely due to the fact that no one comes here but, away, it's still going on. So, is there a future ahead for Swansea and our firm ? The answer is **YES**. The police know it and so do the club otherwise they wouldn't have their mass policing at most games and, if anyone doubts it, then just come on down. You know where we are. Get ready for the next 35 years of football shame ! !

S.R.S - Swansea Riot Squad, No retreat, NEVER surrender.

SCFC Hooligans

Other books by the same Publisher

Football Books

From Shattered Dreams to Wembley Way	Annis Abraham Jnr	£16.99 hardback
Ultras	Roberto Russo & Martin King	£14.99 paperback
Playing Up with Pompey	Bob Beech	£16.99 hardback
Gilly - Running with a pack of Wolves	Gilly Shaw & Martin King	£9.99 paperback
Bully CFC - The Life and Crimes of a Chelsea Head-Hunter	Gaetano Buglioni & Martin King	£16.99 hardback
		£7.99 paperback
Rangers ICF	Davie Carrick & Martin King	£16.99 hardback
		£7.99 paperback
Rivals - Fooball Fans Love-Hate Games	Martin King	£16.99 hardback
		£7.99 paperback
Blue Murder - Chelsea Till I Die	Mark Worrall	£9.99 paperback
Inside The Forest Executive Crew	Gary 'Boatsy' Clarke & Martin King	£7.99 paperback
Well Up For It	Simon Cheetham & Carl Eldridge	£9.99 paperback

Boxing Books

Harry Holland	Harry Holland & Martin King	£16.99 hardback
Blood, Sweat, Tears and Fears	Andy 'Stoneface' Till & Martin King	£16.99 hardback

See www.headhunterbooks.co.uk to order online or at all major Book Sellers.